THE UNSTOPPABLE WASP

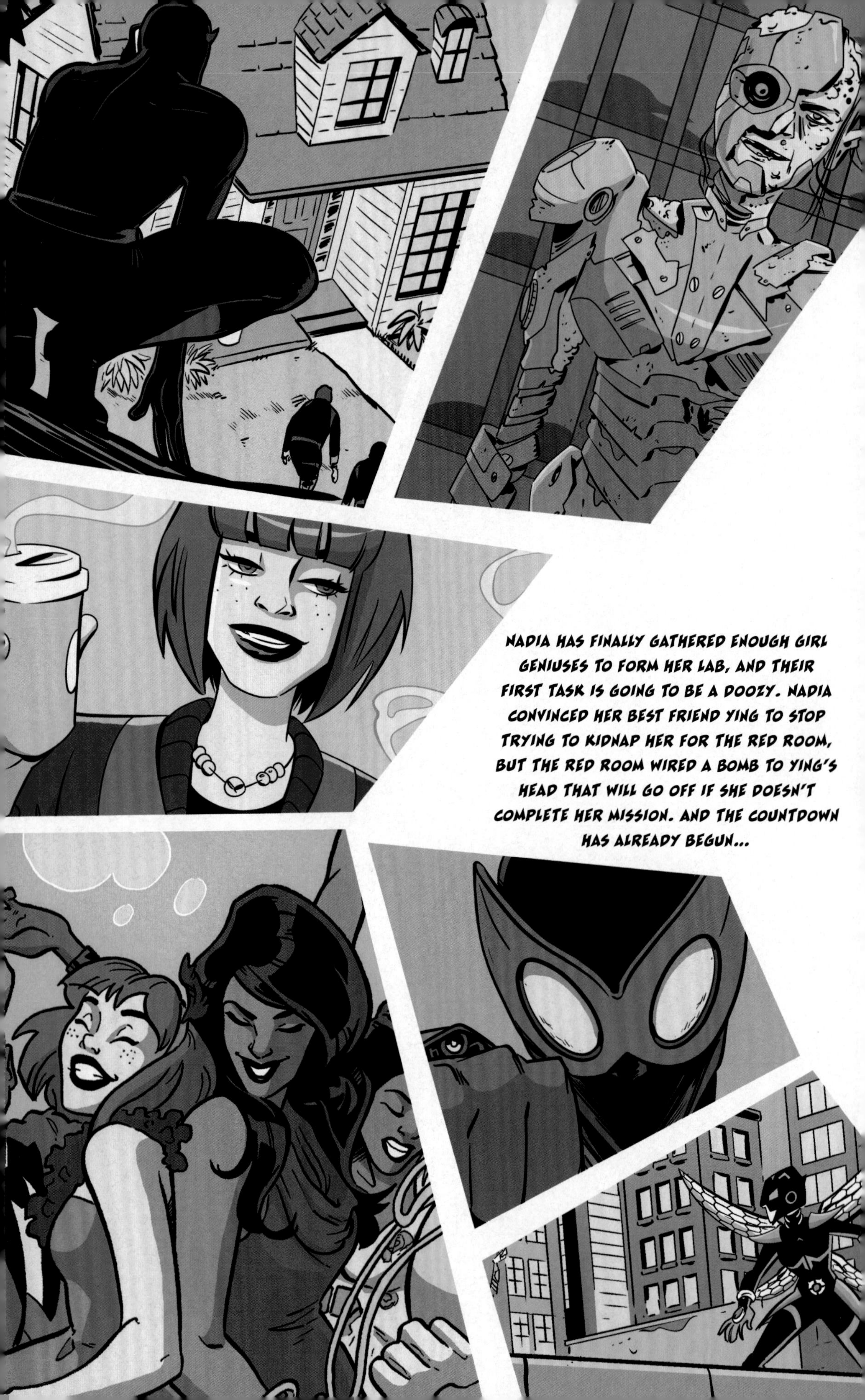
NADIA HAS FINALLY GATHERED ENOUGH GIRL GENIUSES TO FORM HER LAB, AND THEIR FIRST TASK IS GOING TO BE A DOOZY. NADIA CONVINCED HER BEST FRIEND YING TO STOP TRYING TO KIDNAP HER FOR THE RED ROOM, BUT THE RED ROOM WIRED A BOMB TO YING'S HEAD THAT WILL GO OFF IF SHE DOESN'T COMPLETE HER MISSION. AND THE COUNTDOWN HAS ALREADY BEGUN...

THE UNSTOPPABLE WASP

AGENTS OF G.I.R.L.

JEREMY WHITLEY
WRITER

ELSA CHARRETIER (#5-6), **VERONICA FISH** (#7)
AND **RO STEIN & TED BRANDT** (#8)
ARTISTS

MEGAN WILSON
COLOR ARTIST

VC's JOE CARAMAGNA
LETTERER

ELSA CHARRETIER & NICOLAS BANNISTER
COVER ART

ALANNA SMITH
EDITOR

TOM BREVOORT
EXECUTIVE EDITOR

SPECIAL THANKS TO **PREETI CHHIBBER**

WASP CREATED BY **STAN LEE, ERNIE HART & JACK KIRBY**

COLLECTION EDITOR **JENNIFER GRÜNWALD** • ASSISTANT EDITOR **CAITLIN O'CONNELL**
ASSOCIATE MANAGING EDITOR **KATERI WOODY** • EDITOR, SPECIAL PROJECTS **MARK D. BEAZLEY**
VP PRODUCTION & SPECIAL PROJECTS **JEFF YOUNGQUIST** • SVP PRINT, SALES & MARKETING **DAVID GABRIEL**
BOOK DESIGNER **JAY BOWEN**

EDITOR IN CHIEF **C.B. CEBULSKI** • CHIEF CREATIVE OFFICER **JOE QUESADA**
PRESIDENT **DAN BUCKLEY** • EXECUTIVE PRODUCER **ALAN FINE**

THE UNSTOPPABLE WASP VOL. 2: AGENTS OF G.I.R.L. Contains material originally published in magazine form as THE UNSTOPPABLE WASP #5-8 and TALES TO ASTONISH #44. First printing 2018. ISBN 978-1-302-90647-4. Published by MARVEL WORLDWIDE, INC., a subsidiary of MARVEL ENTERTAINMENT, LLC. OFFICE OF PUBLICATION: 135 West 50th Street, New York, NY 10020. **Printed in Canada.** DAN BUCKLEY, President, Marvel Entertainment; JOE QUESADA, Chief Creative Officer; TOM BREVOORT, SVP of Publishing; DAVID BOGART, SVP of Business Affairs & Operations, Publishing & Partnership; DAVID GABRIEL, SVP of Sales & Marketing, Publishing; JEFF YOUNGQUIST, VP of Production & Special Projects; DAN CARR, Executive Director of Publishing Technology; ALEX MORALES, Director of Publishing Operations; SUSAN CRESPI, Production Manager; STAN LEE, Chairman Emeritus. For information regarding advertising in Marvel Comics or on Marvel.com, please contact Vit DeBellis, Custom Solutions & Integrated Advertising Manager, at vdebellis@marvel.com. For Marvel subscription inquiries, please call 888-511-5480. **Manufactured between 1/5/2018 and 2/6/2018 by SOLISCO PRINTERS, SCOTT, QC, CANADA.**

10 9 8 7 6 5 4 3 2 1

5

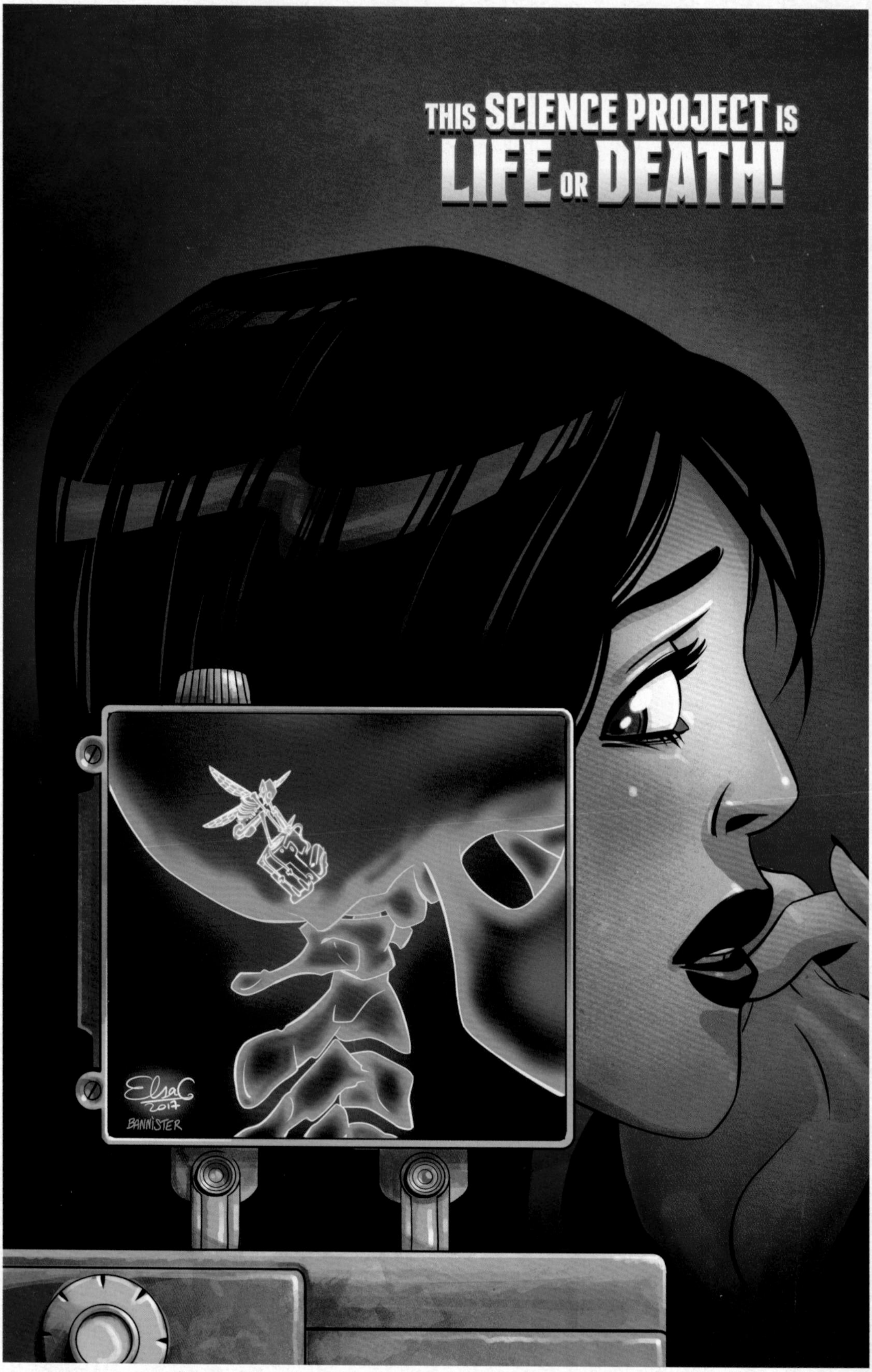
THIS SCIENCE PROJECT IS
LIFE OR DEATH!
ElsaC 2017
BANNISTER

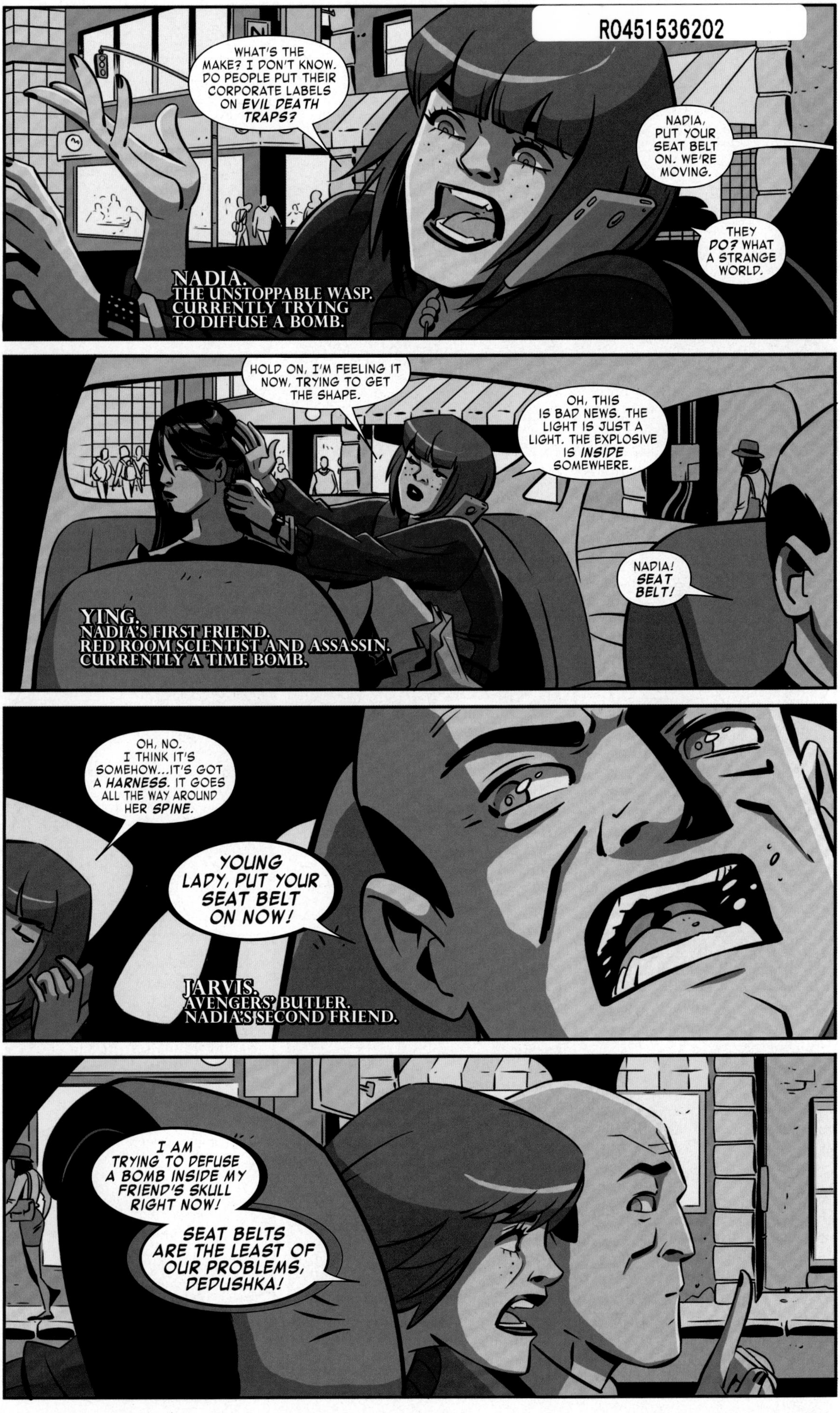
NADIA.
THE UNSTOPPABLE WASP.
CURRENTLY TRYING
TO DIFFUSE A BOMB.
WHAT'S THE MAKE? I DON'T KNOW. DO PEOPLE PUT THEIR CORPORATE LABELS ON EVIL DEATH TRAPS?
NADIA, PUT YOUR SEAT BELT ON. WE'RE MOVING.
THEY DO? WHAT A STRANGE WORLD.
YING.
NADIA'S FIRST FRIEND.
RED ROOM SCIENTIST AND ASSASSIN.
CURRENTLY A TIME BOMB.
HOLD ON, I'M FEELING IT NOW, TRYING TO GET THE SHAPE.
OH, THIS IS BAD NEWS. THE LIGHT IS JUST A LIGHT. THE EXPLOSIVE IS INSIDE SOMEWHERE.
NADIA! SEAT BELT!
JARVIS.
AVENGERS' BUTLER.
NADIA'S SECOND FRIEND.
OH, NO. I THINK IT'S SOMEHOW...IT'S GOT A HARNESS. IT GOES ALL THE WAY AROUND HER SPINE.
YOUNG LADY, PUT YOUR SEAT BELT ON NOW!
I AM TRYING TO DEFUSE A BOMB INSIDE MY FRIEND'S SKULL RIGHT NOW!
SEAT BELTS ARE THE LEAST OF OUR PROBLEMS, DEDUSHKA!

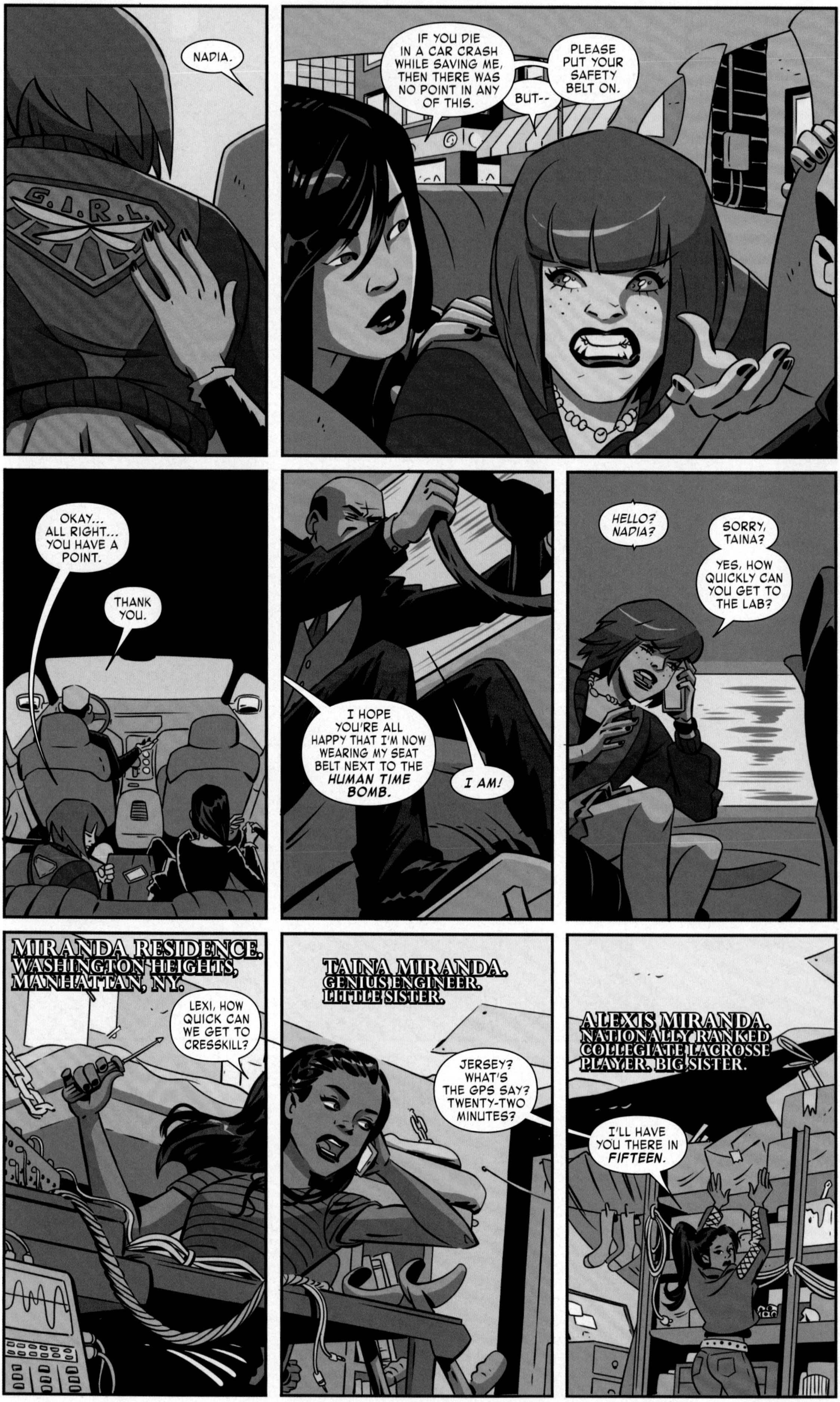
NADIA.
IF YOU DIE IN A CAR CRASH WHILE SAVING ME, THEN THERE WAS NO POINT IN ANY OF THIS.
BUT--
PLEASE PUT YOUR SAFETY BELT ON.
OKAY... ALL RIGHT... YOU HAVE A POINT.
THANK YOU.
I HOPE YOU'RE ALL HAPPY THAT I'M NOW WEARING MY SEAT BELT NEXT TO THE HUMAN TIME BOMB.
I AM!
HELLO? NADIA?
SORRY, TAINA?
YES, HOW QUICKLY CAN YOU GET TO THE LAB?
MIRANDA RESIDENCE. WASHINGTON HEIGHTS, MANHATTAN, NY.
LEXI, HOW QUICK CAN WE GET TO CRESSKILL?
TAINA MIRANDA. GENIUS ENGINEER. LITTLE SISTER.
JERSEY? WHAT'S THE GPS SAY? TWENTY-TWO MINUTES?
ALEXIS MIRANDA. NATIONALLY RANKED COLLEGIATE LACROSSE PLAYER. BIG SISTER.
I'LL HAVE YOU THERE IN FIFTEEN.

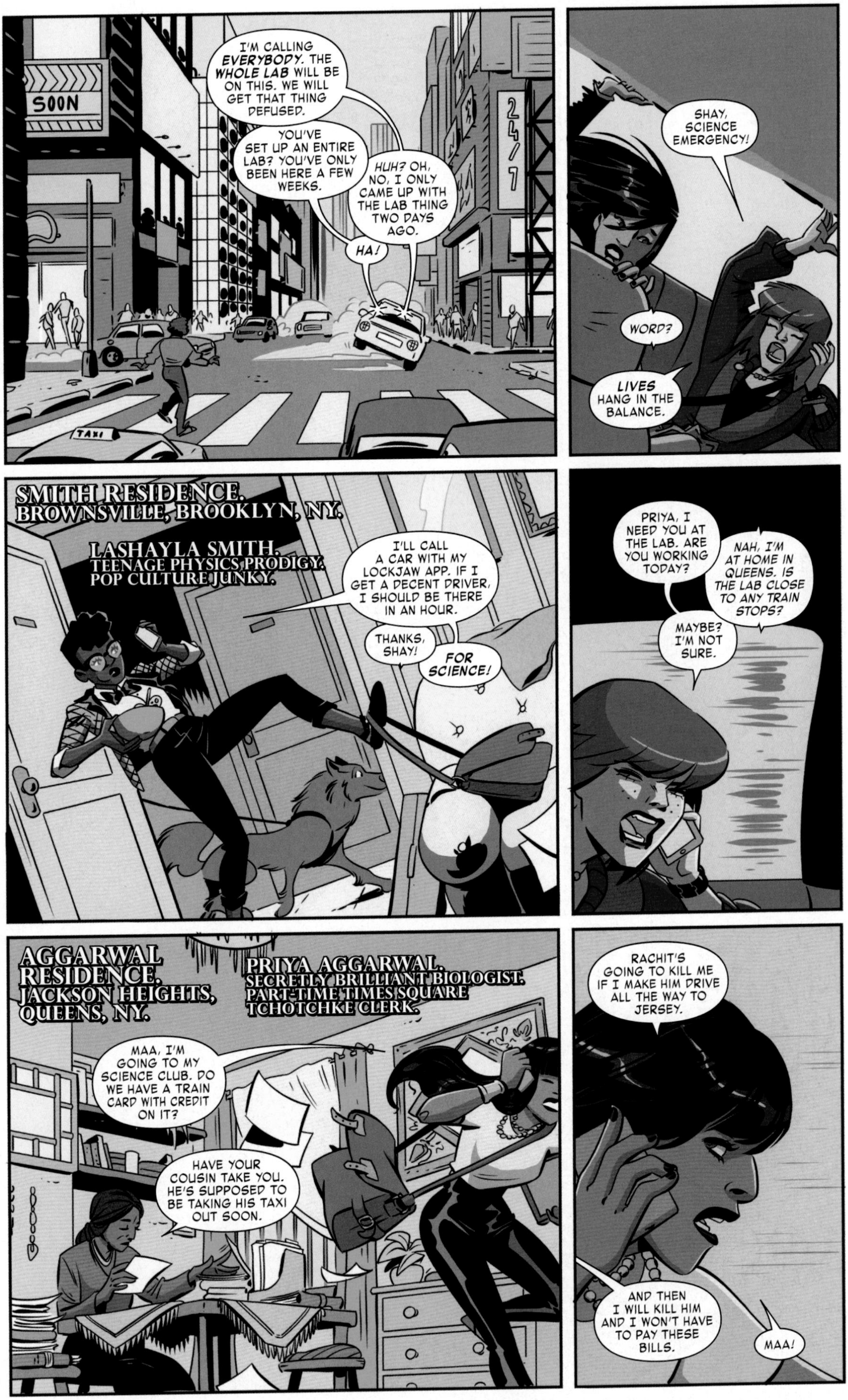
SOON
I'M CALLING EVERYBODY. THE WHOLE LAB WILL BE ON THIS. WE WILL GET THAT THING DEFUSED.
YOU'VE SET UP AN ENTIRE LAB? YOU'VE ONLY BEEN HERE A FEW WEEKS.
HUH? OH, NO, I ONLY CAME UP WITH THE LAB THING TWO DAYS AGO.
HA!
24/7
TAXI
SHAY, SCIENCE EMERGENCY!
WORD?
LIVES HANG IN THE BALANCE.
SMITH RESIDENCE. BROWNSVILLE, BROOKLYN, NY.
LASHAYLA SMITH. TEENAGE PHYSICS PRODIGY. POP CULTURE JUNKY.
I'LL CALL A CAR WITH MY LOCKJAW APP. IF I GET A DECENT DRIVER, I SHOULD BE THERE IN AN HOUR.
THANKS, SHAY!
FOR SCIENCE!
PRIYA, I NEED YOU AT THE LAB. ARE YOU WORKING TODAY?
NAH, I'M AT HOME IN QUEENS. IS THE LAB CLOSE TO ANY TRAIN STOPS?
MAYBE? I'M NOT SURE.
AGGARWAL RESIDENCE. JACKSON HEIGHTS, QUEENS, NY.
PRIYA AGGARWAL. SECRETLY BRILLIANT BIOLOGIST. PART-TIME TIMES SQUARE TCHOTCHKE CLERK.
MAA, I'M GOING TO MY SCIENCE CLUB. DO WE HAVE A TRAIN CARD WITH CREDIT ON IT?
HAVE YOUR COUSIN TAKE YOU. HE'S SUPPOSED TO BE TAKING HIS TAXI OUT SOON.
RACHIT'S GOING TO KILL ME IF I MAKE HIM DRIVE ALL THE WAY TO JERSEY.
AND THEN I WILL KILL HIM AND I WON'T HAVE TO PAY THESE BILLS.
MAA!

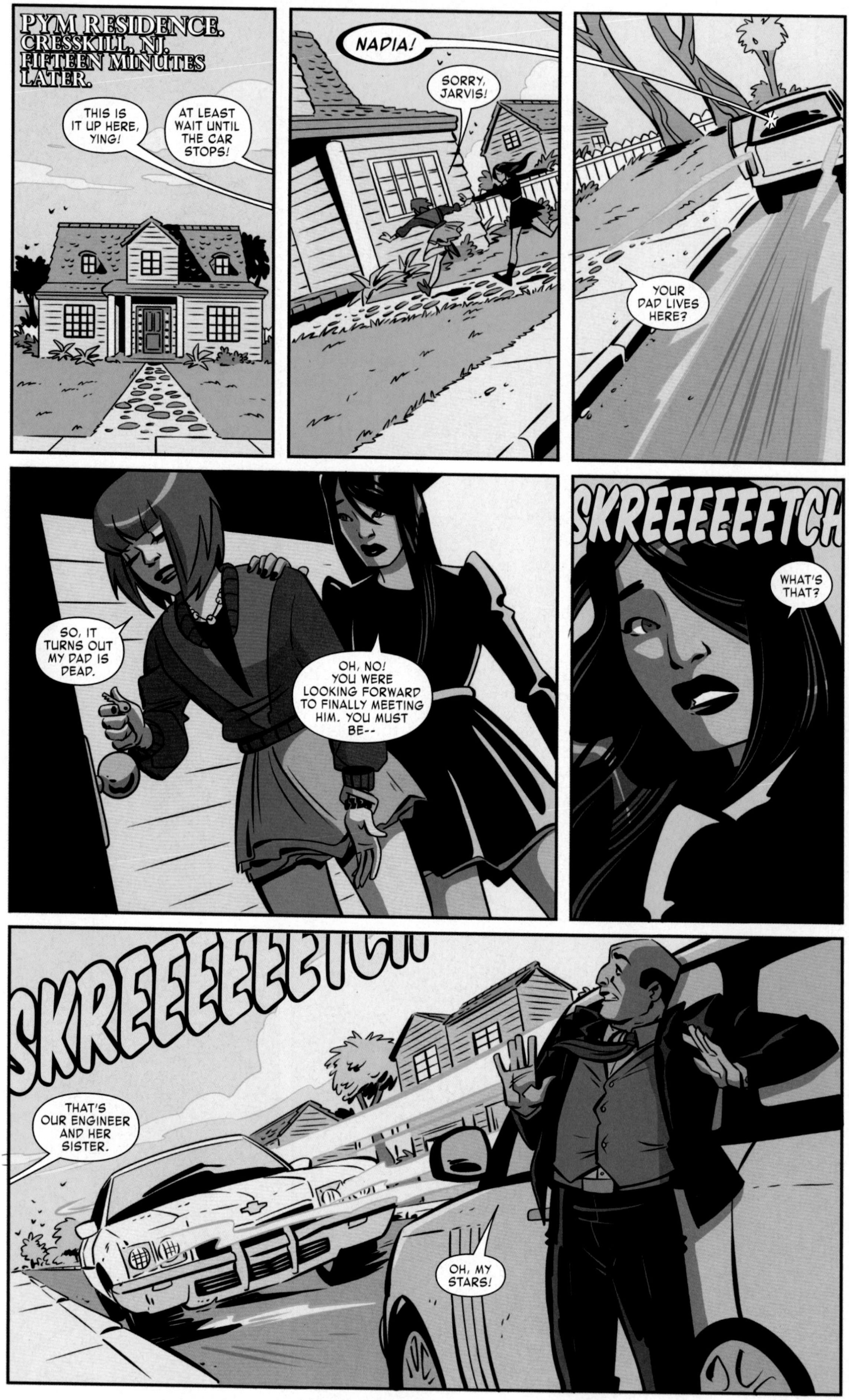
PYM RESIDENCE. CRESSKILL, NJ. FIFTEEN MINUTES LATER.
THIS IS IT UP HERE, YING!
AT LEAST WAIT UNTIL THE CAR STOPS!
NADIA!
SORRY, JARVIS!
YOUR DAD LIVES HERE?
SO, IT TURNS OUT MY DAD IS DEAD.
OH, NO! YOU WERE LOOKING FORWARD TO FINALLY MEETING HIM. YOU MUST BE--
SKREEEEEEETCH
WHAT'S THAT?
SKREEEEEEETCH
THAT'S OUR ENGINEER AND HER SISTER.
OH, MY STARS!

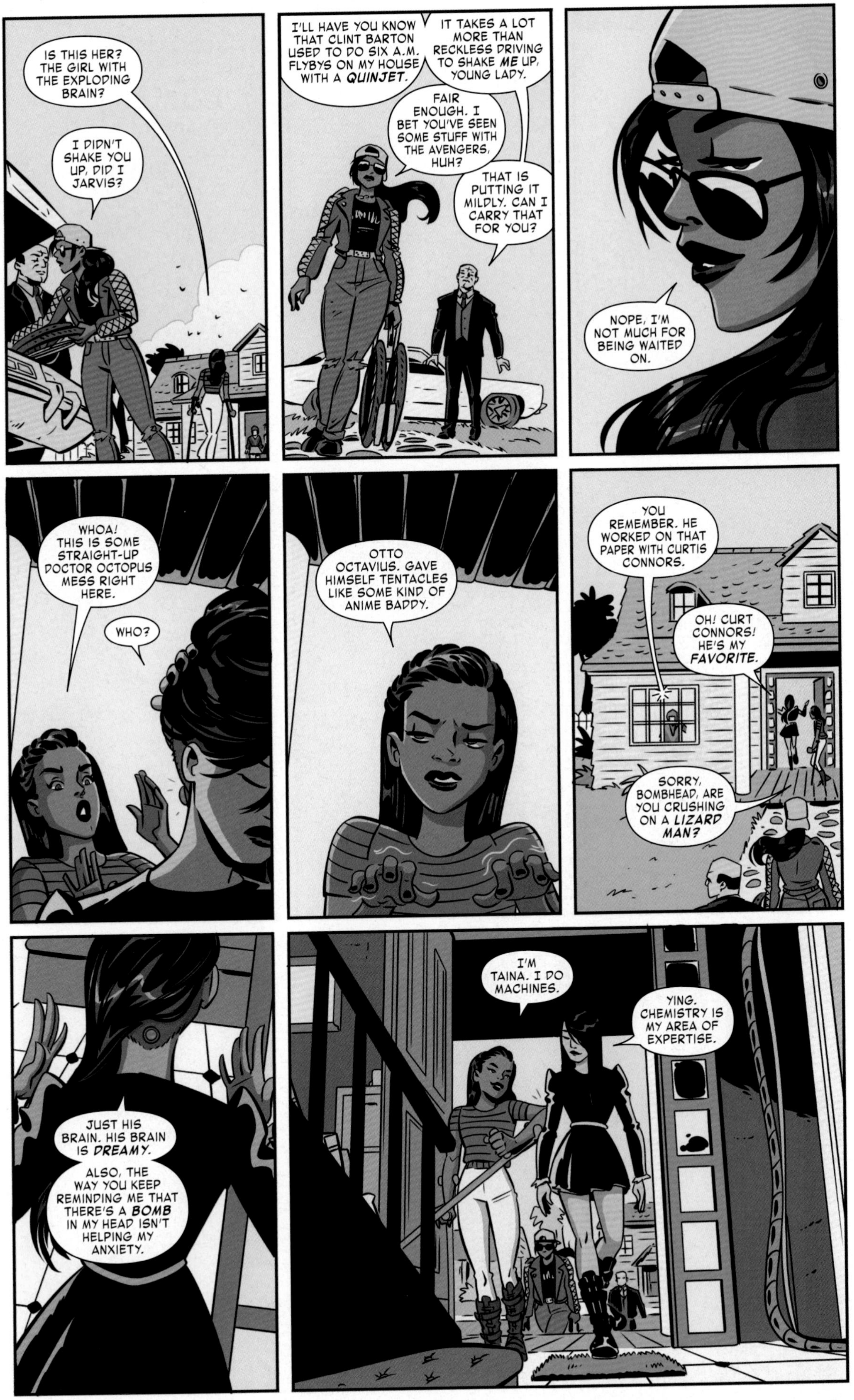
IS THIS HER? THE GIRL WITH THE EXPLODING BRAIN?
I DIDN'T SHAKE YOU UP, DID I JARVIS?
I'LL HAVE YOU KNOW THAT CLINT BARTON USED TO DO SIX A.M. FLYBYS ON MY HOUSE WITH A QUINJET.
IT TAKES A LOT MORE THAN RECKLESS DRIVING TO SHAKE ME UP, YOUNG LADY.
FAIR ENOUGH. I BET YOU'VE SEEN SOME STUFF WITH THE AVENGERS, HUH?
THAT IS PUTTING IT MILDLY. CAN I CARRY THAT FOR YOU?
NOPE, I'M NOT MUCH FOR BEING WAITED ON.
WHOA! THIS IS SOME STRAIGHT-UP DOCTOR OCTOPUS MESS RIGHT HERE.
WHO?
OTTO OCTAVIUS. GAVE HIMSELF TENTACLES LIKE SOME KIND OF ANIME BADDY.
YOU REMEMBER. HE WORKED ON THAT PAPER WITH CURTIS CONNORS.
OH! CURT CONNORS! HE'S MY FAVORITE.
SORRY, BOMBHEAD, ARE YOU CRUSHING ON A LIZARD MAN?
JUST HIS BRAIN. HIS BRAIN IS DREAMY.
ALSO, THE WAY YOU KEEP REMINDING ME THAT THERE'S A BOMB IN MY HEAD ISN'T HELPING MY ANXIETY.
I'M TAINA. I DO MACHINES.
YING. CHEMISTRY IS MY AREA OF EXPERTISE.

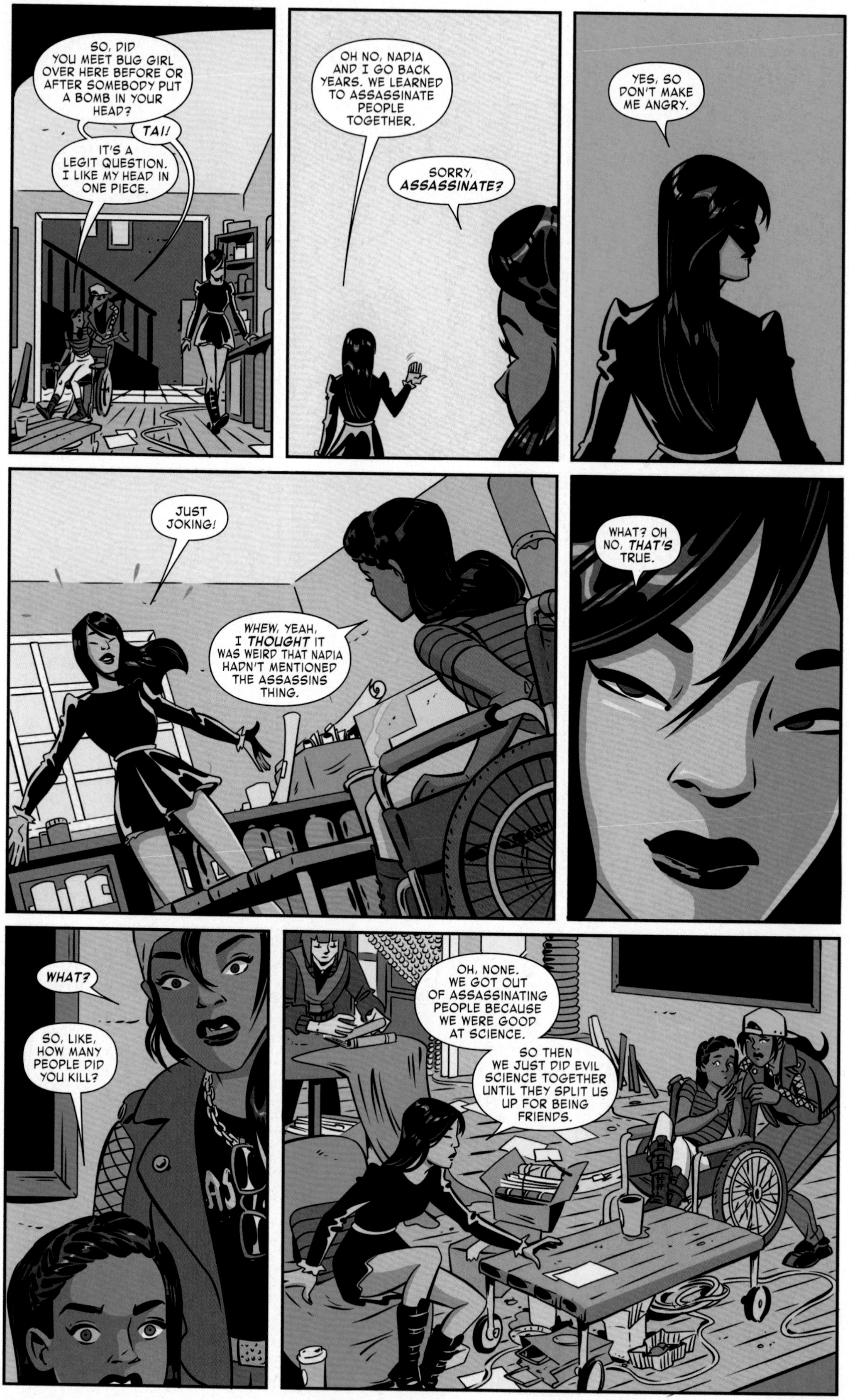
SO, DID YOU MEET BUG GIRL OVER HERE BEFORE OR AFTER SOMEBODY PUT A BOMB IN YOUR HEAD?
TAI!
IT'S A LEGIT QUESTION. I LIKE MY HEAD IN ONE PIECE.
OH NO, NADIA AND I GO BACK YEARS. WE LEARNED TO ASSASSINATE PEOPLE TOGETHER.
SORRY, ASSASSINATE?
YES, SO DON'T MAKE ME ANGRY.
JUST JOKING!
WHEW, YEAH, I THOUGHT IT WAS WEIRD THAT NADIA HADN'T MENTIONED THE ASSASSINS THING.
WHAT? OH NO, THAT'S TRUE.
WHAT?
SO, LIKE, HOW MANY PEOPLE DID YOU KILL?
OH, NONE. WE GOT OUT OF ASSASSINATING PEOPLE BECAUSE WE WERE GOOD AT SCIENCE.
SO THEN WE JUST DID EVIL SCIENCE TOGETHER UNTIL THEY SPLIT US UP FOR BEING FRIENDS.

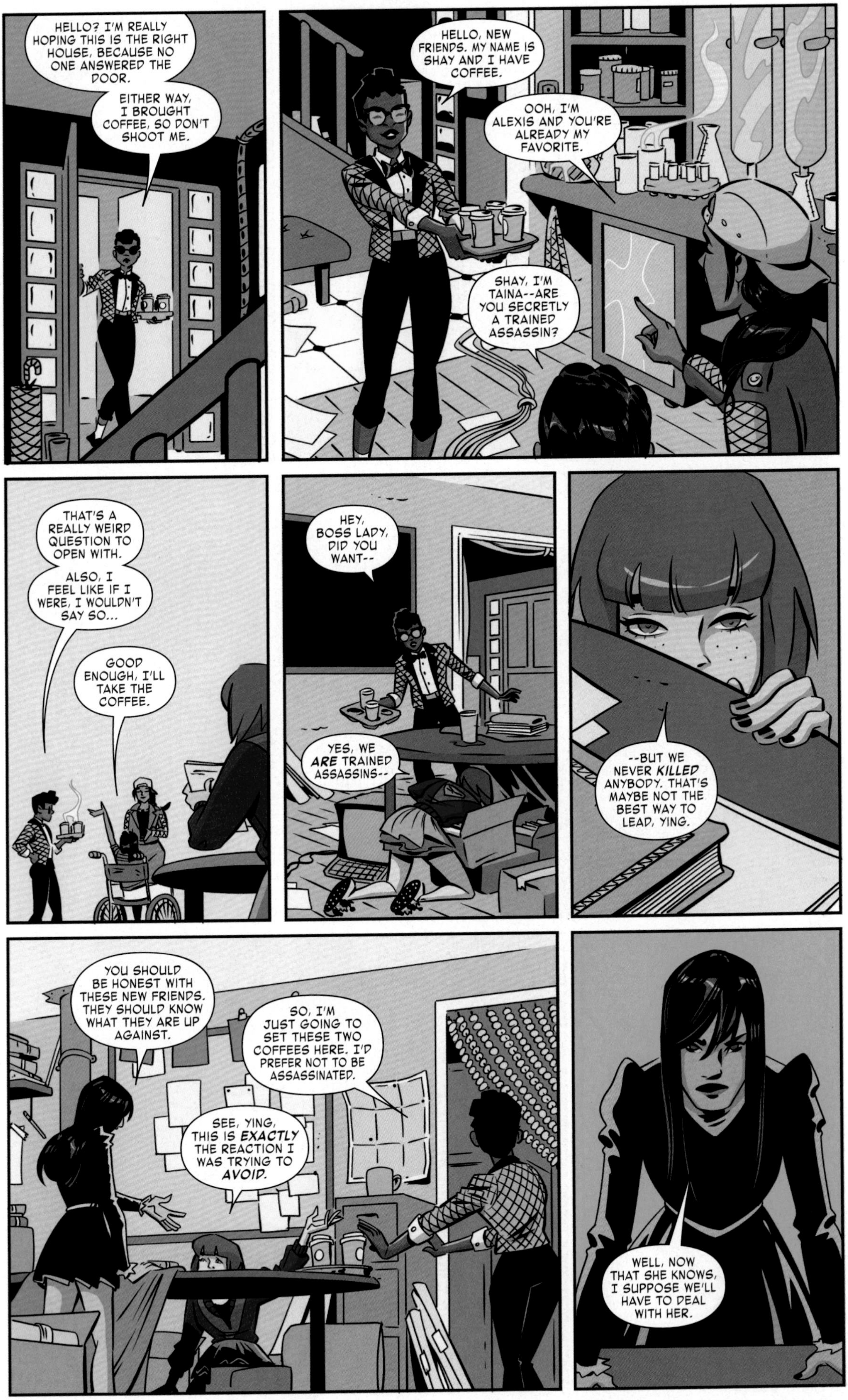
HELLO? I'M REALLY HOPING THIS IS THE RIGHT HOUSE, BECAUSE NO ONE ANSWERED THE DOOR.
EITHER WAY, I BROUGHT COFFEE, SO DON'T SHOOT ME.
HELLO, NEW FRIENDS. MY NAME IS SHAY AND I HAVE COFFEE.
OOH, I'M ALEXIS AND YOU'RE ALREADY MY FAVORITE.
SHAY, I'M TAINA--ARE YOU SECRETLY A TRAINED ASSASSIN?
THAT'S A REALLY WEIRD QUESTION TO OPEN WITH.
ALSO, I FEEL LIKE IF I WERE, I WOULDN'T SAY SO...
GOOD ENOUGH, I'LL TAKE THE COFFEE.
HEY, BOSS LADY, DID YOU WANT--
YES, WE ARE TRAINED ASSASSINS--
--BUT WE NEVER KILLED ANYBODY. THAT'S MAYBE NOT THE BEST WAY TO LEAD, YING.
YOU SHOULD BE HONEST WITH THESE NEW FRIENDS. THEY SHOULD KNOW WHAT THEY ARE UP AGAINST.
SO, I'M JUST GOING TO SET THESE TWO COFFEES HERE. I'D PREFER NOT TO BE ASSASSINATED.
SEE, YING, THIS IS EXACTLY THE REACTION I WAS TRYING TO AVOID.
WELL, NOW THAT SHE KNOWS, I SUPPOSE WE'LL HAVE TO DEAL WITH HER.

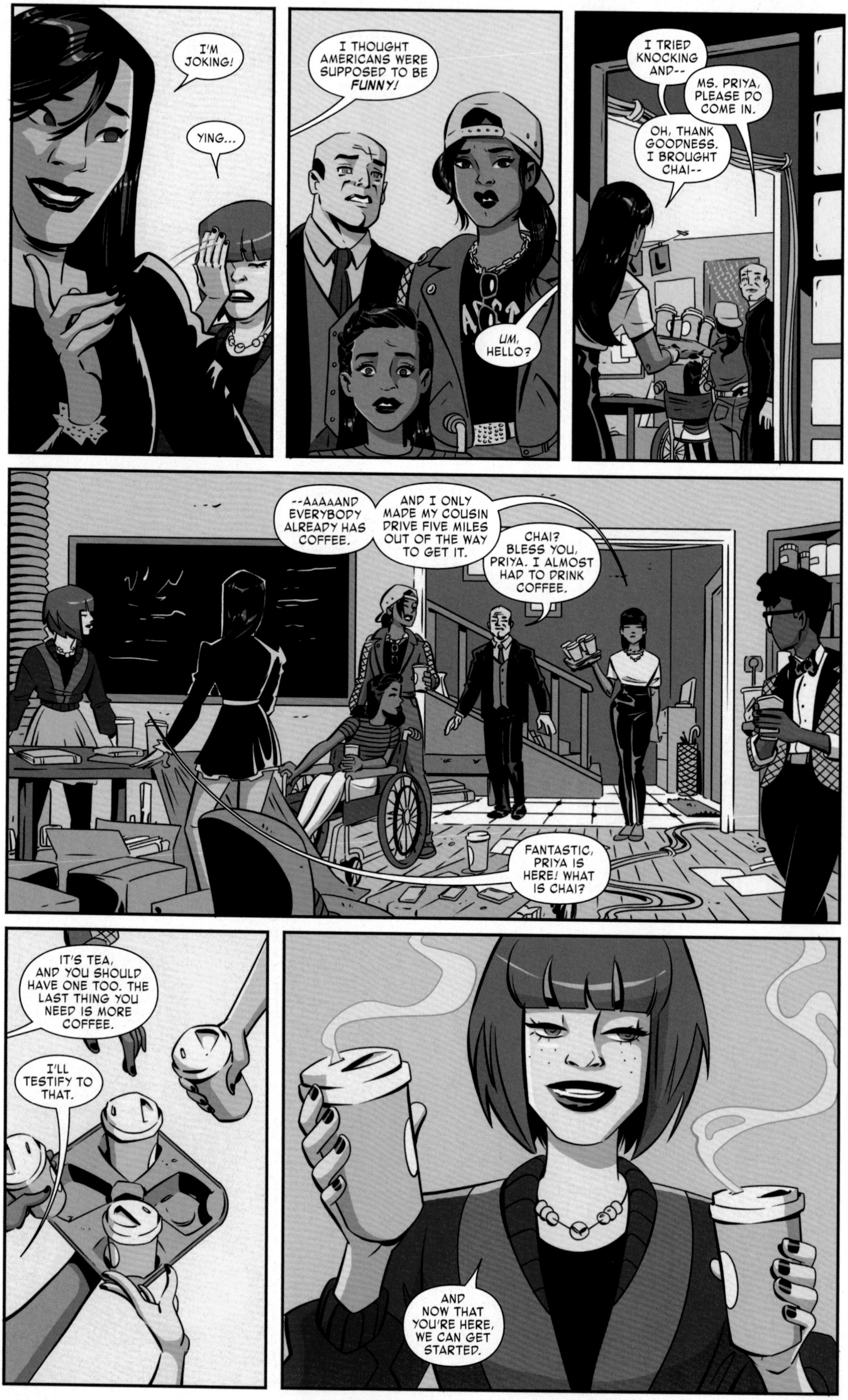
I'M JOKING!
YING...
I THOUGHT AMERICANS WERE SUPPOSED TO BE FUNNY!
UM, HELLO?
I TRIED KNOCKING AND--
MS. PRIYA, PLEASE DO COME IN.
OH, THANK GOODNESS. I BROUGHT CHAI--
--AAAAAND EVERYBODY ALREADY HAS COFFEE.
AND I ONLY MADE MY COUSIN DRIVE FIVE MILES OUT OF THE WAY TO GET IT.
CHAI? BLESS YOU, PRIYA. I ALMOST HAD TO DRINK COFFEE.
FANTASTIC, PRIYA IS HERE! WHAT IS CHAI?
IT'S TEA, AND YOU SHOULD HAVE ONE TOO. THE LAST THING YOU NEED IS MORE COFFEE.
I'LL TESTIFY TO THAT.
AND NOW THAT YOU'RE HERE, WE CAN GET STARTED.

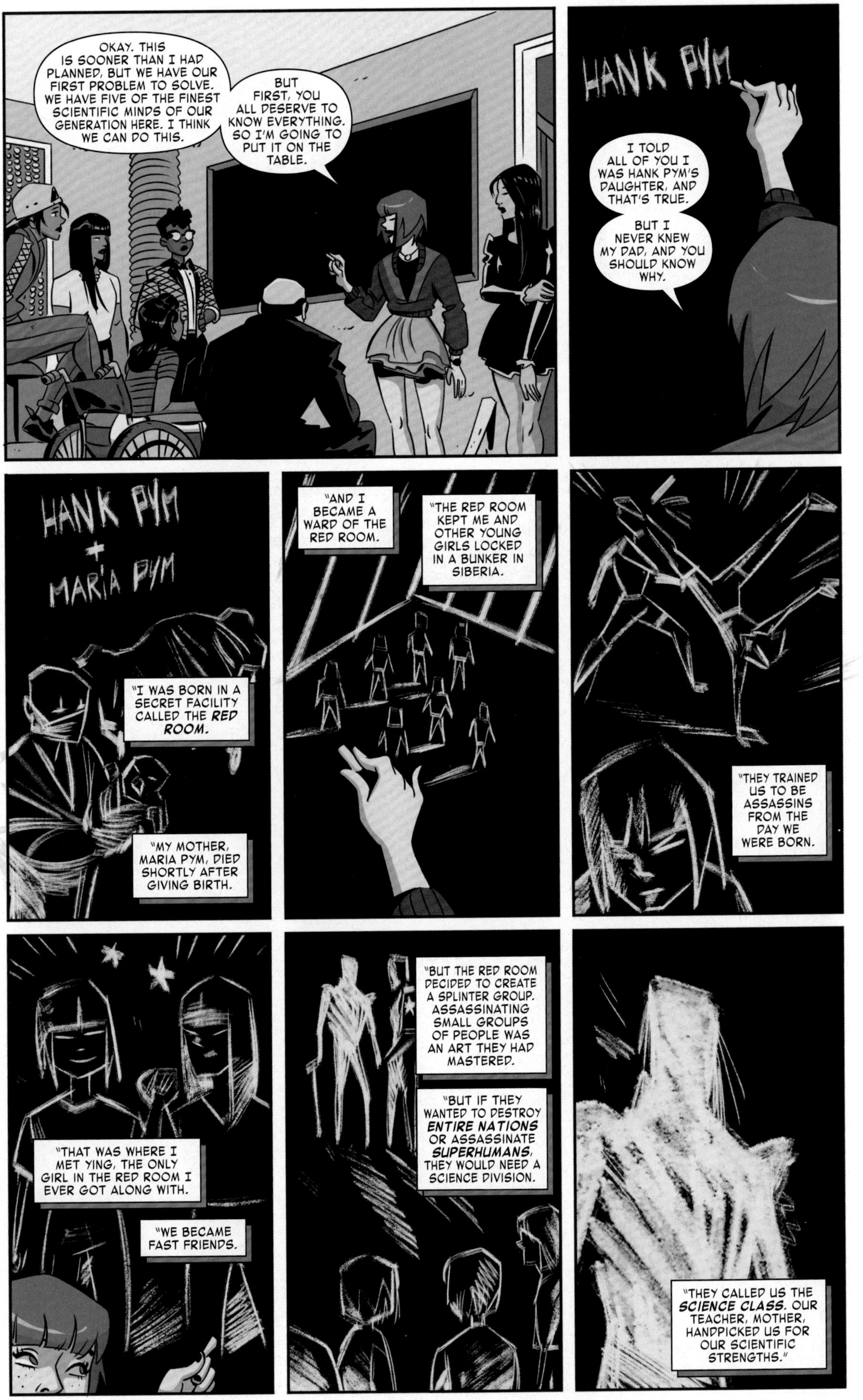
OKAY. THIS IS SOONER THAN I HAD PLANNED, BUT WE HAVE OUR FIRST PROBLEM TO SOLVE. WE HAVE FIVE OF THE FINEST SCIENTIFIC MINDS OF OUR GENERATION HERE. I THINK WE CAN DO THIS.
BUT FIRST, YOU ALL DESERVE TO KNOW EVERYTHING. SO I'M GOING TO PUT IT ON THE TABLE.
HANK PYM
I TOLD ALL OF YOU I WAS HANK PYM'S DAUGHTER, AND THAT'S TRUE.
BUT I NEVER KNEW MY DAD, AND YOU SHOULD KNOW WHY.
HANK PYM + MARIA PYM
"I WAS BORN IN A SECRET FACILITY CALLED THE *RED ROOM.*
"MY MOTHER, MARIA PYM, DIED SHORTLY AFTER GIVING BIRTH.
"AND I BECAME A WARD OF THE RED ROOM.
"THE RED ROOM KEPT ME AND OTHER YOUNG GIRLS LOCKED IN A BUNKER IN SIBERIA.
"THEY TRAINED US TO BE ASSASSINS FROM THE DAY WE WERE BORN.
"THAT WAS WHERE I MET YING, THE ONLY GIRL IN THE RED ROOM I EVER GOT ALONG WITH.
"WE BECAME FAST FRIENDS.
"BUT THE RED ROOM DECIDED TO CREATE A SPLINTER GROUP. ASSASSINATING SMALL GROUPS OF PEOPLE WAS AN ART THEY HAD MASTERED.
"BUT IF THEY WANTED TO DESTROY *ENTIRE NATIONS* OR ASSASSINATE *SUPERHUMANS*, THEY WOULD NEED A SCIENCE DIVISION.
"THEY CALLED US THE *SCIENCE CLASS*. OUR TEACHER, MOTHER, HANDPICKED US FOR OUR SCIENTIFIC STRENGTHS."

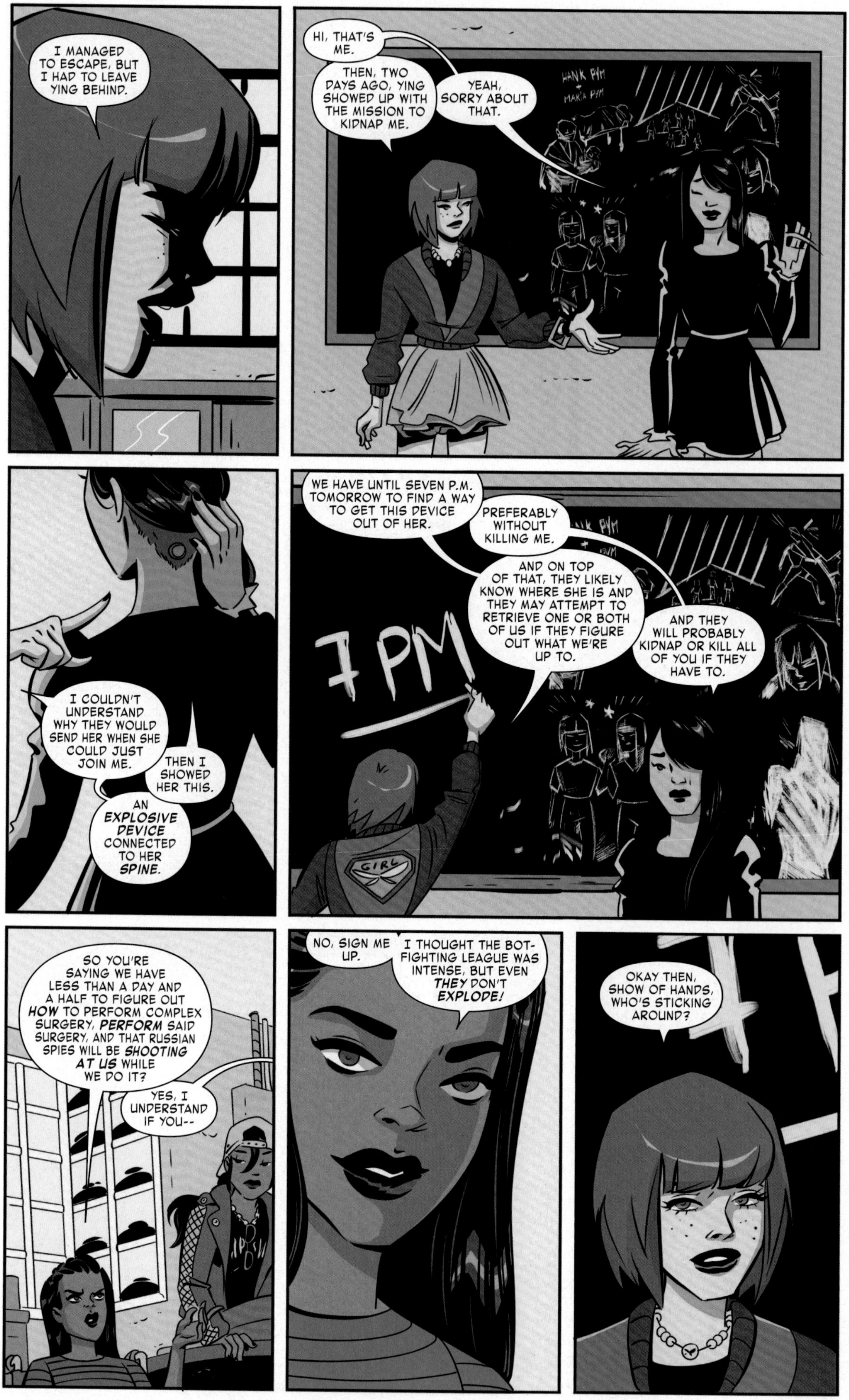
I MANAGED TO ESCAPE, BUT I HAD TO LEAVE YING BEHIND.
HI, THAT'S ME.
THEN, TWO DAYS AGO, YING SHOWED UP WITH THE MISSION TO KIDNAP ME.
YEAH, SORRY ABOUT THAT.
HANK PYM + MARIA PYM
I COULDN'T UNDERSTAND WHY THEY WOULD SEND HER WHEN SHE COULD JUST JOIN ME.
THEN I SHOWED HER THIS.
AN EXPLOSIVE DEVICE CONNECTED TO HER SPINE.
WE HAVE UNTIL SEVEN P.M. TOMORROW TO FIND A WAY TO GET THIS DEVICE OUT OF HER.
PREFERABLY WITHOUT KILLING ME.
AND ON TOP OF THAT, THEY LIKELY KNOW WHERE SHE IS AND THEY MAY ATTEMPT TO RETRIEVE ONE OR BOTH OF US IF THEY FIGURE OUT WHAT WE'RE UP TO.
AND THEY WILL PROBABLY KIDNAP OR KILL ALL OF YOU IF THEY HAVE TO.
7 PM
GIRL
SO YOU'RE SAYING WE HAVE LESS THAN A DAY AND A HALF TO FIGURE OUT HOW TO PERFORM COMPLEX SURGERY, PERFORM SAID SURGERY, AND THAT RUSSIAN SPIES WILL BE SHOOTING AT US WHILE WE DO IT?
YES, I UNDERSTAND IF YOU--
NO, SIGN ME UP.
I THOUGHT THE BOT-FIGHTING LEAGUE WAS INTENSE, BUT EVEN THEY DON'T EXPLODE!
OKAY THEN, SHOW OF HANDS, WHO'S STICKING AROUND?

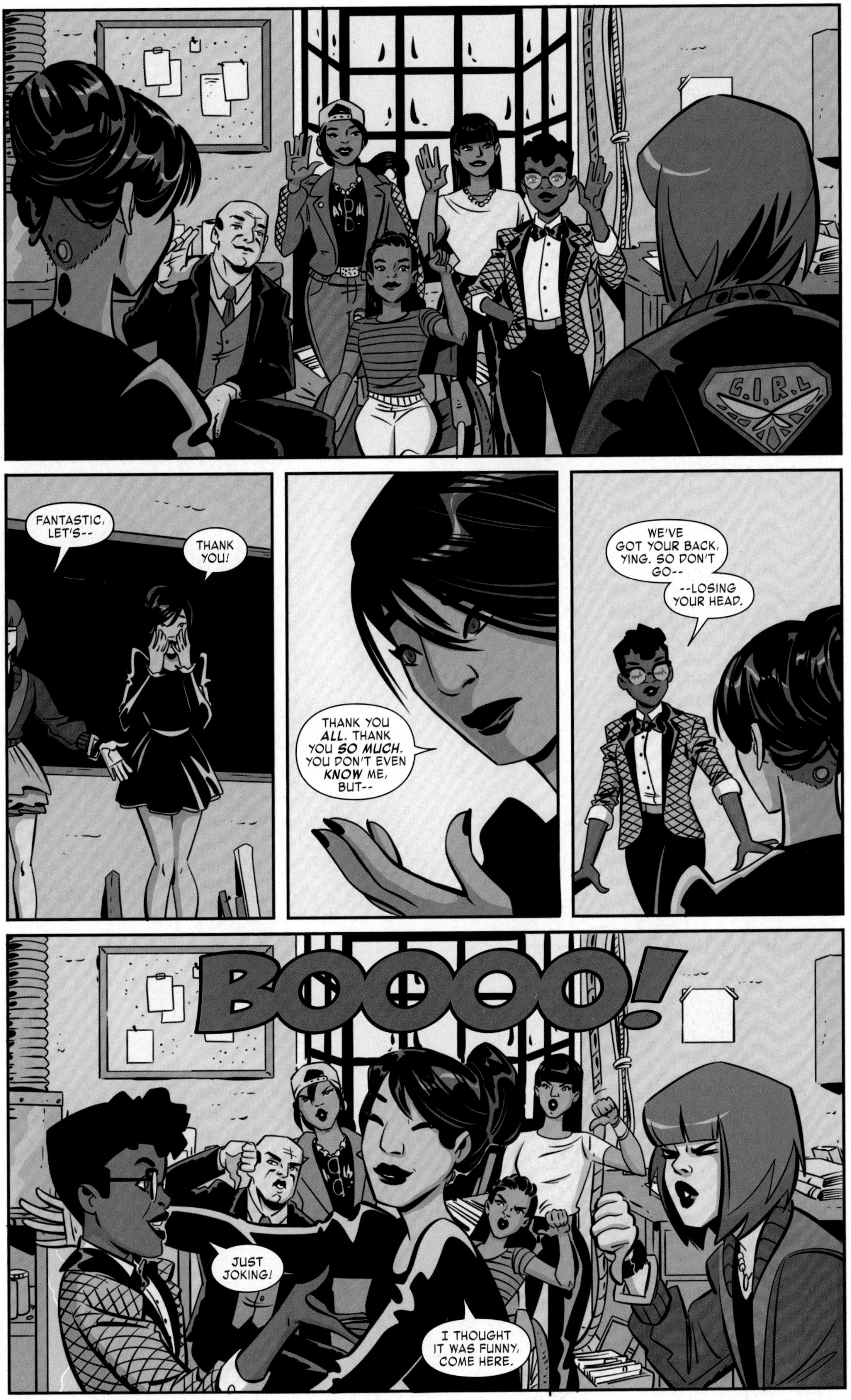
FANTASTIC, LET'S--
THANK YOU!
THANK YOU ALL. THANK YOU SO MUCH. YOU DON'T EVEN KNOW ME, BUT--
WE'VE GOT YOUR BACK, YING. SO DON'T GO--
--LOSING YOUR HEAD.
BOOOO!
JUST JOKING!
I THOUGHT IT WAS FUNNY, COME HERE.

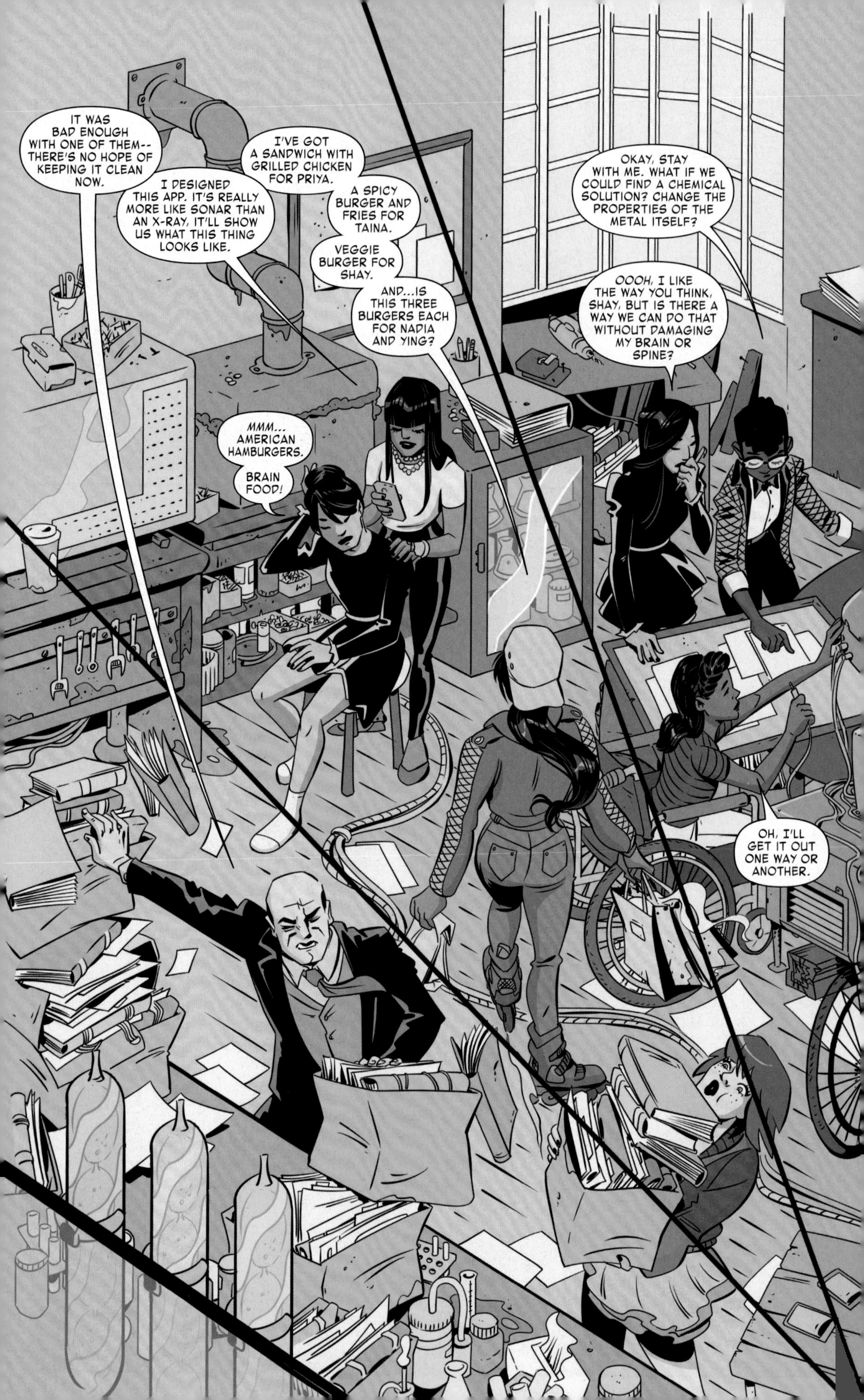
IT WAS BAD ENOUGH WITH ONE OF THEM-- THERE'S NO HOPE OF KEEPING IT CLEAN NOW.
I DESIGNED THIS APP. IT'S REALLY MORE LIKE SONAR THAN AN X-RAY. IT'LL SHOW US WHAT THIS THING LOOKS LIKE.
I'VE GOT A SANDWICH WITH GRILLED CHICKEN FOR PRIYA.
A SPICY BURGER AND FRIES FOR TAINA.
VEGGIE BURGER FOR SHAY.
AND...IS THIS THREE BURGERS EACH FOR NADIA AND YING?
MMM... AMERICAN HAMBURGERS.
BRAIN FOOD!
OKAY, STAY WITH ME. WHAT IF WE COULD FIND A CHEMICAL SOLUTION? CHANGE THE PROPERTIES OF THE METAL ITSELF?
OOOH, I LIKE THE WAY YOU THINK, SHAY, BUT IS THERE A WAY WE CAN DO THAT WITHOUT DAMAGING MY BRAIN OR SPINE?
OH, I'LL GET IT OUT ONE WAY OR ANOTHER.

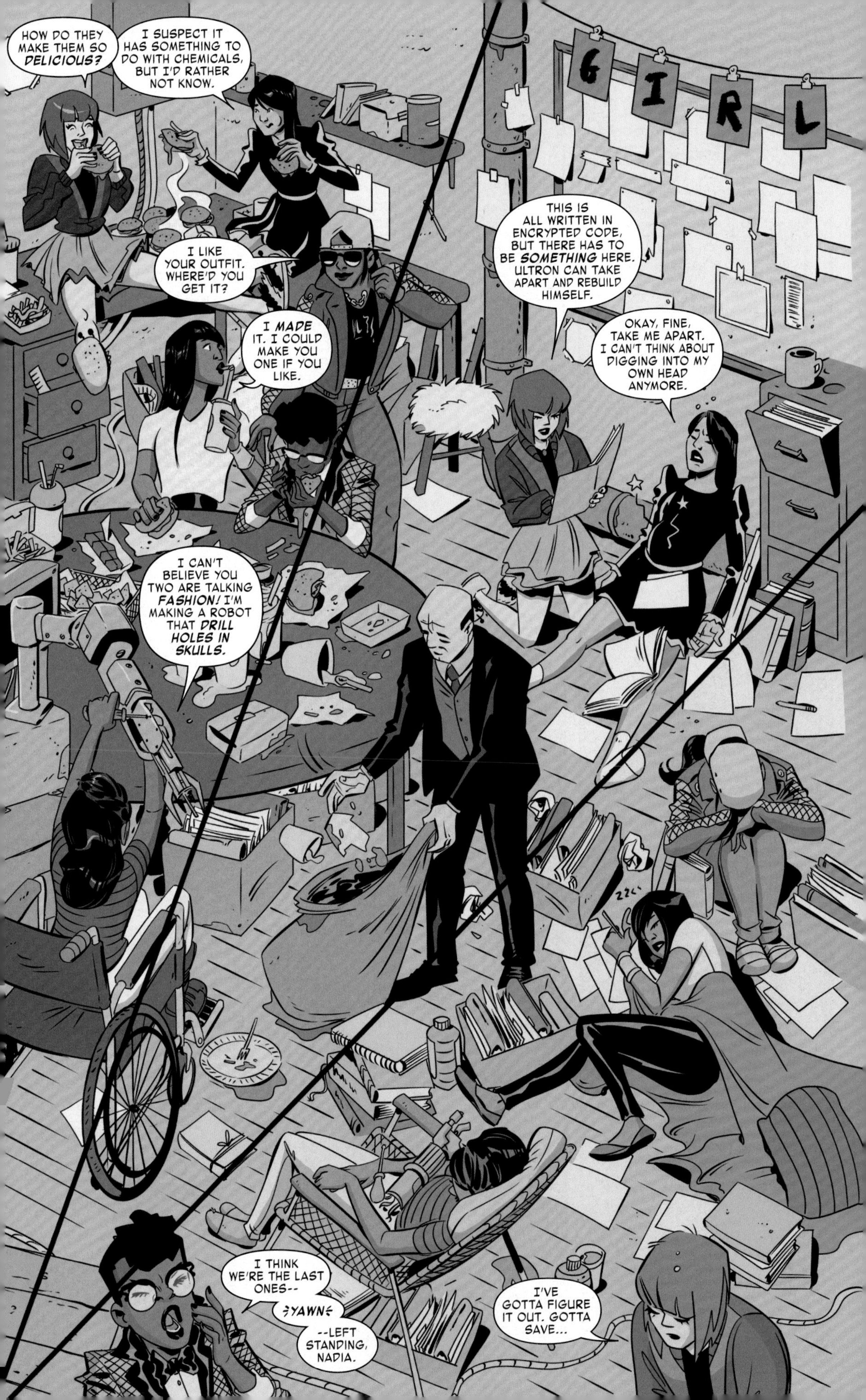
HOW DO THEY MAKE THEM SO DELICIOUS?
I SUSPECT IT HAS SOMETHING TO DO WITH CHEMICALS, BUT I'D RATHER NOT KNOW.
I LIKE YOUR OUTFIT. WHERE'D YOU GET IT?
I MADE IT. I COULD MAKE YOU ONE IF YOU LIKE.
THIS IS ALL WRITTEN IN ENCRYPTED CODE, BUT THERE HAS TO BE SOMETHING HERE. ULTRON CAN TAKE APART AND REBUILD HIMSELF.
OKAY, FINE, TAKE ME APART. I CAN'T THINK ABOUT DIGGING INTO MY OWN HEAD ANYMORE.
I CAN'T BELIEVE YOU TWO ARE TALKING FASHION! I'M MAKING A ROBOT THAT DRILL HOLES IN SKULLS.
ZZZ
I THINK WE'RE THE LAST ONES--
YAWN
--LEFT STANDING, NADIA.
I'VE GOTTA FIGURE IT OUT. GOTTA SAVE...

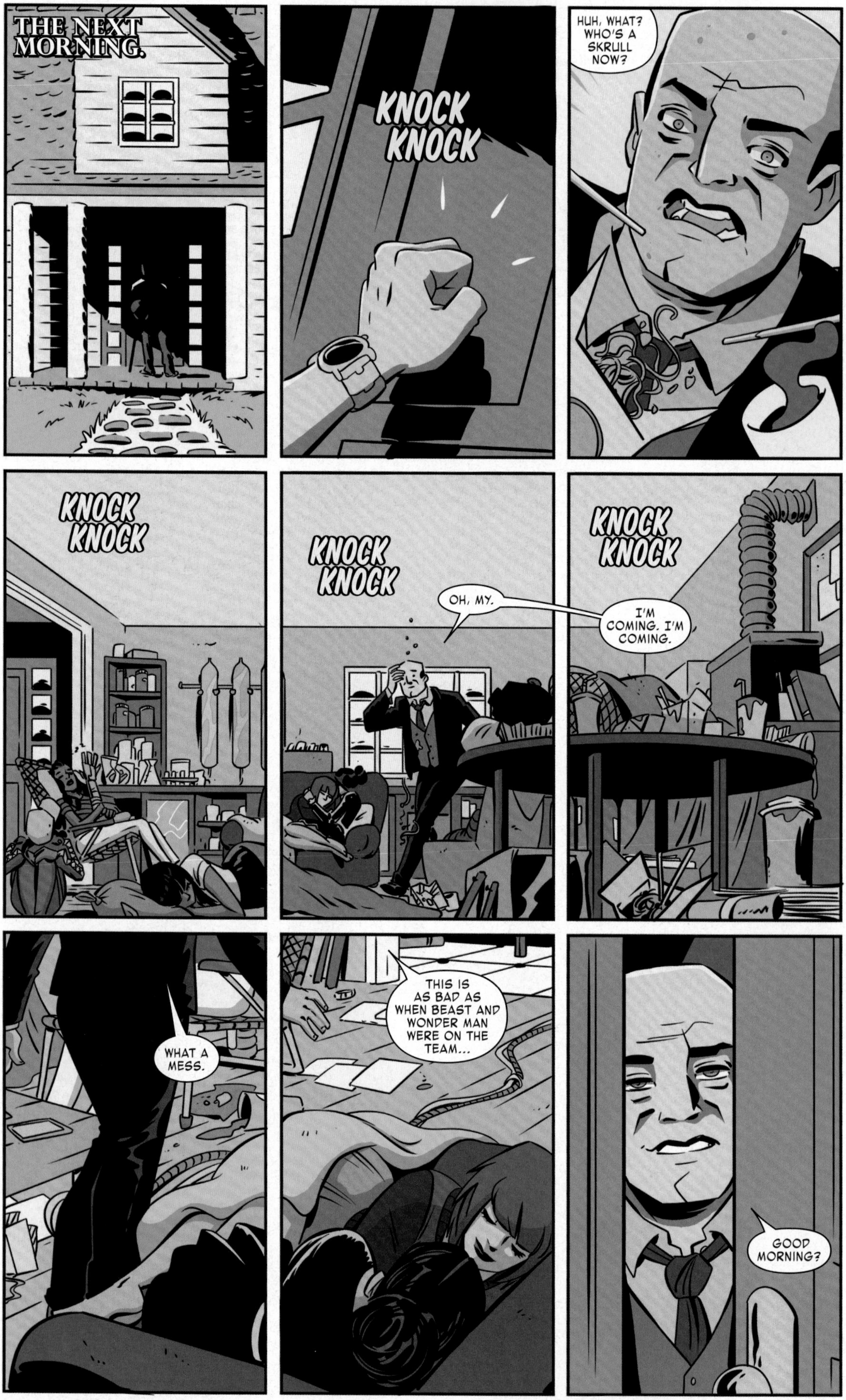
THE NEXT MORNING.
KNOCK KNOCK
HUH, WHAT? WHO'S A SKRULL NOW?
KNOCK KNOCK
KNOCK KNOCK
OH, MY.
KNOCK KNOCK
I'M COMING. I'M COMING.
WHAT A MESS.
THIS IS AS BAD AS WHEN BEAST AND WONDER MAN WERE ON THE TEAM...
GOOD MORNING?

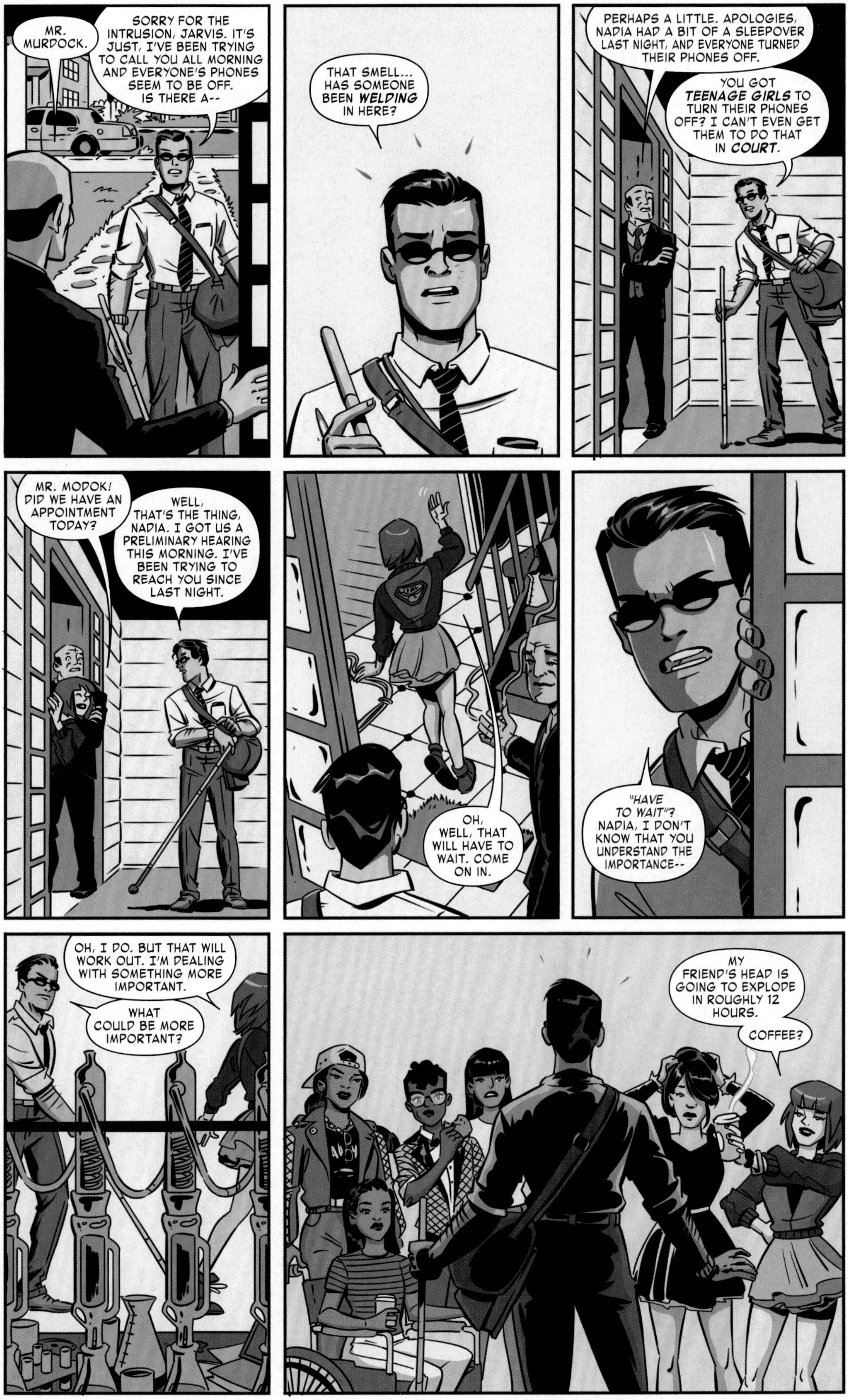
MR. MURDOCK.
SORRY FOR THE INTRUSION, JARVIS. IT'S JUST, I'VE BEEN TRYING TO CALL YOU ALL MORNING AND EVERYONE'S PHONES SEEM TO BE OFF. IS THERE A--
THAT SMELL... HAS SOMEONE BEEN WELDING IN HERE?
PERHAPS A LITTLE. APOLOGIES, NADIA HAD A BIT OF A SLEEPOVER LAST NIGHT, AND EVERYONE TURNED THEIR PHONES OFF.
YOU GOT TEENAGE GIRLS TO TURN THEIR PHONES OFF? I CAN'T EVEN GET THEM TO DO THAT IN COURT.
MR. MODOK! DID WE HAVE AN APPOINTMENT TODAY?
WELL, THAT'S THE THING, NADIA. I GOT US A PRELIMINARY HEARING THIS MORNING. I'VE BEEN TRYING TO REACH YOU SINCE LAST NIGHT.
OH, WELL, THAT WILL HAVE TO WAIT. COME ON IN.
"HAVE TO WAIT"? NADIA, I DON'T KNOW THAT YOU UNDERSTAND THE IMPORTANCE--
OH, I DO. BUT THAT WILL WORK OUT. I'M DEALING WITH SOMETHING MORE IMPORTANT.
WHAT COULD BE MORE IMPORTANT?
MY FRIEND'S HEAD IS GOING TO EXPLODE IN ROUGHLY 12 HOURS.
COFFEE?

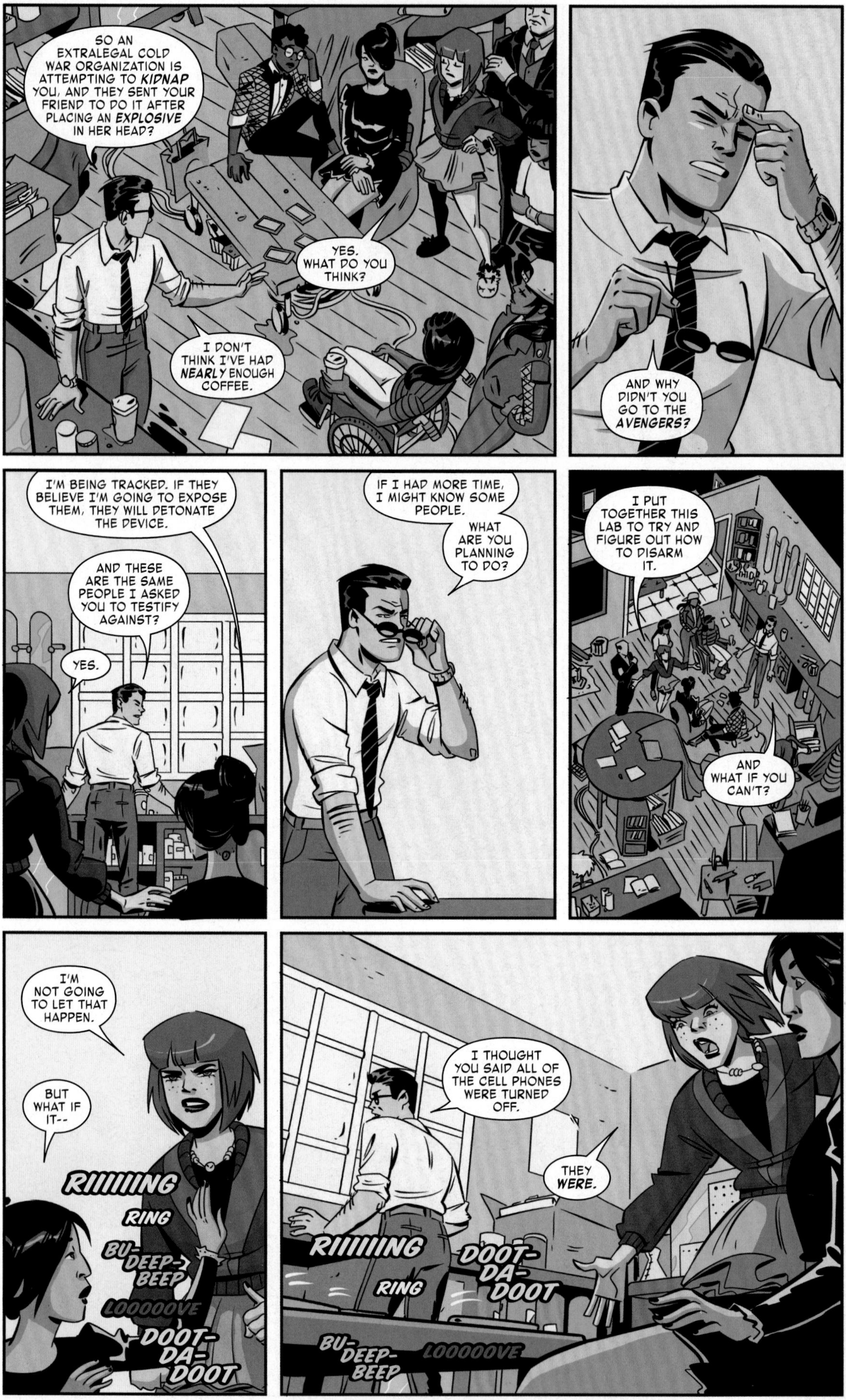
SO AN EXTRALEGAL COLD WAR ORGANIZATION IS ATTEMPTING TO *KIDNAP* YOU, AND THEY SENT YOUR FRIEND TO DO IT AFTER PLACING AN *EXPLOSIVE* IN HER HEAD?
YES. WHAT DO YOU THINK?
I DON'T THINK I'VE HAD *NEARLY* ENOUGH COFFEE.
AND WHY DIDN'T YOU GO TO THE *AVENGERS?*
I'M BEING TRACKED. IF THEY BELIEVE I'M GOING TO EXPOSE THEM, THEY WILL DETONATE THE DEVICE.
AND THESE ARE THE SAME PEOPLE I ASKED YOU TO TESTIFY AGAINST?
YES.
IF I HAD MORE TIME, I MIGHT KNOW SOME PEOPLE.
WHAT ARE YOU PLANNING TO DO?
I PUT TOGETHER THIS LAB TO TRY AND FIGURE OUT HOW TO DISARM IT.
AND WHAT IF YOU CAN'T?
I'M NOT GOING TO LET THAT HAPPEN.
BUT WHAT IF IT--
RIIIIIING
RING
BU-DEEP-BEEP
LOOOOOVE
DOOT-DA-DOOT
I THOUGHT YOU SAID ALL OF THE CELL PHONES WERE TURNED OFF.
THEY *WERE.*
RIIIIIING
RING
DOOT-DA-DOOT
BU-DEEP-BEEP
LOOOOOVE

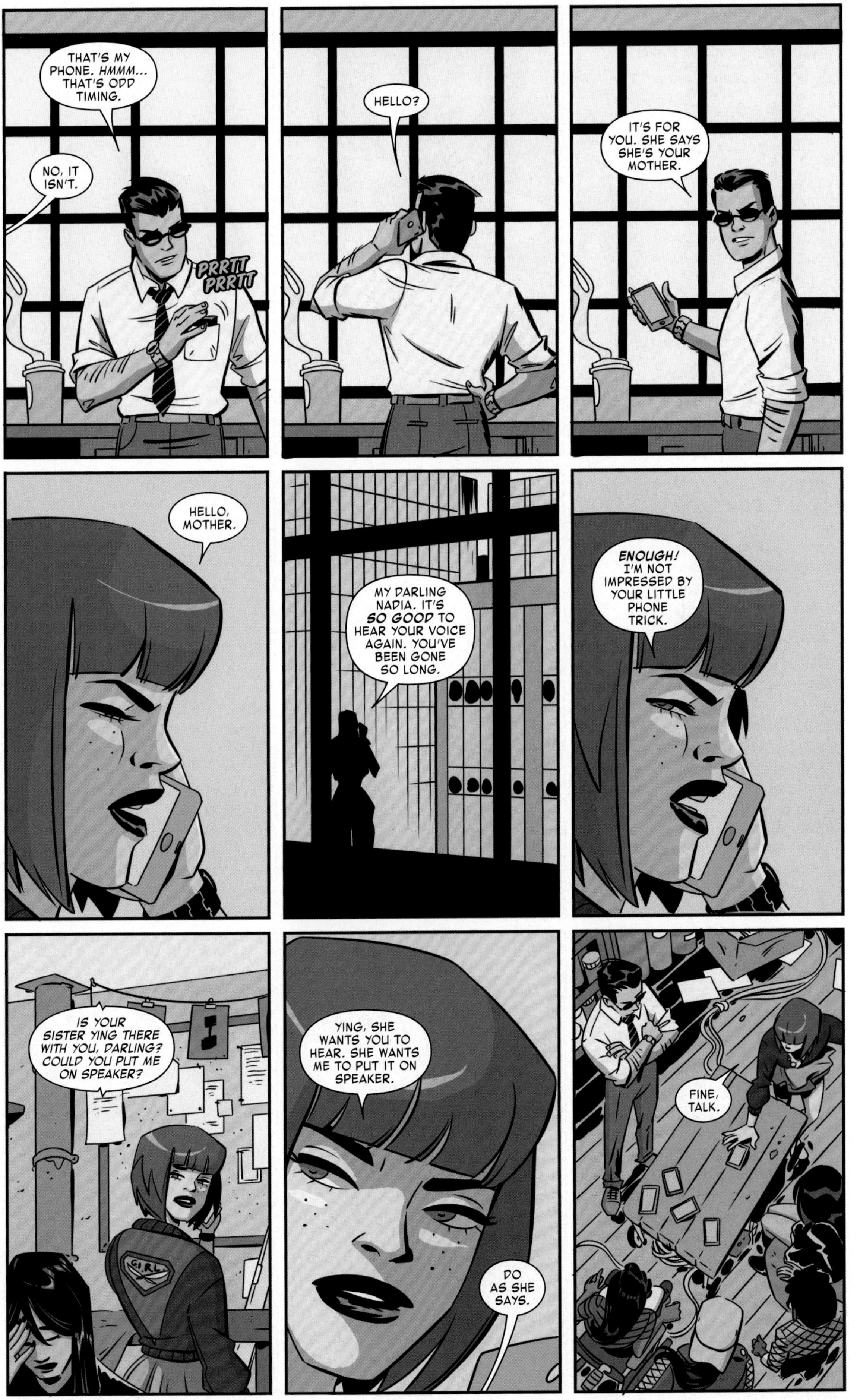
THAT'S MY PHONE. HMMM... THAT'S ODD TIMING.
NO, IT ISN'T.
PRRTT PRRTT
HELLO?
IT'S FOR YOU. SHE SAYS SHE'S YOUR MOTHER.
HELLO, MOTHER.
MY DARLING NADIA. IT'S SO GOOD TO HEAR YOUR VOICE AGAIN. YOU'VE BEEN GONE SO LONG.
ENOUGH! I'M NOT IMPRESSED BY YOUR LITTLE PHONE TRICK.
IS YOUR SISTER YING THERE WITH YOU, DARLING? COULD YOU PUT ME ON SPEAKER?
G.I.R.L.
YING, SHE WANTS YOU TO HEAR. SHE WANTS ME TO PUT IT ON SPEAKER.
DO AS SHE SAYS.
FINE, TALK.

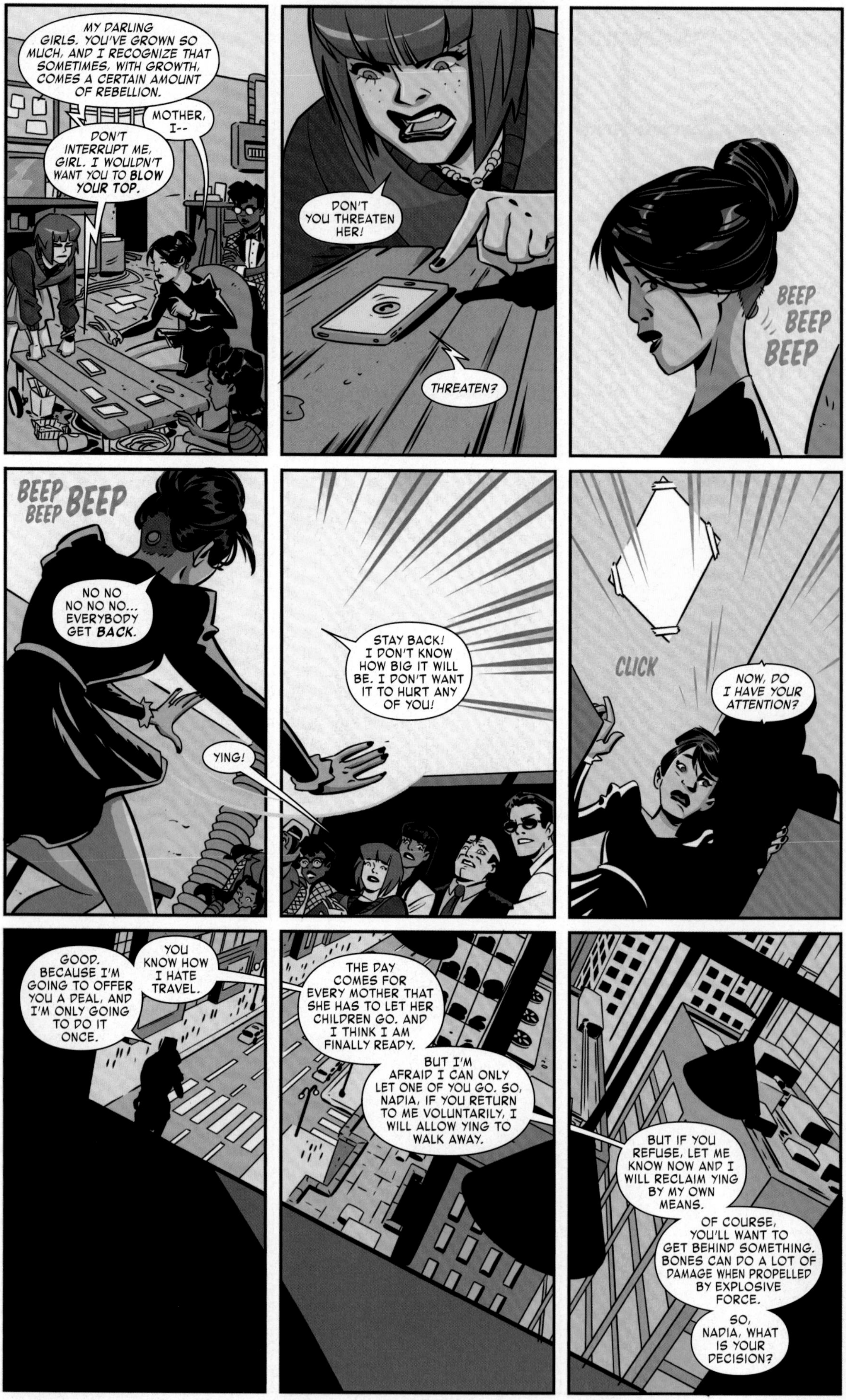
MY DARLING GIRLS. YOU'VE GROWN SO MUCH, AND I RECOGNIZE THAT SOMETIMES, WITH GROWTH, COMES A CERTAIN AMOUNT OF REBELLION.
MOTHER, I--
DON'T INTERRUPT ME, GIRL. I WOULDN'T WANT YOU TO BLOW YOUR TOP.
DON'T YOU THREATEN HER!
THREATEN?
BEEP BEEP BEEP
BEEP BEEP BEEP
NO NO NO NO NO... EVERYBODY GET BACK.
YING!
STAY BACK! I DON'T KNOW HOW BIG IT WILL BE. I DON'T WANT IT TO HURT ANY OF YOU!
CLICK
NOW, DO I HAVE YOUR ATTENTION?
GOOD. BECAUSE I'M GOING TO OFFER YOU A DEAL, AND I'M ONLY GOING TO DO IT ONCE.
YOU KNOW HOW I HATE TRAVEL.
THE DAY COMES FOR EVERY MOTHER THAT SHE HAS TO LET HER CHILDREN GO. AND I THINK I AM FINALLY READY.
BUT I'M AFRAID I CAN ONLY LET ONE OF YOU GO. SO, NADIA, IF YOU RETURN TO ME VOLUNTARILY, I WILL ALLOW YING TO WALK AWAY.
BUT IF YOU REFUSE, LET ME KNOW NOW AND I WILL RECLAIM YING BY MY OWN MEANS.
OF COURSE, YOU'LL WANT TO GET BEHIND SOMETHING. BONES CAN DO A LOT OF DAMAGE WHEN PROPELLED BY EXPLOSIVE FORCE.
SO, NADIA, WHAT IS YOUR DECISION?

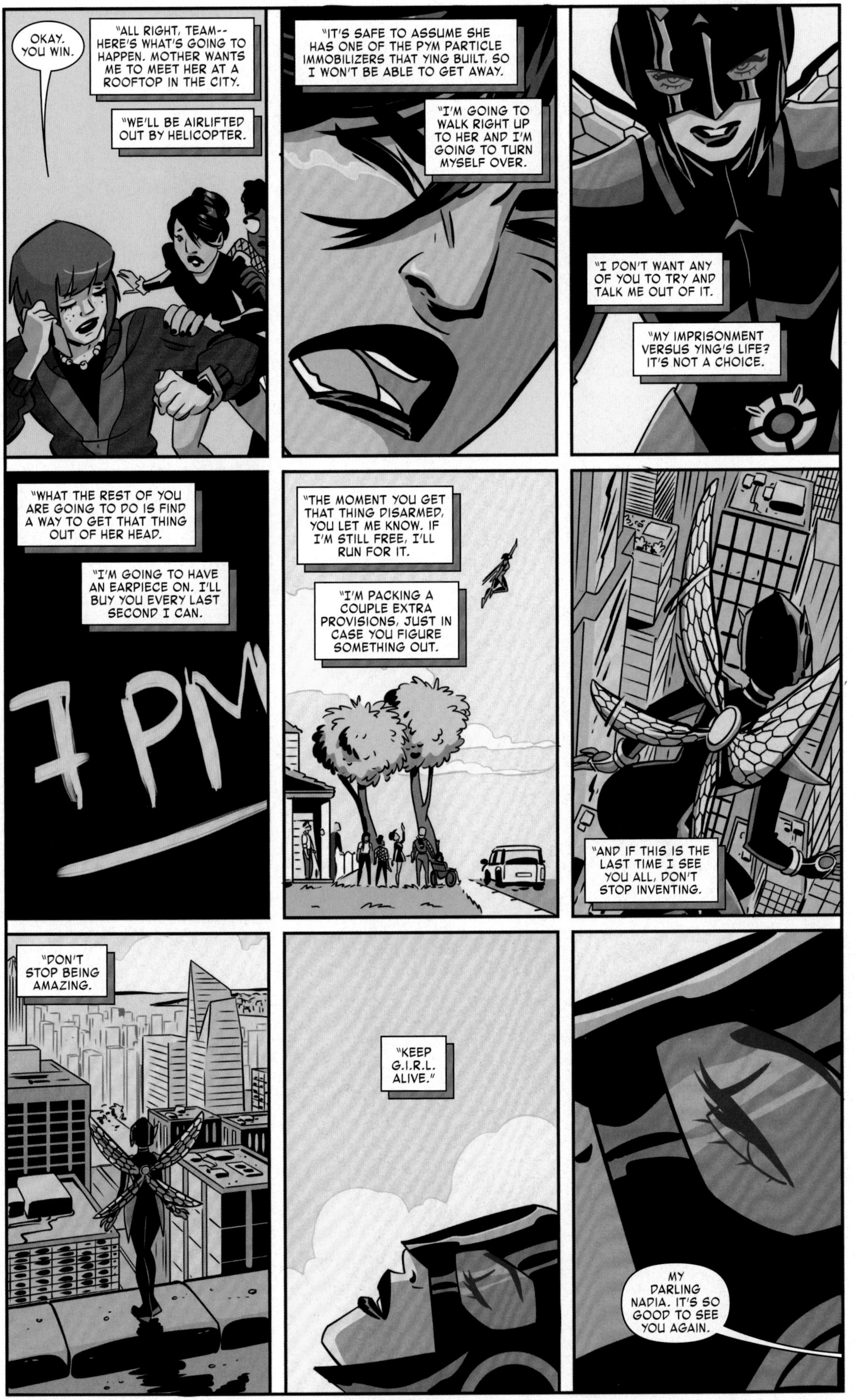
OKAY. YOU WIN.
"ALL RIGHT, TEAM-- HERE'S WHAT'S GOING TO HAPPEN. MOTHER WANTS ME TO MEET HER AT A ROOFTOP IN THE CITY.
"WE'LL BE AIRLIFTED OUT BY HELICOPTER.
"IT'S SAFE TO ASSUME SHE HAS ONE OF THE PYM PARTICLE IMMOBILIZERS THAT YING BUILT, SO I WON'T BE ABLE TO GET AWAY.
"I'M GOING TO WALK RIGHT UP TO HER AND I'M GOING TO TURN MYSELF OVER.
"I DON'T WANT ANY OF YOU TO TRY AND TALK ME OUT OF IT.
"MY IMPRISONMENT VERSUS YING'S LIFE? IT'S NOT A CHOICE.
"WHAT THE REST OF YOU ARE GOING TO DO IS FIND A WAY TO GET THAT THING OUT OF HER HEAD.
"I'M GOING TO HAVE AN EARPIECE ON. I'LL BUY YOU EVERY LAST SECOND I CAN.
7 PM
"THE MOMENT YOU GET THAT THING DISARMED, YOU LET ME KNOW. IF I'M STILL FREE, I'LL RUN FOR IT.
"I'M PACKING A COUPLE EXTRA PROVISIONS, JUST IN CASE YOU FIGURE SOMETHING OUT.
"AND IF THIS IS THE LAST TIME I SEE YOU ALL, DON'T STOP INVENTING.
"DON'T STOP BEING AMAZING.
"KEEP G.I.R.L. ALIVE."
MY DARLING NADIA. IT'S SO GOOD TO SEE YOU AGAIN.

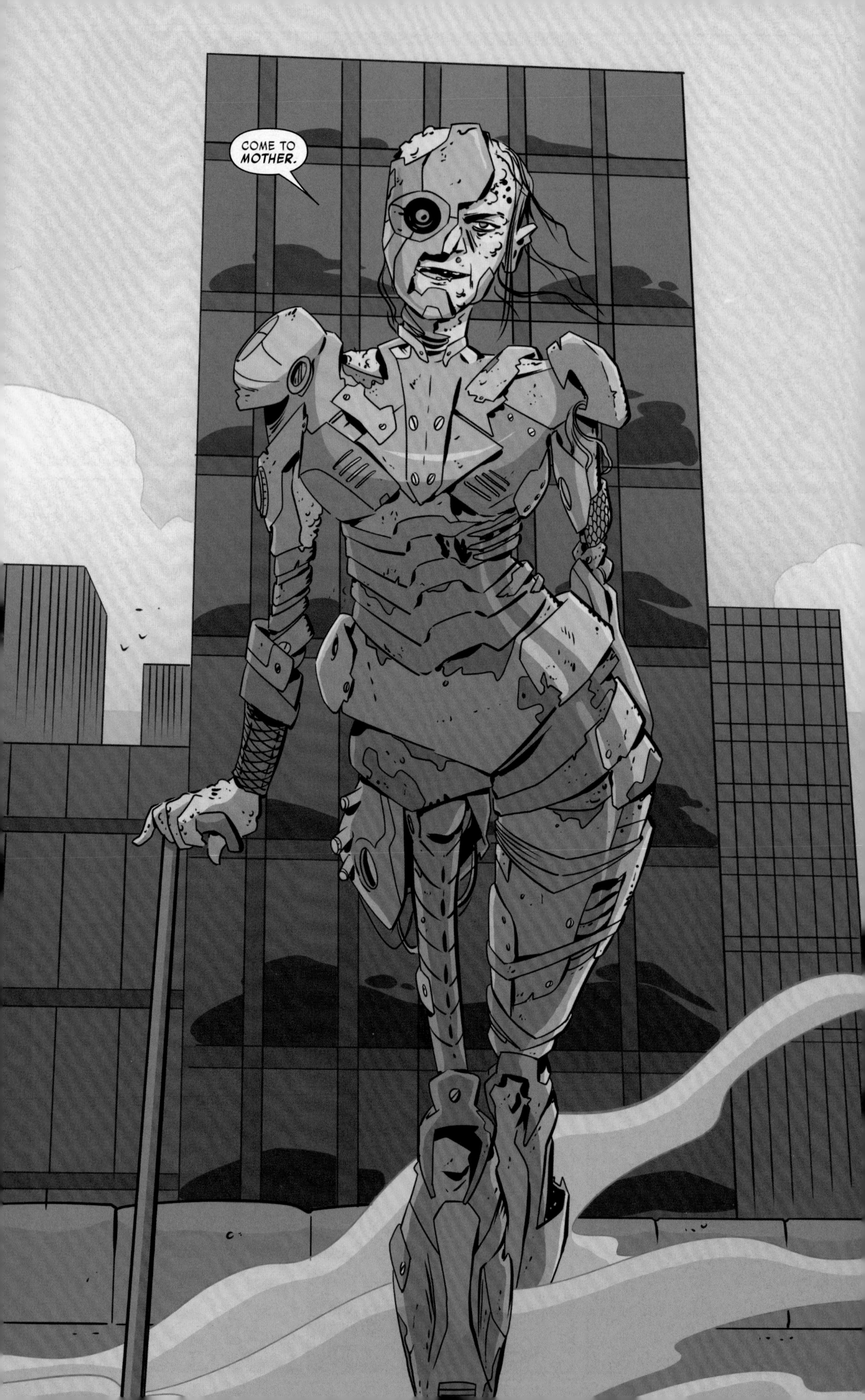
COME TO MOTHER.

6

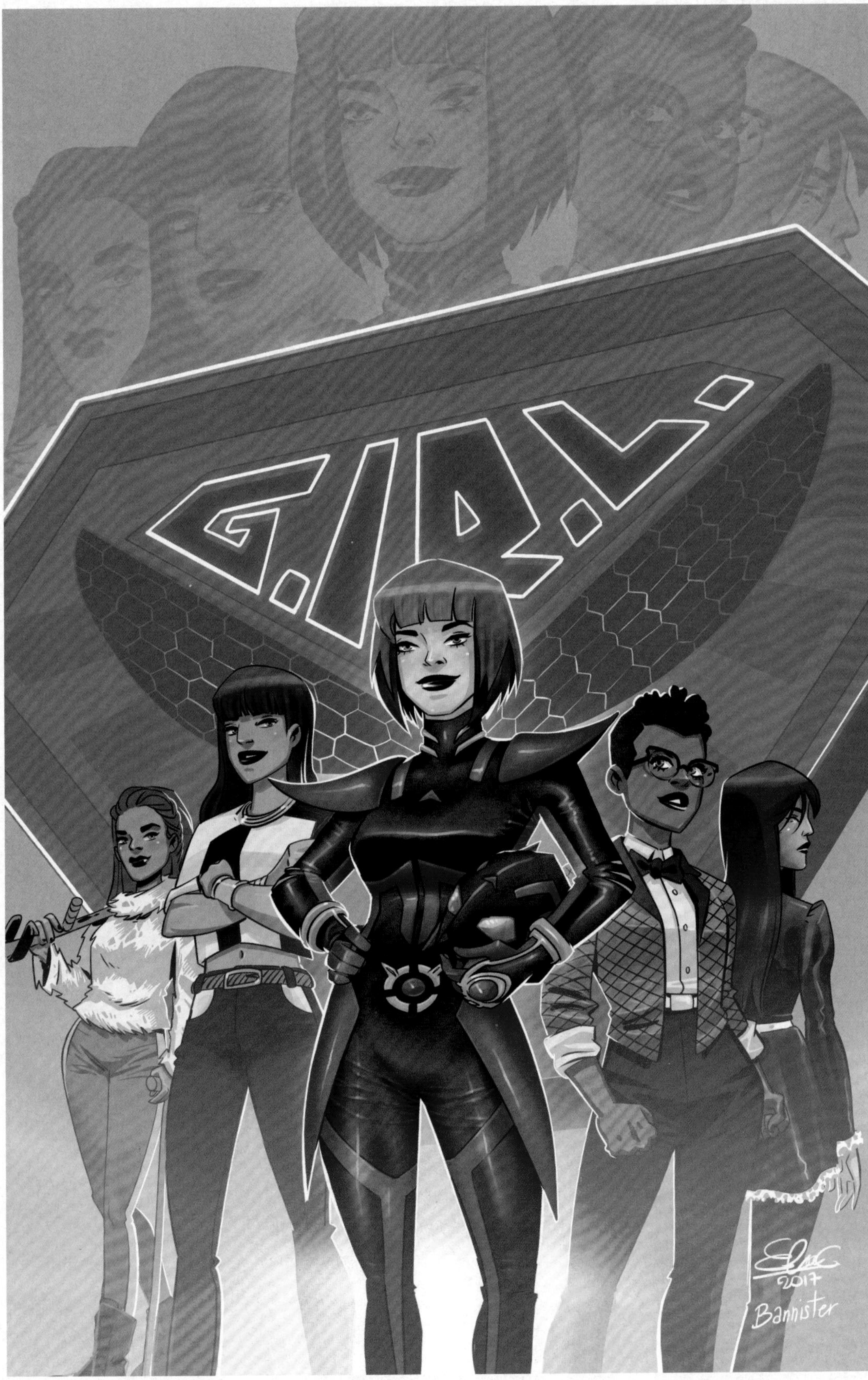
G.I.R.L.
2017
Bannister

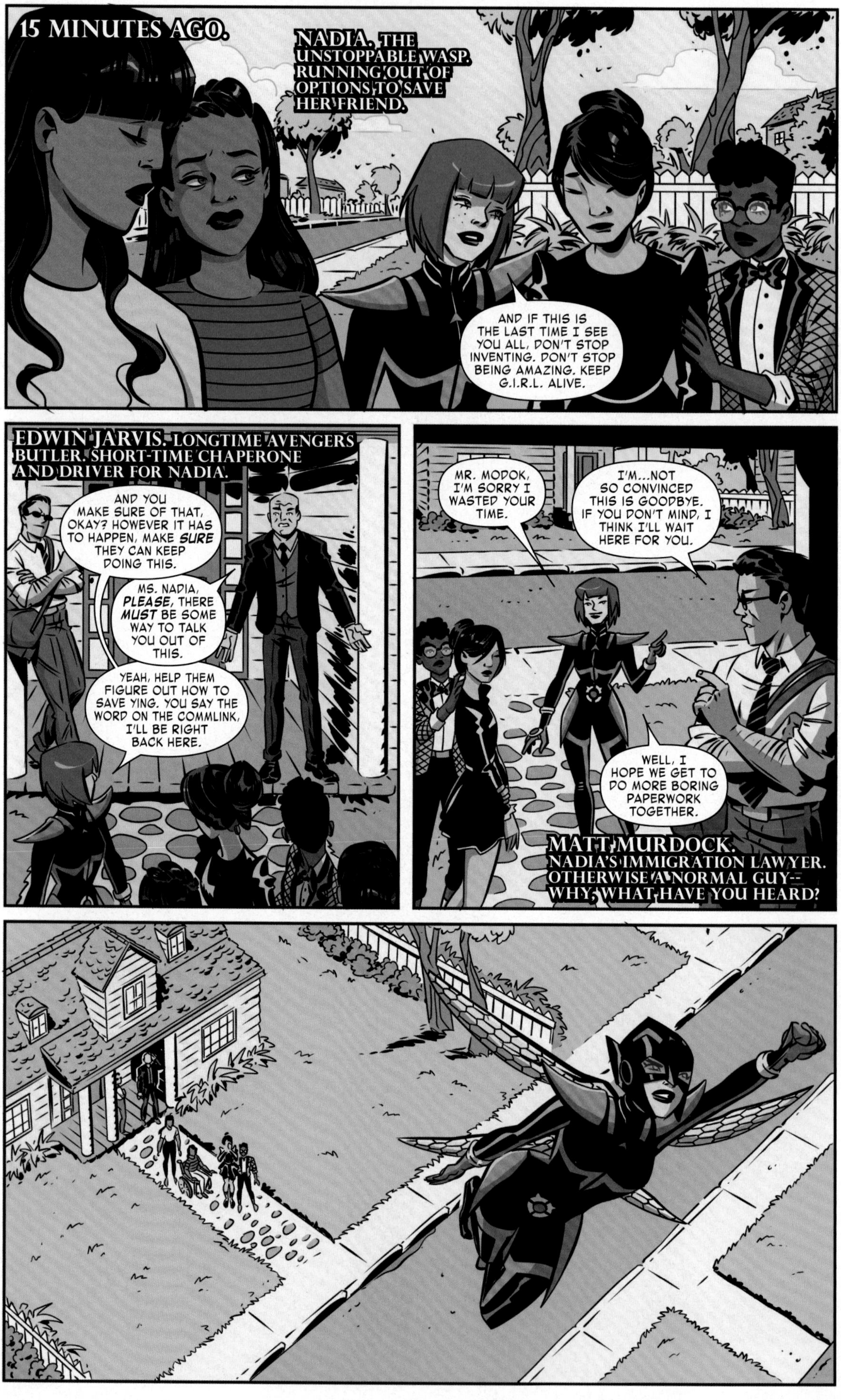

15 MINUTES AGO.
NADIA. THE UNSTOPPABLE WASP. RUNNING OUT OF OPTIONS TO SAVE HER FRIEND.
AND IF THIS IS THE LAST TIME I SEE YOU ALL, DON'T STOP INVENTING. DON'T STOP BEING AMAZING. KEEP G.I.R.L. ALIVE.
EDWIN JARVIS. LONGTIME AVENGERS BUTLER. SHORT-TIME CHAPERONE AND DRIVER FOR NADIA.
AND YOU MAKE SURE OF THAT, OKAY? HOWEVER IT HAS TO HAPPEN, MAKE SURE THEY CAN KEEP DOING THIS.
MS. NADIA, PLEASE, THERE MUST BE SOME WAY TO TALK YOU OUT OF THIS.
YEAH, HELP THEM FIGURE OUT HOW TO SAVE YING. YOU SAY THE WORD ON THE COMMLINK, I'LL BE RIGHT BACK HERE.
MR. MODOK, I'M SORRY I WASTED YOUR TIME.
I'M...NOT SO CONVINCED THIS IS GOODBYE. IF YOU DON'T MIND, I THINK I'LL WAIT HERE FOR YOU.
WELL, I HOPE WE GET TO DO MORE BORING PAPERWORK TOGETHER.
MATT MURDOCK. NADIA'S IMMIGRATION LAWYER. OTHERWISE A NORMAL GUY-- WHY, WHAT HAVE YOU HEARD?

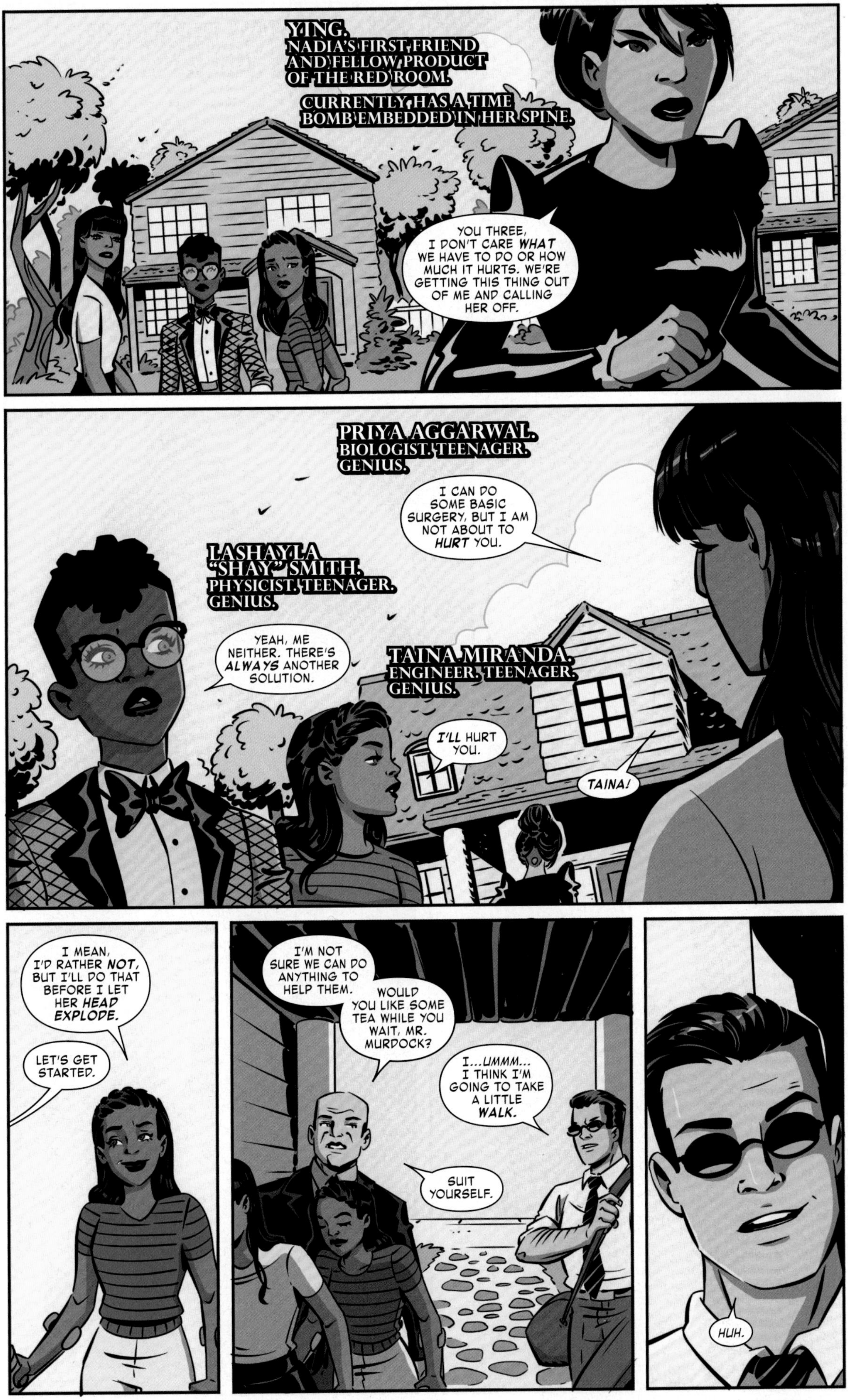

YING.
NADIA'S FIRST FRIEND AND FELLOW PRODUCT OF THE RED ROOM.
CURRENTLY HAS A TIME BOMB EMBEDDED IN HER SPINE.
YOU THREE, I DON'T CARE WHAT WE HAVE TO DO OR HOW MUCH IT HURTS. WE'RE GETTING THIS THING OUT OF ME AND CALLING HER OFF.
PRIYA AGGARWAL.
BIOLOGIST. TEENAGER. GENIUS.
I CAN DO SOME BASIC SURGERY, BUT I AM NOT ABOUT TO HURT YOU.
LASHAYLA "SHAY" SMITH.
PHYSICIST. TEENAGER. GENIUS.
YEAH, ME NEITHER. THERE'S ALWAYS ANOTHER SOLUTION.
TAINA MIRANDA.
ENGINEER. TEENAGER. GENIUS.
I'LL HURT YOU.
TAINA!
I MEAN, I'D RATHER NOT, BUT I'LL DO THAT BEFORE I LET HER HEAD EXPLODE.
LET'S GET STARTED.
I'M NOT SURE WE CAN DO ANYTHING TO HELP THEM.
WOULD YOU LIKE SOME TEA WHILE YOU WAIT, MR. MURDOCK?
I...UMMM... I THINK I'M GOING TO TAKE A LITTLE WALK.
SUIT YOURSELF.
HUH.

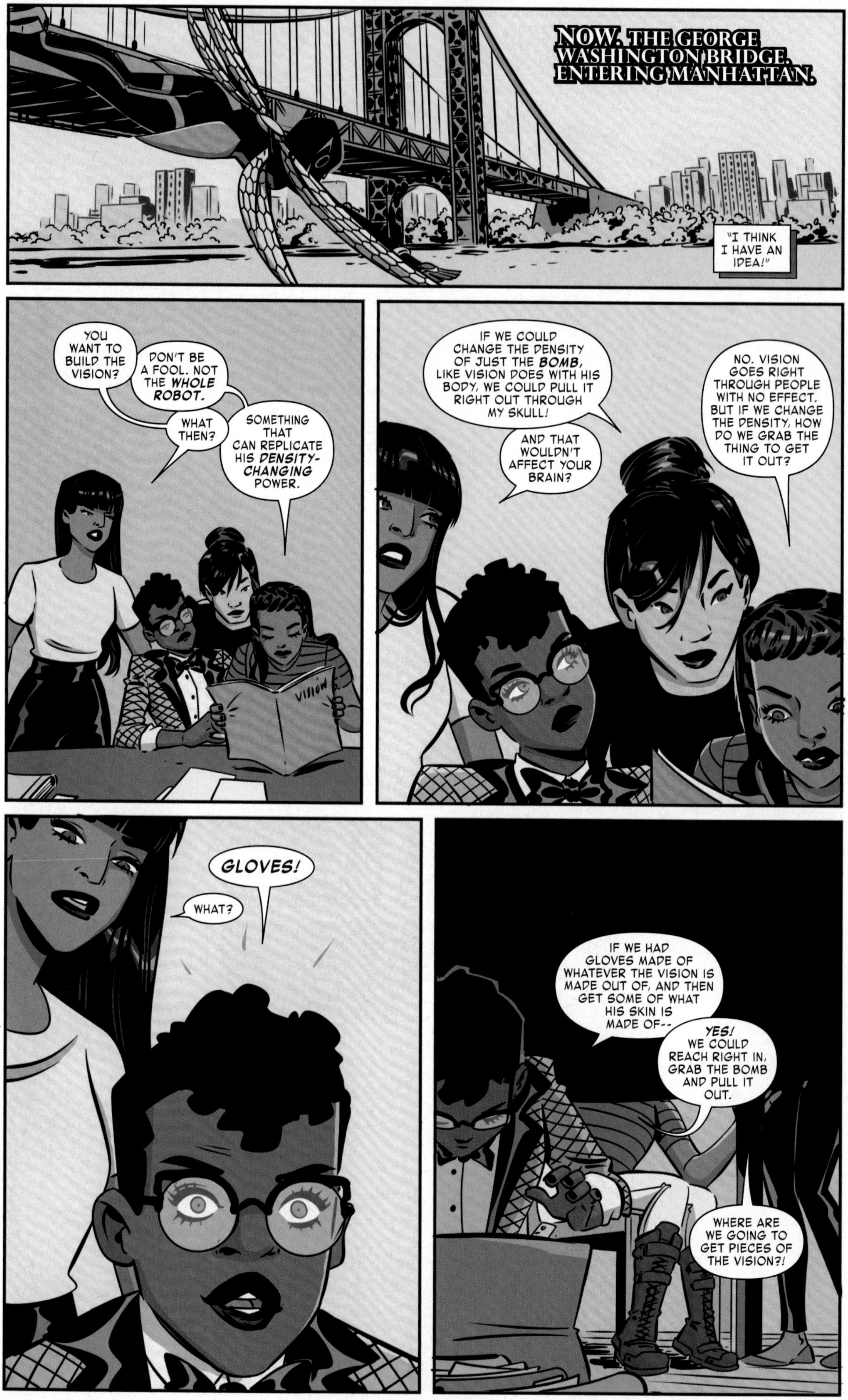
NOW. THE GEORGE WASHINGTON BRIDGE. ENTERING MANHATTAN.
"I THINK I HAVE AN IDEA!"
YOU WANT TO BUILD THE VISION?
DON'T BE A FOOL. NOT THE WHOLE ROBOT.
WHAT THEN?
SOMETHING THAT CAN REPLICATE HIS DENSITY-CHANGING POWER.
VISION
IF WE COULD CHANGE THE DENSITY OF JUST THE BOMB, LIKE VISION DOES WITH HIS BODY, WE COULD PULL IT RIGHT OUT THROUGH MY SKULL!
AND THAT WOULDN'T AFFECT YOUR BRAIN?
NO. VISION GOES RIGHT THROUGH PEOPLE WITH NO EFFECT. BUT IF WE CHANGE THE DENSITY, HOW DO WE GRAB THE THING TO GET IT OUT?
GLOVES!
WHAT?
IF WE HAD GLOVES MADE OF WHATEVER THE VISION IS MADE OUT OF, AND THEN GET SOME OF WHAT HIS SKIN IS MADE OF--
YES! WE COULD REACH RIGHT IN, GRAB THE BOMB AND PULL IT OUT.
WHERE ARE WE GOING TO GET PIECES OF THE VISION?!

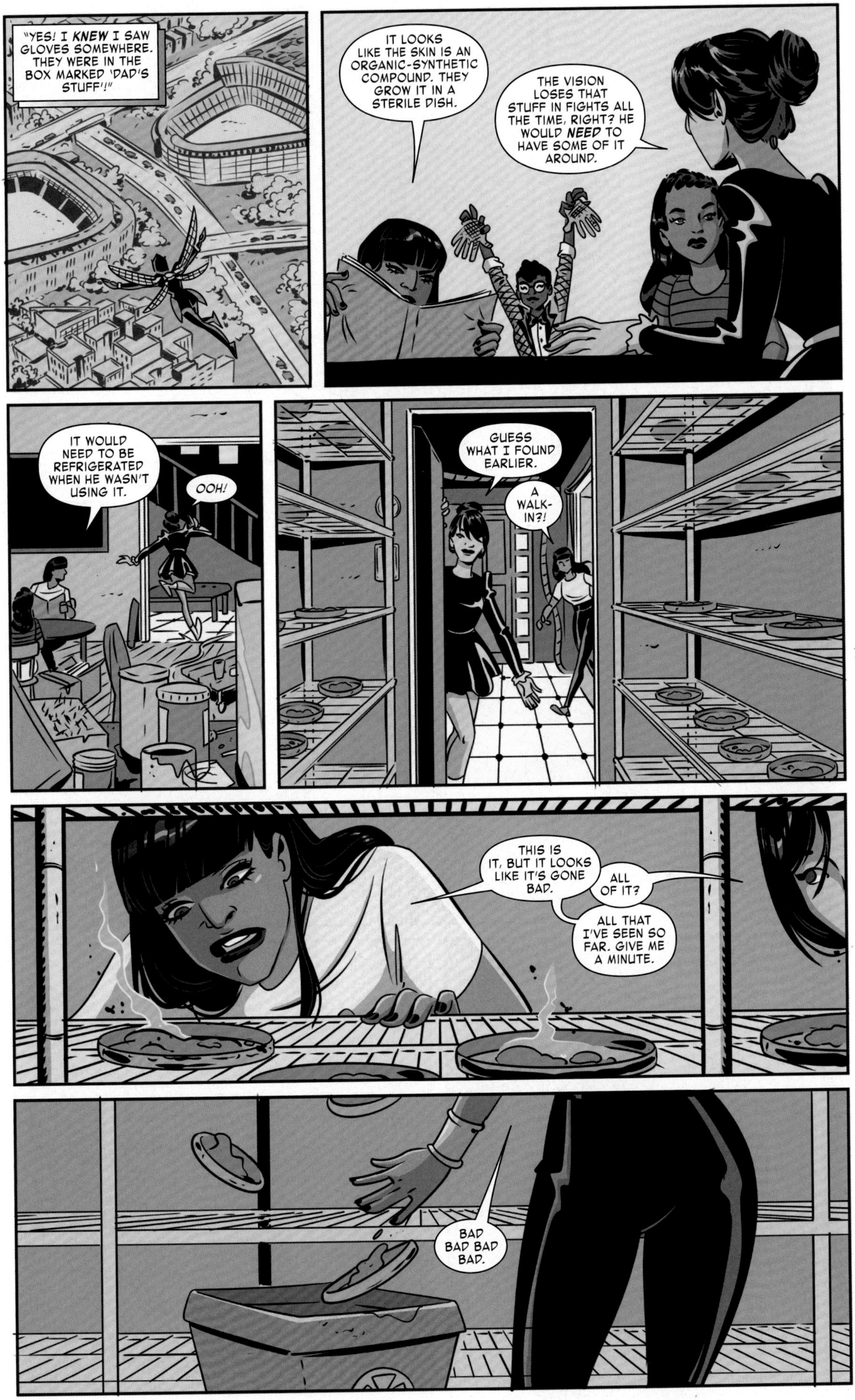
"YES! I KNEW I SAW GLOVES SOMEWHERE. THEY WERE IN THE BOX MARKED 'DAD'S STUFF'!"
IT LOOKS LIKE THE SKIN IS AN ORGANIC-SYNTHETIC COMPOUND. THEY GROW IT IN A STERILE DISH.
THE VISION LOSES THAT STUFF IN FIGHTS ALL THE TIME, RIGHT? HE WOULD NEED TO HAVE SOME OF IT AROUND.
IT WOULD NEED TO BE REFRIGERATED WHEN HE WASN'T USING IT.
OOH!
GUESS WHAT I FOUND EARLIER.
A WALK-IN?!
THIS IS IT, BUT IT LOOKS LIKE IT'S GONE BAD.
ALL OF IT?
ALL THAT I'VE SEEN SO FAR. GIVE ME A MINUTE.
BAD BAD BAD BAD.

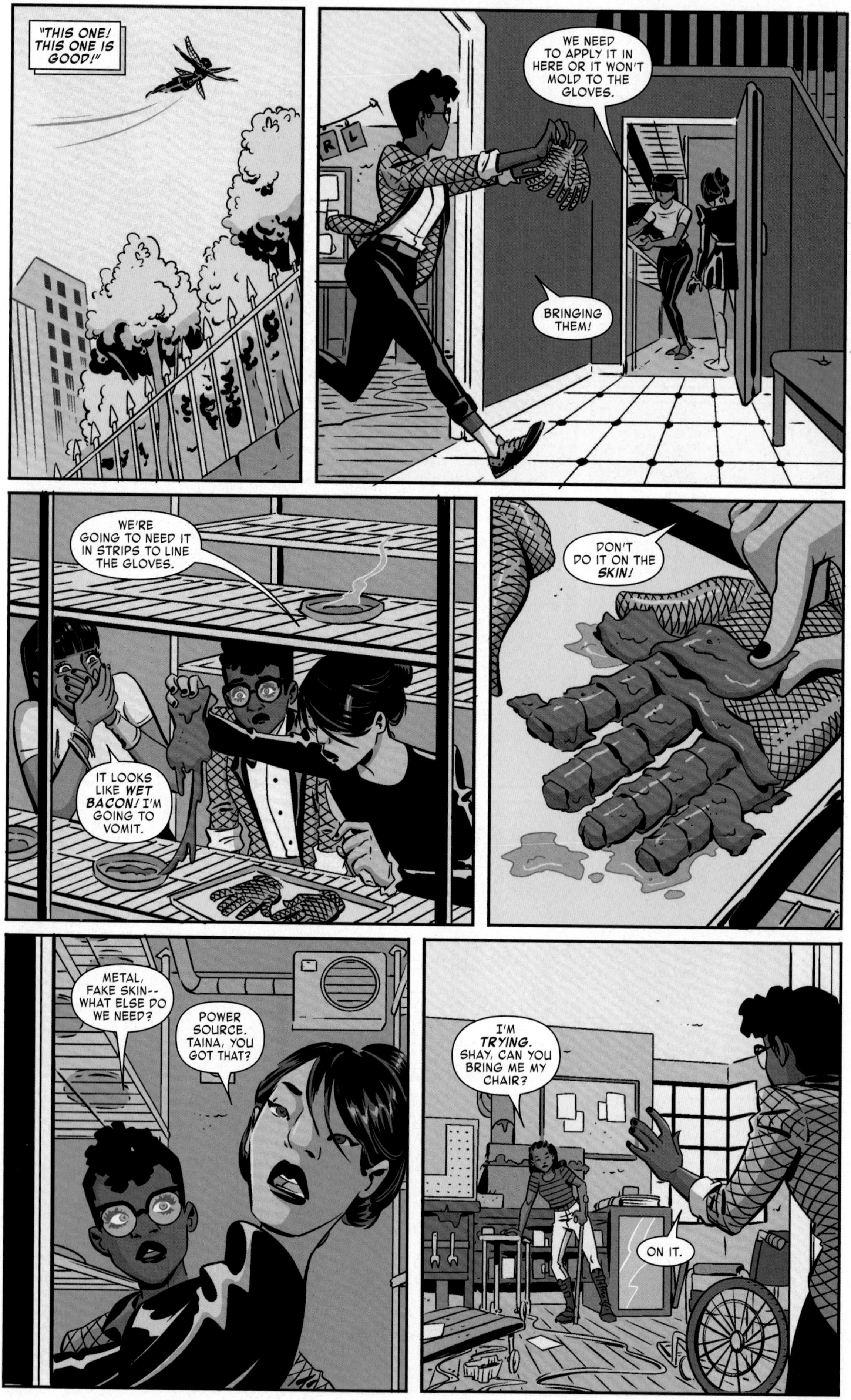
"THIS ONE! THIS ONE IS GOOD!"
WE NEED TO APPLY IT IN HERE OR IT WON'T MOLD TO THE GLOVES.
BRINGING THEM!
WE'RE GOING TO NEED IT IN STRIPS TO LINE THE GLOVES.
IT LOOKS LIKE WET BACON! I'M GOING TO VOMIT.
DON'T DO IT ON THE SKIN!
METAL, FAKE SKIN-- WHAT ELSE DO WE NEED?
POWER SOURCE. TAINA, YOU GOT THAT?
I'M TRYING. SHAY, CAN YOU BRING ME MY CHAIR?
ON IT.

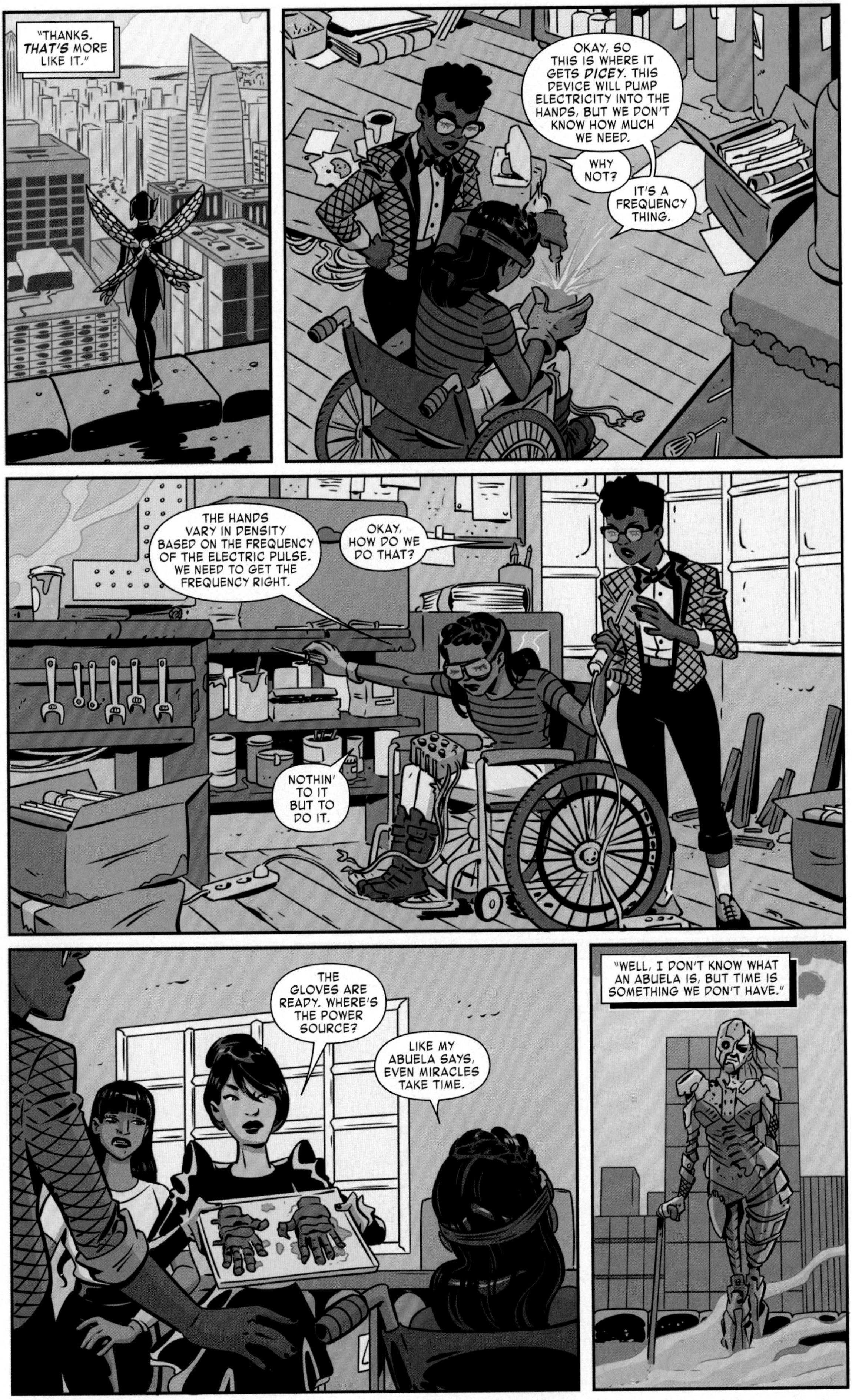
"THANKS. THAT'S MORE LIKE IT."
OKAY, SO THIS IS WHERE IT GETS DICEY. THIS DEVICE WILL PUMP ELECTRICITY INTO THE HANDS, BUT WE DON'T KNOW HOW MUCH WE NEED.
WHY NOT?
IT'S A FREQUENCY THING.
THE HANDS VARY IN DENSITY BASED ON THE FREQUENCY OF THE ELECTRIC PULSE. WE NEED TO GET THE FREQUENCY RIGHT.
OKAY, HOW DO WE DO THAT?
NOTHIN' TO IT BUT TO DO IT.
THE GLOVES ARE READY. WHERE'S THE POWER SOURCE?
LIKE MY ABUELA SAYS, EVEN MIRACLES TAKE TIME.
"WELL, I DON'T KNOW WHAT AN ABUELA IS, BUT TIME IS SOMETHING WE DON'T HAVE."

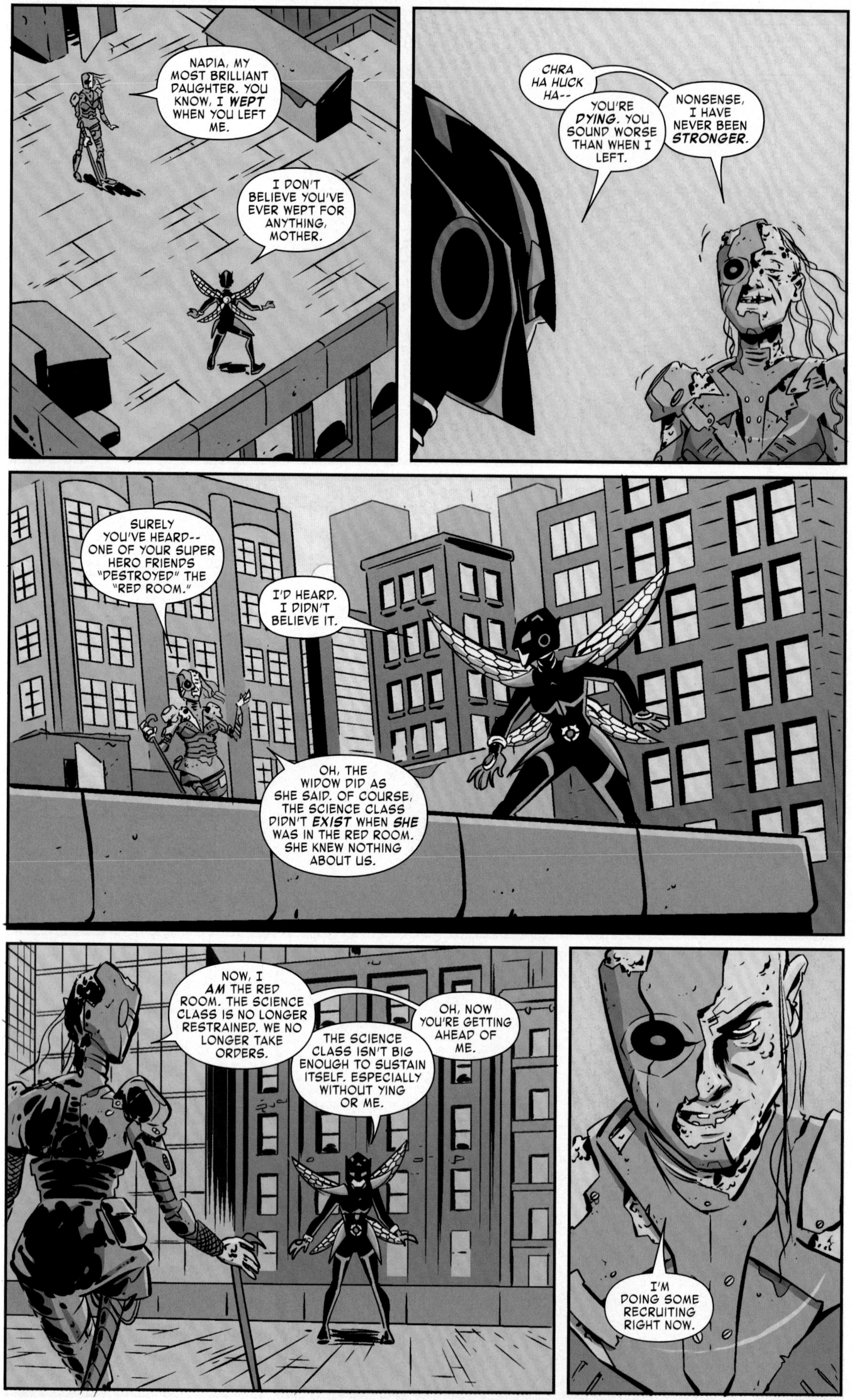

NADIA, MY MOST BRILLIANT DAUGHTER. YOU KNOW, I WEPT WHEN YOU LEFT ME.
I DON'T BELIEVE YOU'VE EVER WEPT FOR ANYTHING, MOTHER.
CHRA HA HUCK HA--
YOU'RE DYING. YOU SOUND WORSE THAN WHEN I LEFT.
NONSENSE, I HAVE NEVER BEEN STRONGER.
SURELY YOU'VE HEARD-- ONE OF YOUR SUPER HERO FRIENDS "DESTROYED" THE "RED ROOM."
I'D HEARD. I DIDN'T BELIEVE IT.
OH, THE WIDOW DID AS SHE SAID. OF COURSE, THE SCIENCE CLASS DIDN'T EXIST WHEN SHE WAS IN THE RED ROOM. SHE KNEW NOTHING ABOUT US.
NOW, I AM THE RED ROOM. THE SCIENCE CLASS IS NO LONGER RESTRAINED. WE NO LONGER TAKE ORDERS.
THE SCIENCE CLASS ISN'T BIG ENOUGH TO SUSTAIN ITSELF. ESPECIALLY WITHOUT YING OR ME.
OH, NOW YOU'RE GETTING AHEAD OF ME.
I'M DOING SOME RECRUITING RIGHT NOW.

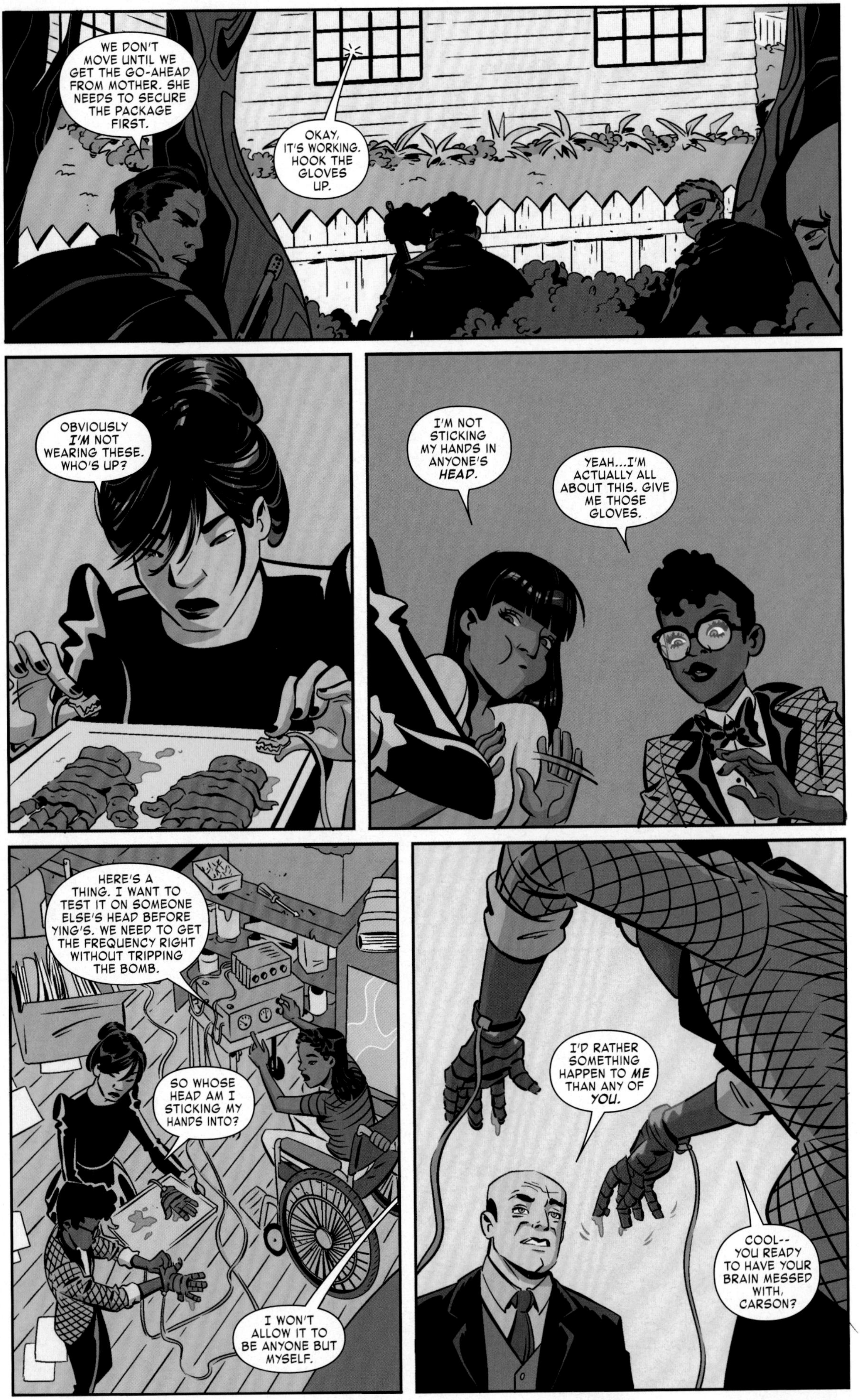
WE DON'T MOVE UNTIL WE GET THE GO-AHEAD FROM MOTHER. SHE NEEDS TO SECURE THE PACKAGE FIRST.
OKAY, IT'S WORKING. HOOK THE GLOVES UP.
OBVIOUSLY I'M NOT WEARING THESE. WHO'S UP?
I'M NOT STICKING MY HANDS IN ANYONE'S HEAD.
YEAH...I'M ACTUALLY ALL ABOUT THIS. GIVE ME THOSE GLOVES.
HERE'S A THING. I WANT TO TEST IT ON SOMEONE ELSE'S HEAD BEFORE YING'S. WE NEED TO GET THE FREQUENCY RIGHT WITHOUT TRIPPING THE BOMB.
SO WHOSE HEAD AM I STICKING MY HANDS INTO?
I WON'T ALLOW IT TO BE ANYONE BUT MYSELF.
I'D RATHER SOMETHING HAPPEN TO ME THAN ANY OF YOU.
COOL-- YOU READY TO HAVE YOUR BRAIN MESSED WITH, CARSON?

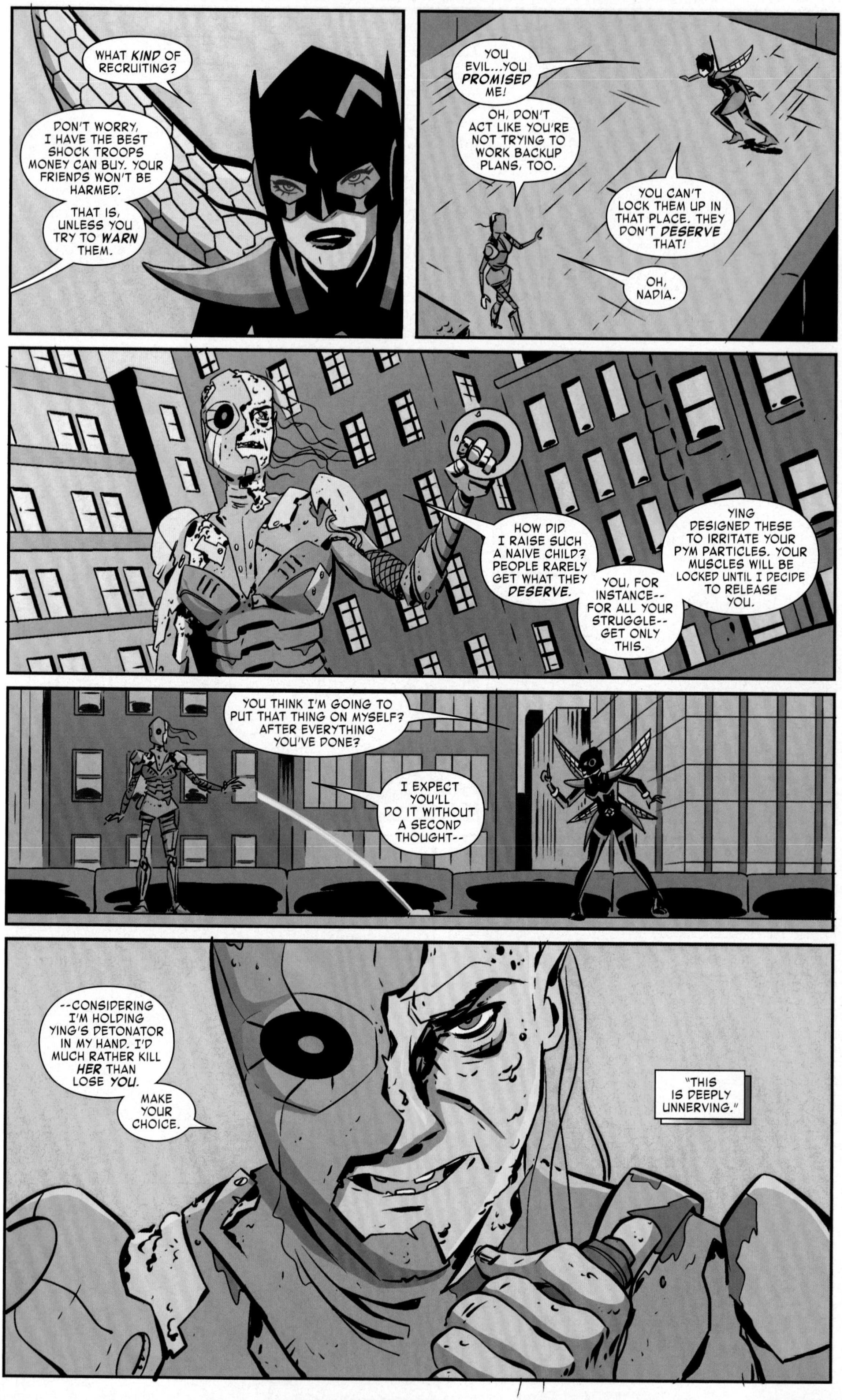
WHAT *KIND* OF RECRUITING?
DON'T WORRY, I HAVE THE BEST SHOCK TROOPS MONEY CAN BUY. YOUR FRIENDS WON'T BE HARMED.
THAT IS, UNLESS YOU TRY TO *WARN* THEM.
YOU EVIL...YOU *PROMISED* ME!
OH, DON'T ACT LIKE YOU'RE NOT TRYING TO WORK BACKUP PLANS, TOO.
YOU CAN'T LOCK THEM UP IN THAT PLACE. THEY DON'T *DESERVE* THAT!
OH, NADIA.
HOW DID I RAISE SUCH A NAIVE CHILD? PEOPLE RARELY GET WHAT THEY *DESERVE.*
YOU, FOR INSTANCE-- FOR ALL YOUR STRUGGLE-- GET ONLY THIS.
YING DESIGNED THESE TO IRRITATE YOUR PYM PARTICLES. YOUR MUSCLES WILL BE LOCKED UNTIL I DECIDE TO RELEASE YOU.
YOU THINK I'M GOING TO PUT THAT THING ON MYSELF? AFTER EVERYTHING YOU'VE DONE?
I EXPECT YOU'LL DO IT WITHOUT A SECOND THOUGHT--
--CONSIDERING I'M HOLDING YING'S DETONATOR IN MY HAND. I'D MUCH RATHER KILL *HER* THAN LOSE *YOU*.
MAKE YOUR CHOICE.
"THIS IS DEEPLY UNNERVING."

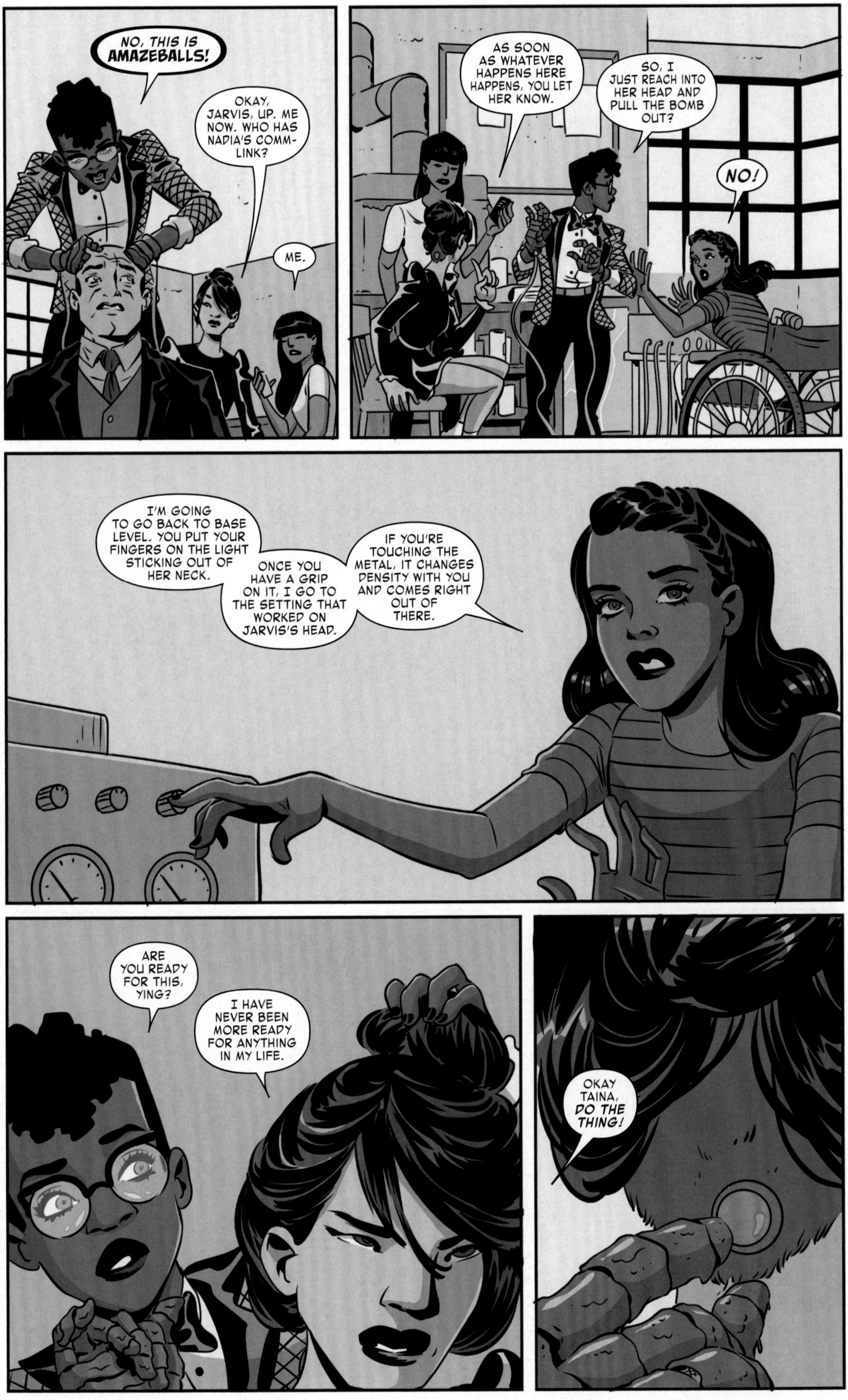
NO, THIS IS AMAZEBALLS!
OKAY, JARVIS, UP. ME NOW. WHO HAS NADIA'S COMM-LINK?
ME.
AS SOON AS WHATEVER HAPPENS HERE HAPPENS, YOU LET HER KNOW.
SO, I JUST REACH INTO HER HEAD AND PULL THE BOMB OUT?
NO!
I'M GOING TO GO BACK TO BASE LEVEL. YOU PUT YOUR FINGERS ON THE LIGHT STICKING OUT OF HER NECK.
ONCE YOU HAVE A GRIP ON IT, I GO TO THE SETTING THAT WORKED ON JARVIS'S HEAD.
IF YOU'RE TOUCHING THE METAL, IT CHANGES DENSITY WITH YOU AND COMES RIGHT OUT OF THERE.
ARE YOU READY FOR THIS, YING?
I HAVE NEVER BEEN MORE READY FOR ANYTHING IN MY LIFE.
OKAY TAINA, DO THE THING!

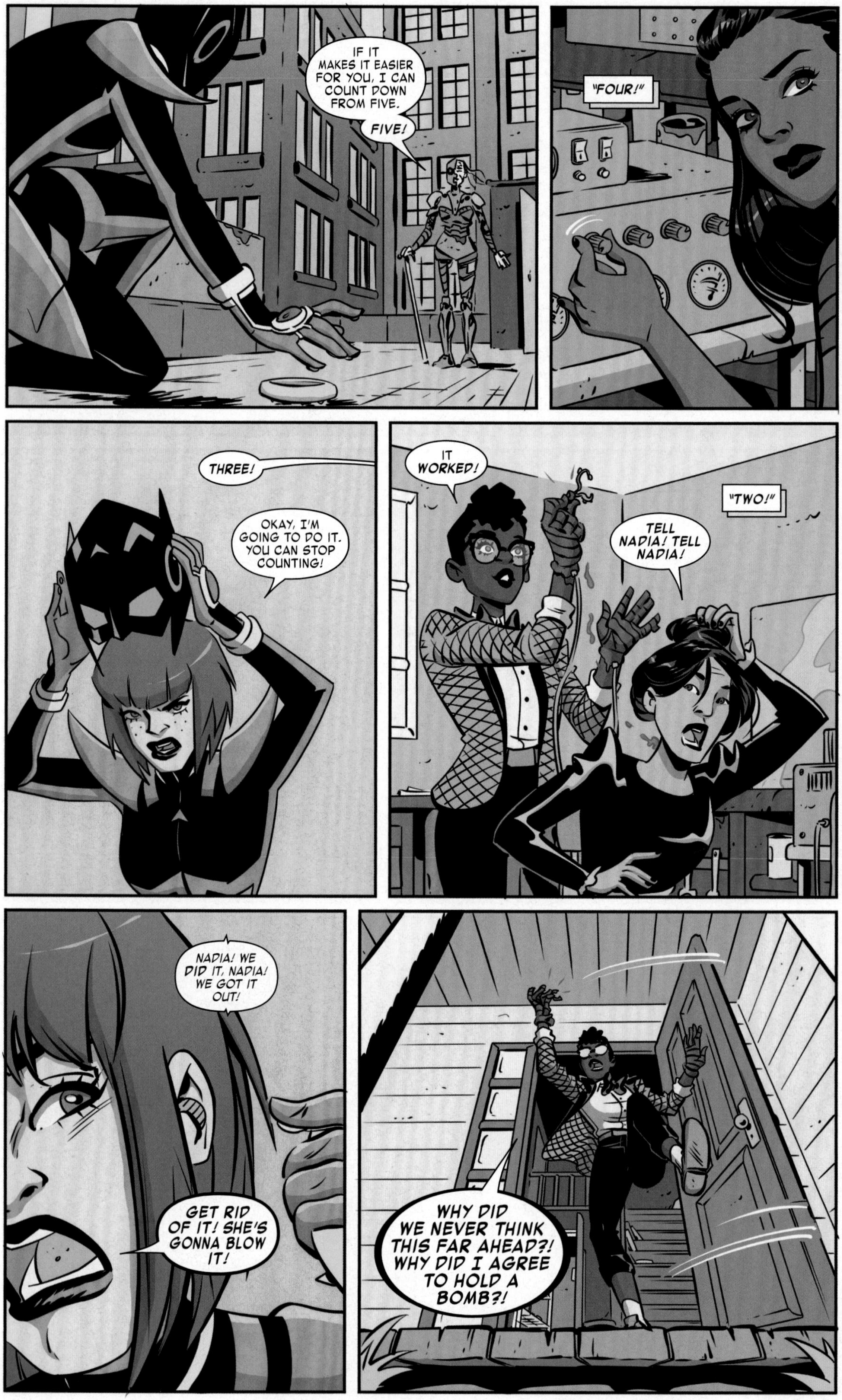
IF IT MAKES IT EASIER FOR YOU, I CAN COUNT DOWN FROM FIVE.
FIVE!
"FOUR!"
THREE!
OKAY, I'M GOING TO DO IT. YOU CAN STOP COUNTING!
IT WORKED!
"TWO!"
TELL NADIA! TELL NADIA!
NADIA! WE DID IT, NADIA! WE GOT IT OUT!
GET RID OF IT! SHE'S GONNA BLOW IT!
WHY DID WE NEVER THINK THIS FAR AHEAD?! WHY DID I AGREE TO HOLD A BOMB?!

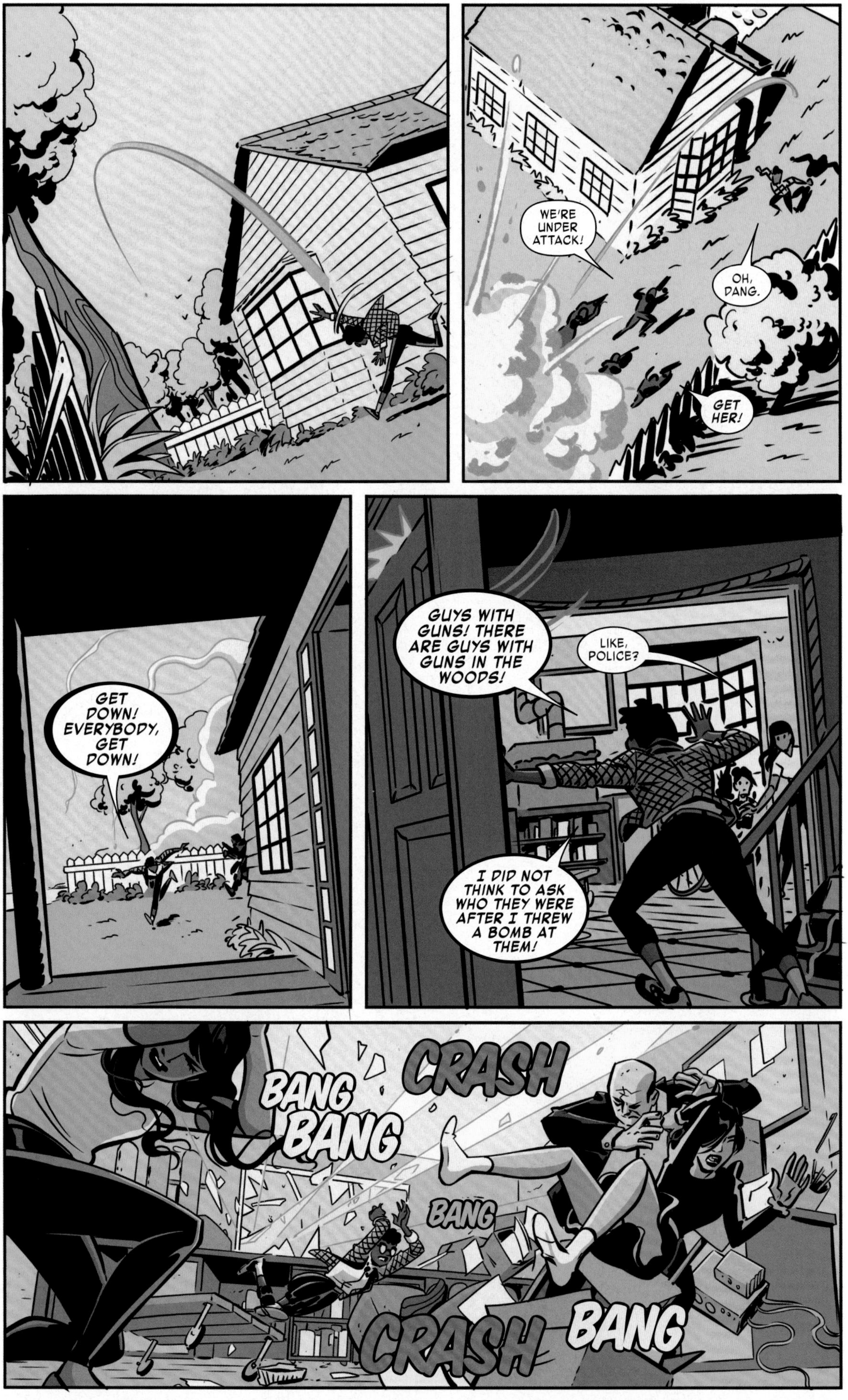
WE'RE UNDER ATTACK!
OH, DANG.
GET HER!
GET DOWN! EVERYBODY, GET DOWN!
GUYS WITH GUNS! THERE ARE GUYS WITH GUNS IN THE WOODS!
LIKE, POLICE?
I DID NOT THINK TO ASK WHO THEY WERE AFTER I THREW A BOMB AT THEM!
CRASH
BANG
BANG
BANG
CRASH
BANG

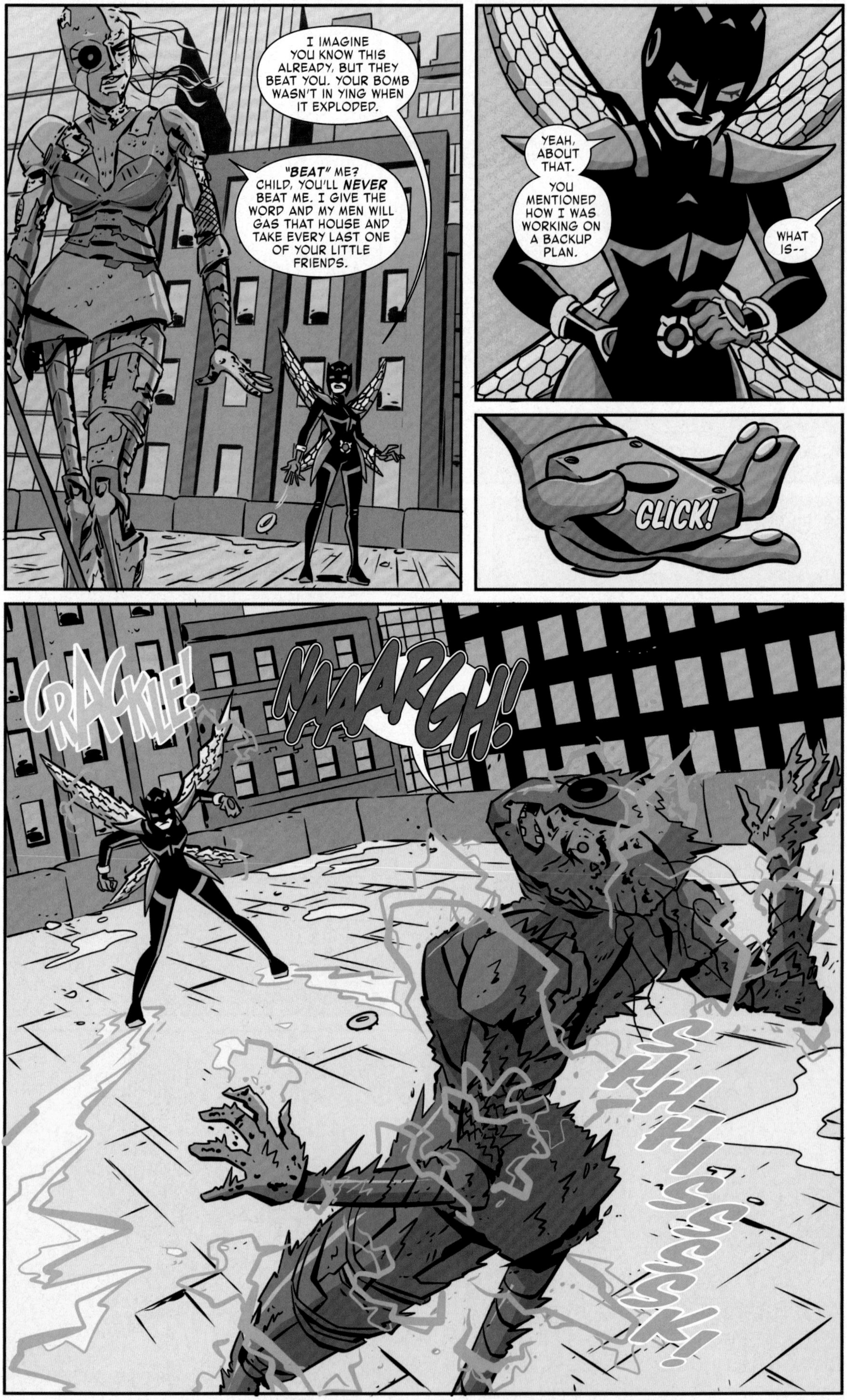
I IMAGINE YOU KNOW THIS ALREADY, BUT THEY BEAT YOU. YOUR BOMB WASN'T IN YING WHEN IT EXPLODED.
"BEAT" ME? CHILD, YOU'LL NEVER BEAT ME. I GIVE THE WORD AND MY MEN WILL GAS THAT HOUSE AND TAKE EVERY LAST ONE OF YOUR LITTLE FRIENDS.
YEAH, ABOUT THAT.
YOU MENTIONED HOW I WAS WORKING ON A BACKUP PLAN.
WHAT IS--
CLICK!
CRACKLE!
NAAARGH!
SHHHISSSSK!

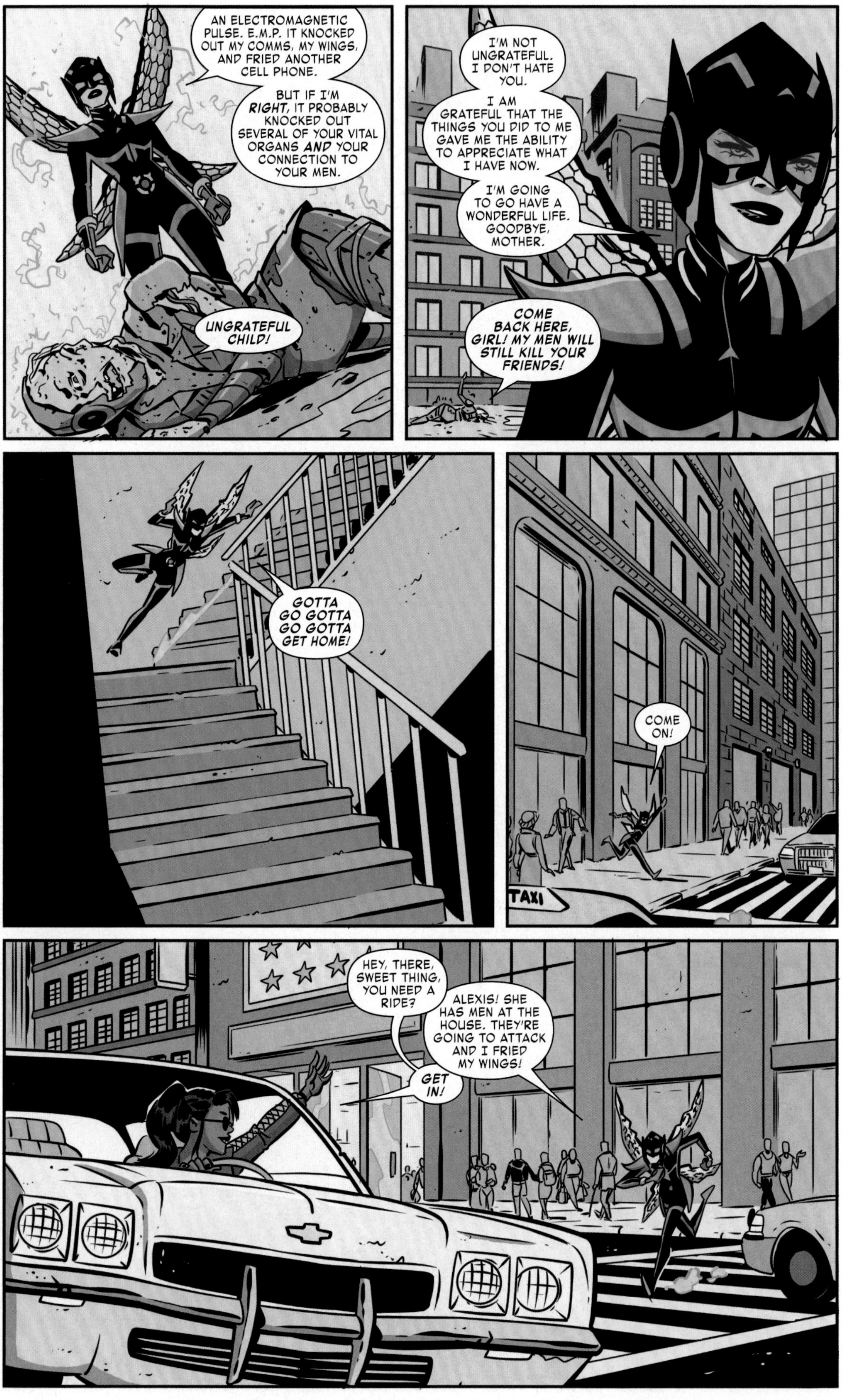
AN ELECTROMAGNETIC PULSE. E.M.P. IT KNOCKED OUT MY COMMS, MY WINGS, AND FRIED ANOTHER CELL PHONE.
BUT IF I'M RIGHT, IT PROBABLY KNOCKED OUT SEVERAL OF YOUR VITAL ORGANS AND YOUR CONNECTION TO YOUR MEN.
UNGRATEFUL CHILD!
I'M NOT UNGRATEFUL. I DON'T HATE YOU.
I AM GRATEFUL THAT THE THINGS YOU DID TO ME GAVE ME THE ABILITY TO APPRECIATE WHAT I HAVE NOW.
I'M GOING TO GO HAVE A WONDERFUL LIFE. GOODBYE, MOTHER.
COME BACK HERE, GIRL! MY MEN WILL STILL KILL YOUR FRIENDS!
GOTTA GO GOTTA GO GOTTA GET HOME!
COME ON!
TAXI
HEY, THERE, SWEET THING, YOU NEED A RIDE?
ALEXIS! SHE HAS MEN AT THE HOUSE. THEY'RE GOING TO ATTACK AND I FRIED MY WINGS!
GET IN!

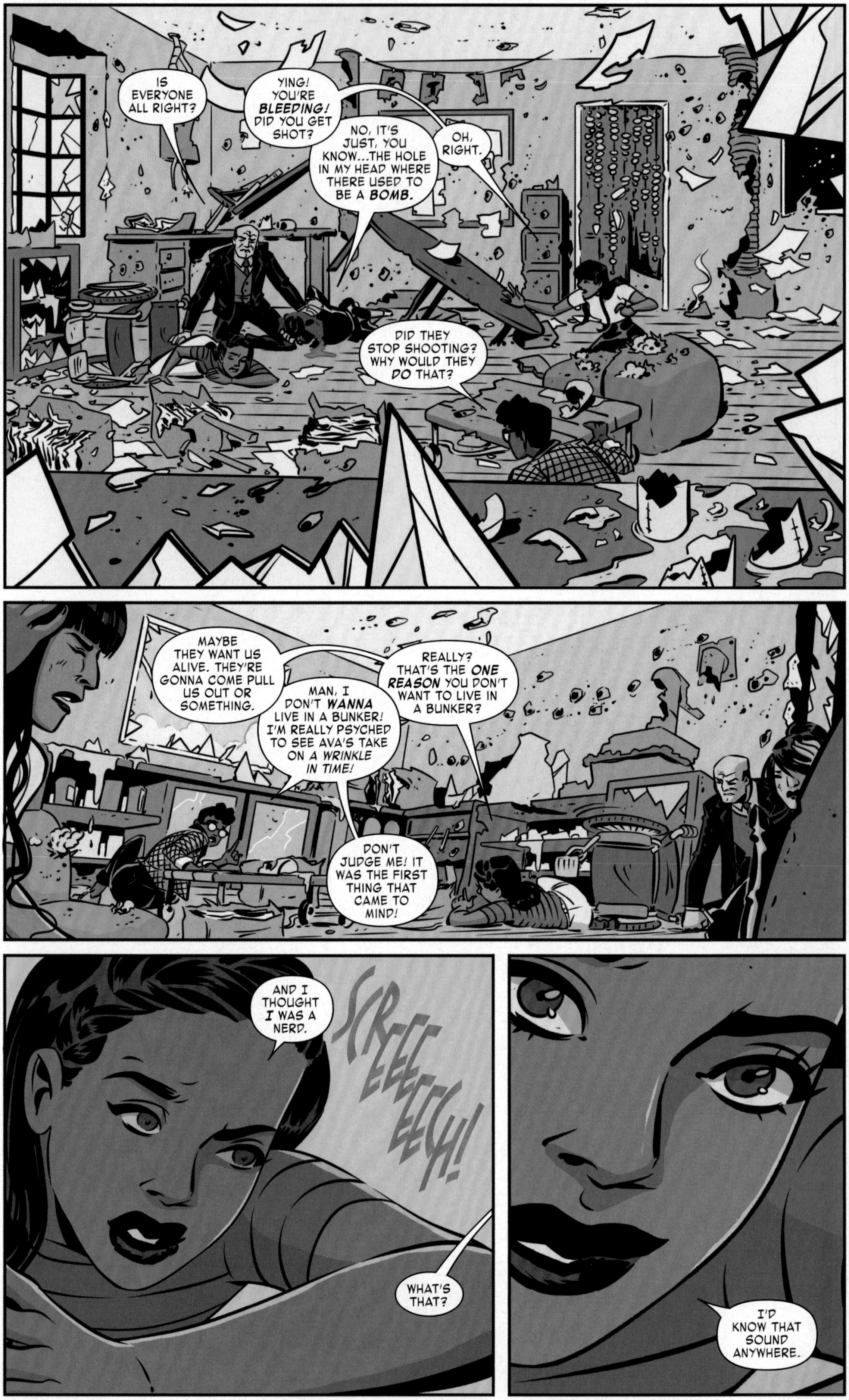
IS EVERYONE ALL RIGHT?
YING! YOU'RE BLEEDING! DID YOU GET SHOT?
NO, IT'S JUST, YOU KNOW...THE HOLE IN MY HEAD WHERE THERE USED TO BE A BOMB.
OH, RIGHT.
DID THEY STOP SHOOTING? WHY WOULD THEY DO THAT?
MAYBE THEY WANT US ALIVE. THEY'RE GONNA COME PULL US OUT OR SOMETHING.
MAN, I DON'T WANNA LIVE IN A BUNKER! I'M REALLY PSYCHED TO SEE AVA'S TAKE ON A WRINKLE IN TIME!
REALLY? THAT'S THE ONE REASON YOU DON'T WANT TO LIVE IN A BUNKER?
DON'T JUDGE ME! IT WAS THE FIRST THING THAT CAME TO MIND!
AND I THOUGHT I WAS A NERD.
SCREEEEEECH!
WHAT'S THAT?
I'D KNOW THAT SOUND ANYWHERE.

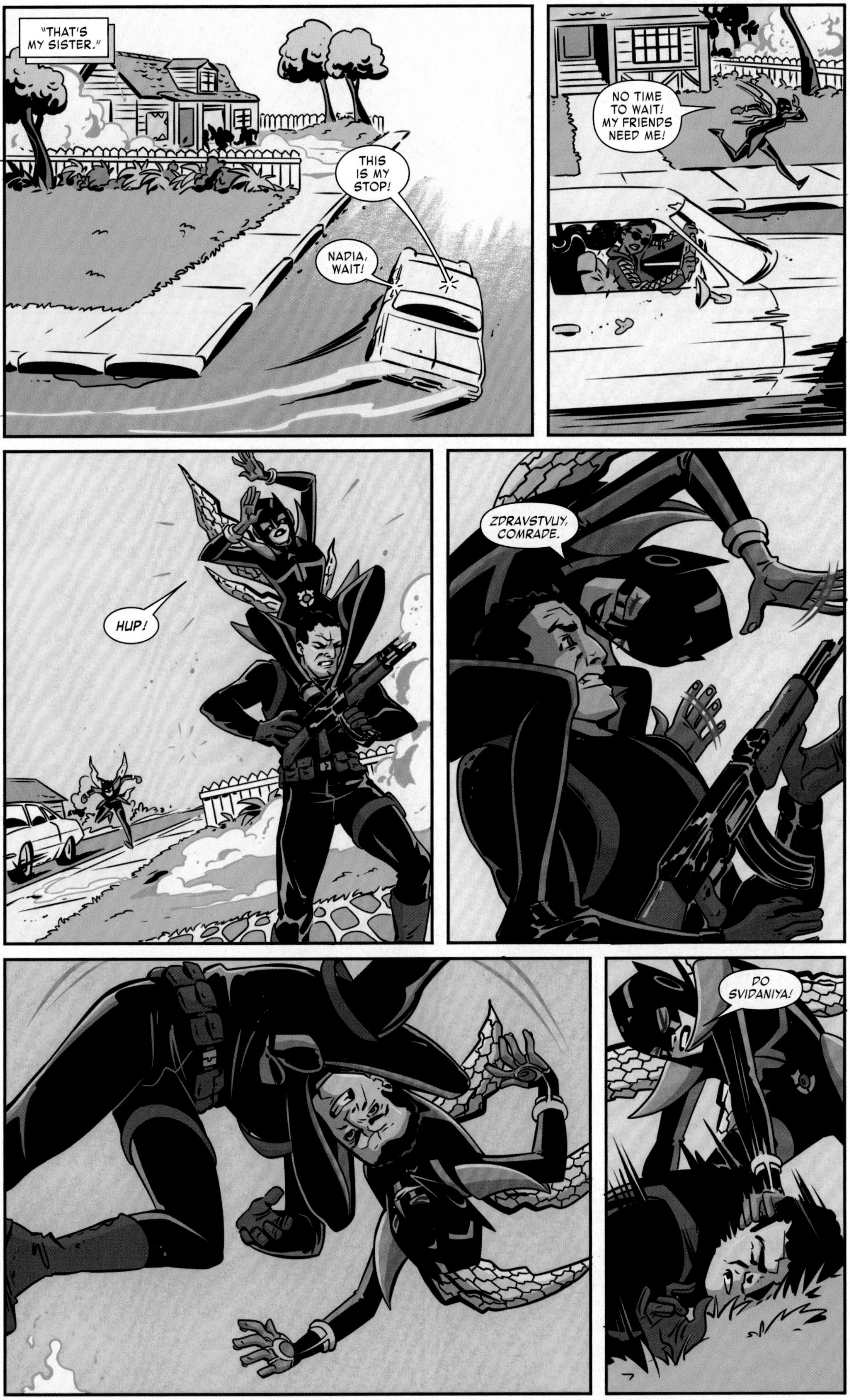
"THAT'S MY SISTER."
THIS IS MY STOP!
NADIA, WAIT!
NO TIME TO WAIT! MY FRIENDS NEED ME!
HUP!
ZDRAVSTVUY, COMRADE.
DO SVIDANIYA!

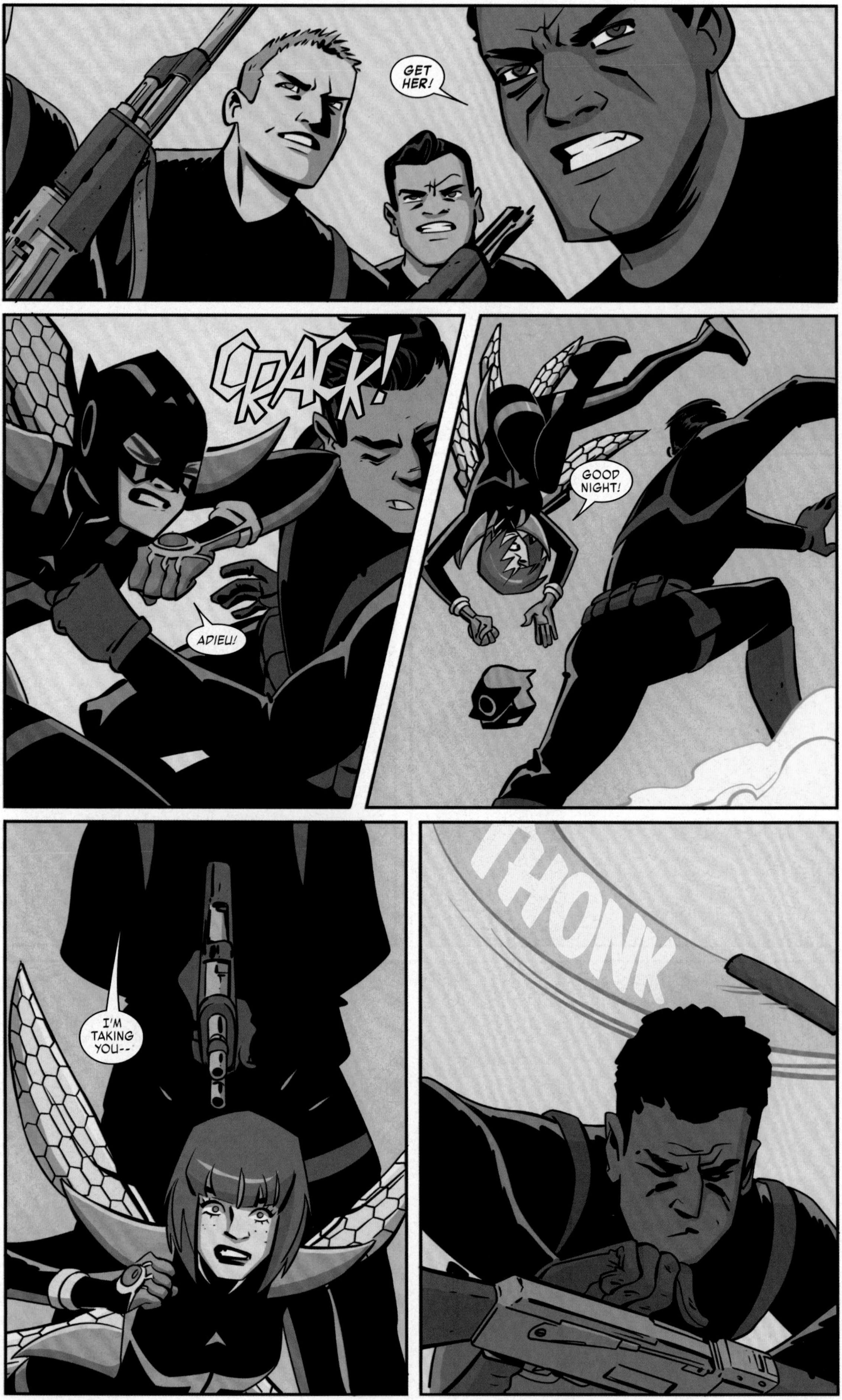
GET HER!
CRACK!
ADIEU!
GOOD NIGHT!
I'M TAKING YOU--
THONK

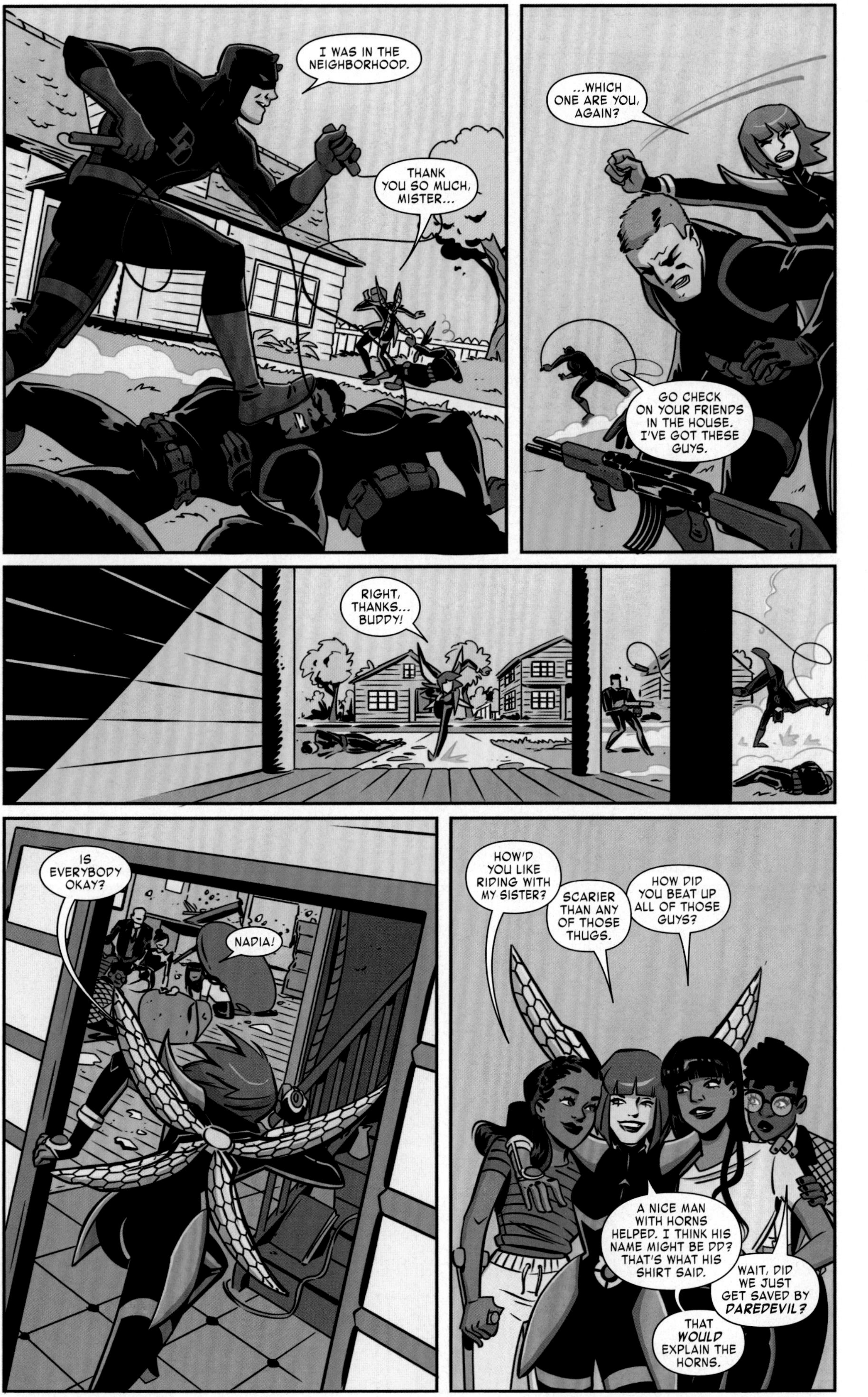
I WAS IN THE NEIGHBORHOOD.
THANK YOU SO MUCH, MISTER...
...WHICH ONE ARE YOU, AGAIN?
GO CHECK ON YOUR FRIENDS IN THE HOUSE. I'VE GOT THESE GUYS.
RIGHT, THANKS... BUDDY!
IS EVERYBODY OKAY?
NADIA!
HOW'D YOU LIKE RIDING WITH MY SISTER?
SCARIER THAN ANY OF THOSE THUGS.
HOW DID YOU BEAT UP ALL OF THOSE GUYS?
A NICE MAN WITH HORNS HELPED. I THINK HIS NAME MIGHT BE DD? THAT'S WHAT HIS SHIRT SAID.
WAIT, DID WE JUST GET SAVED BY DAREDEVIL?
THAT WOULD EXPLAIN THE HORNS.

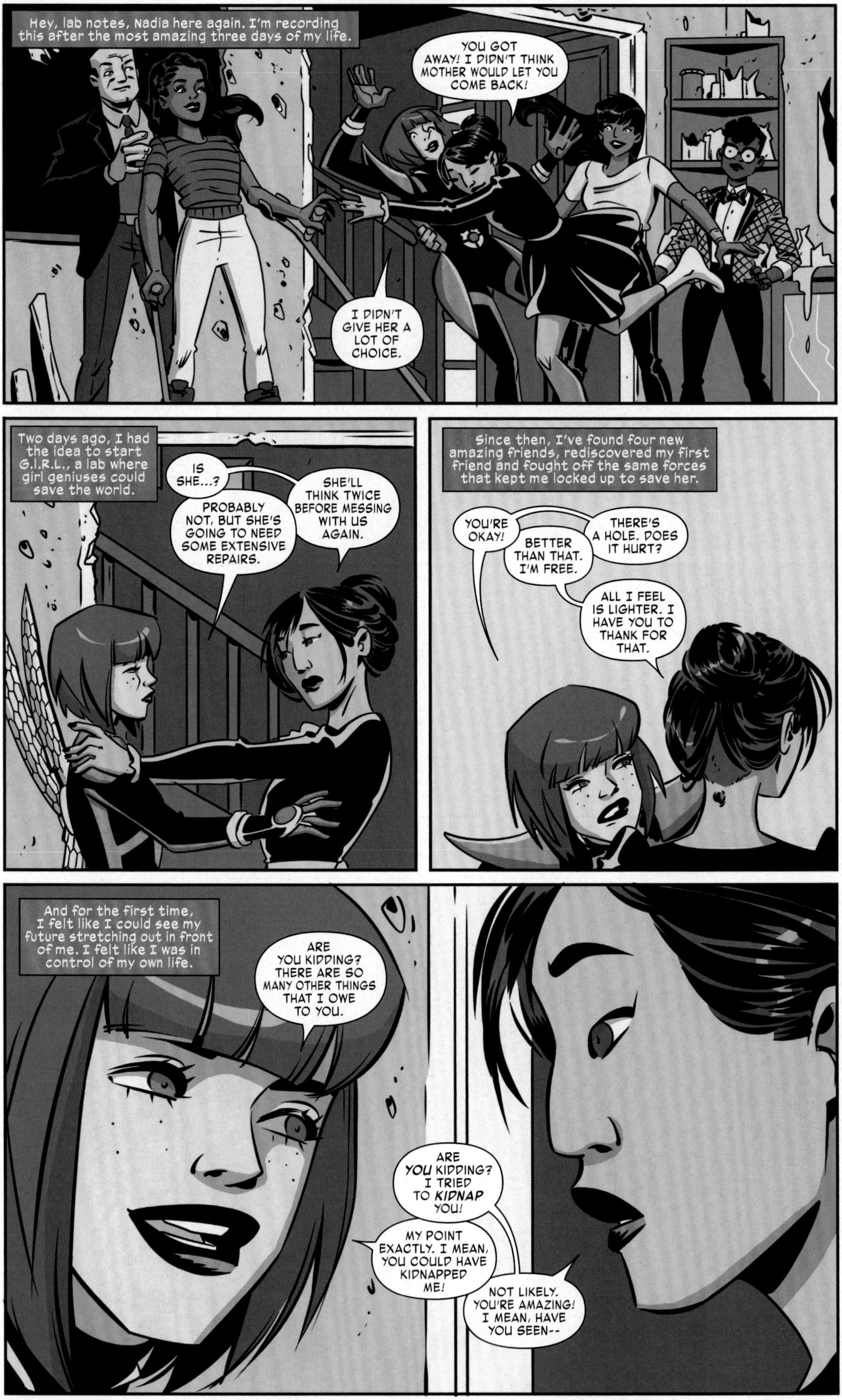

Hey, lab notes, Nadia here again. I'm recording this after the most amazing three days of my life.
YOU GOT AWAY! I DIDN'T THINK MOTHER WOULD LET YOU COME BACK!
I DIDN'T GIVE HER A LOT OF CHOICE.
Two days ago, I had the idea to start G.I.R.L., a lab where girl geniuses could save the world.
IS SHE...?
PROBABLY NOT, BUT SHE'S GOING TO NEED SOME EXTENSIVE REPAIRS.
SHE'LL THINK TWICE BEFORE MESSING WITH US AGAIN.
Since then, I've found four new amazing friends, rediscovered my first friend and fought off the same forces that kept me locked up to save her.
YOU'RE OKAY!
THERE'S A HOLE. DOES IT HURT?
BETTER THAN THAT. I'M FREE.
ALL I FEEL IS LIGHTER. I HAVE YOU TO THANK FOR THAT.
And for the first time, I felt like I could see my future stretching out in front of me. I felt like I was in control of my own life.
ARE YOU KIDDING? THERE ARE SO MANY OTHER THINGS THAT I OWE TO YOU.
ARE YOU KIDDING? I TRIED TO KIDNAP YOU!
MY POINT EXACTLY. I MEAN, YOU COULD HAVE KIDNAPPED ME!
NOT LIKELY. YOU'RE AMAZING! I MEAN, HAVE YOU SEEN--

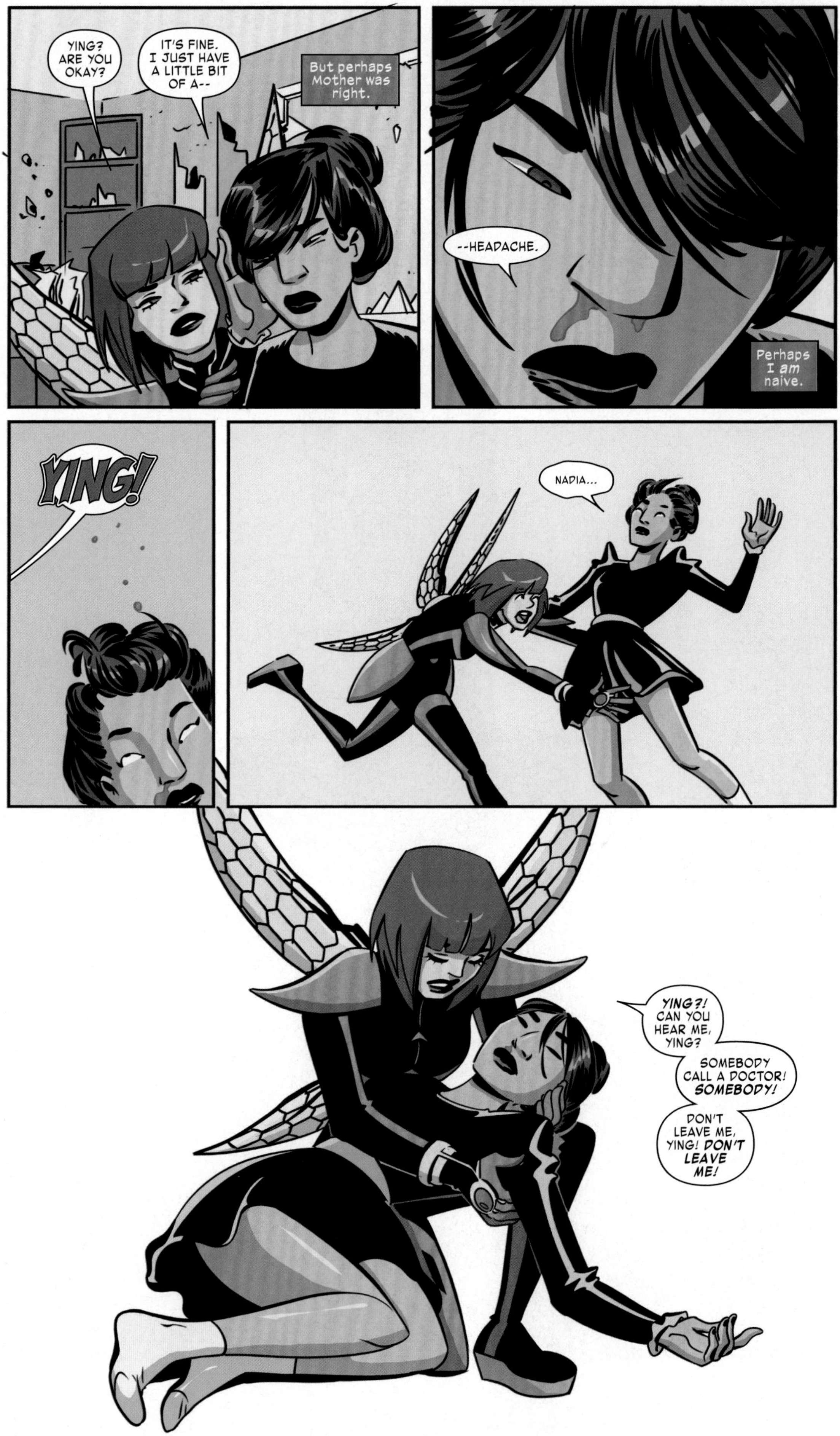
YING? ARE YOU OKAY?
IT'S FINE. I JUST HAVE A LITTLE BIT OF A--
But perhaps Mother was right.
--HEADACHE.
Perhaps I *am* naive.
YING!
NADIA...
YING?! CAN YOU HEAR ME, YING?
SOMEBODY CALL A DOCTOR! ***SOMEBODY!***
DON'T LEAVE ME, YING! ***DON'T LEAVE ME!***

7

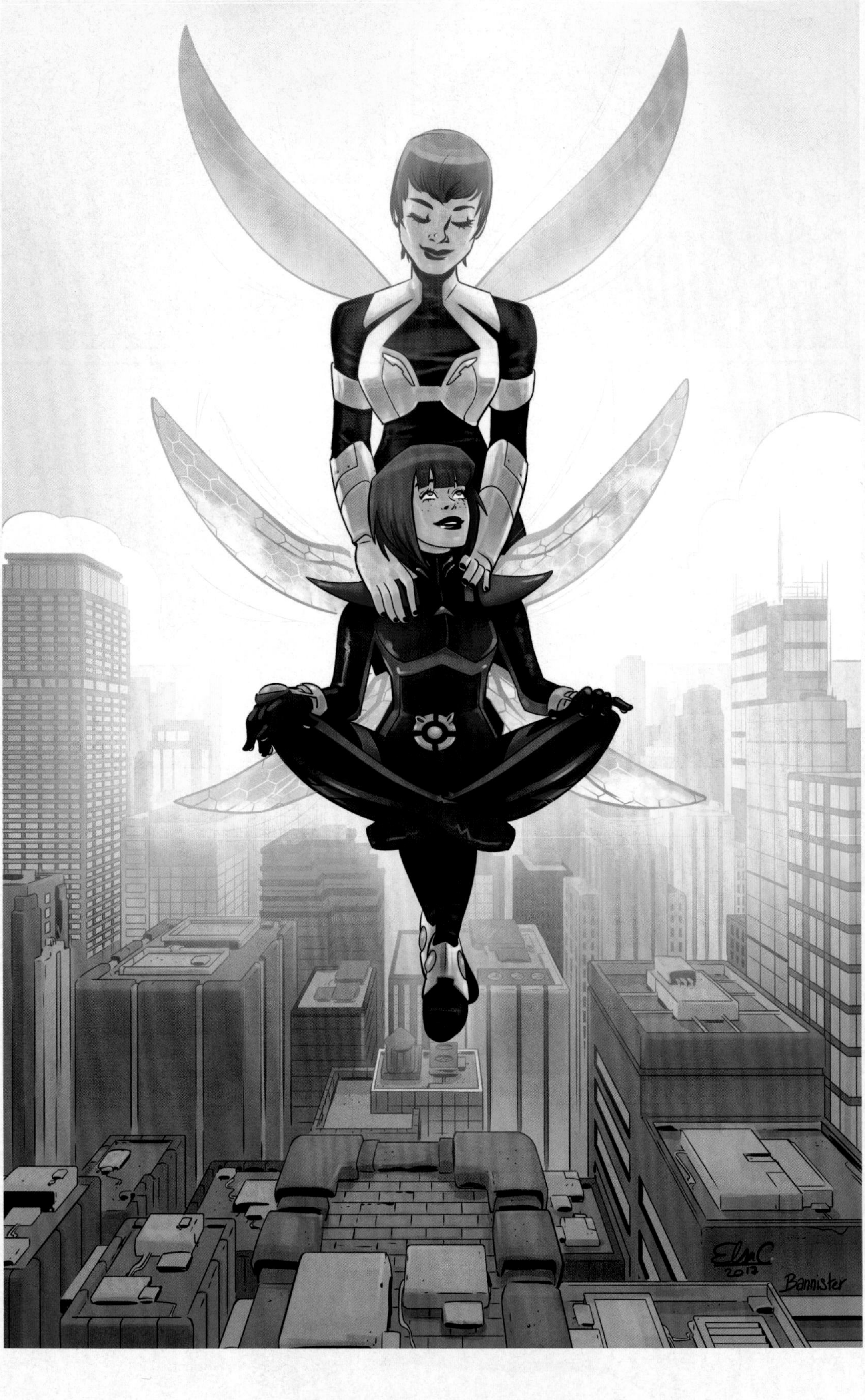

Bannister

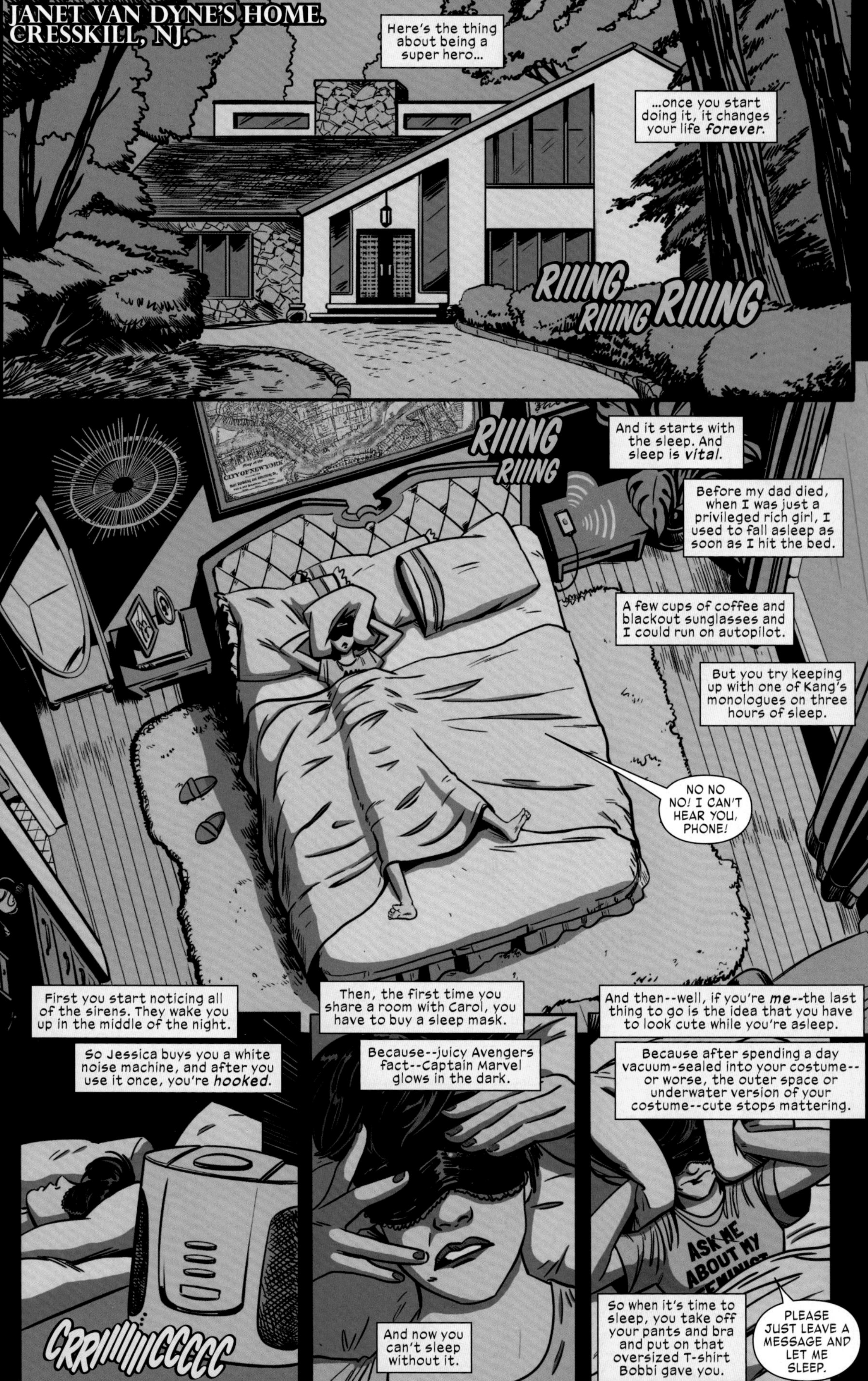

JANET VAN DYNE'S HOME. CRESSKILL, NJ.
Here's the thing about being a super hero...
...once you start doing it, it changes your life *forever*.
RIIING RIIING RIIING
RIIING RIIING
And it starts with the sleep. And sleep is *vital*.
Before my dad died, when I was just a privileged rich girl, I used to fall asleep as soon as I hit the bed.
A few cups of coffee and blackout sunglasses and I could run on autopilot.
But you try keeping up with one of Kang's monologues on three hours of sleep.
NO NO NO! I CAN'T HEAR YOU, PHONE!
First you start noticing all of the sirens. They wake you up in the middle of the night.
So Jessica buys you a white noise machine, and after you use it once, you're *hooked*.
CRRIIIIIIIICCCCC
Then, the first time you share a room with Carol, you have to buy a sleep mask.
Because--juicy Avengers fact--Captain Marvel glows in the dark.
And now you can't sleep without it.
And then--well, if you're *me*--the last thing to go is the idea that you have to look cute while you're asleep.
Because after spending a day vacuum-sealed into your costume--or worse, the outer space or underwater version of your costume--cute stops mattering.
ASK ME ABOUT MY
So when it's time to sleep, you take off your pants and bra and put on that oversized T-shirt Bobbi gave you.
PLEASE JUST LEAVE A MESSAGE AND LET ME SLEEP.

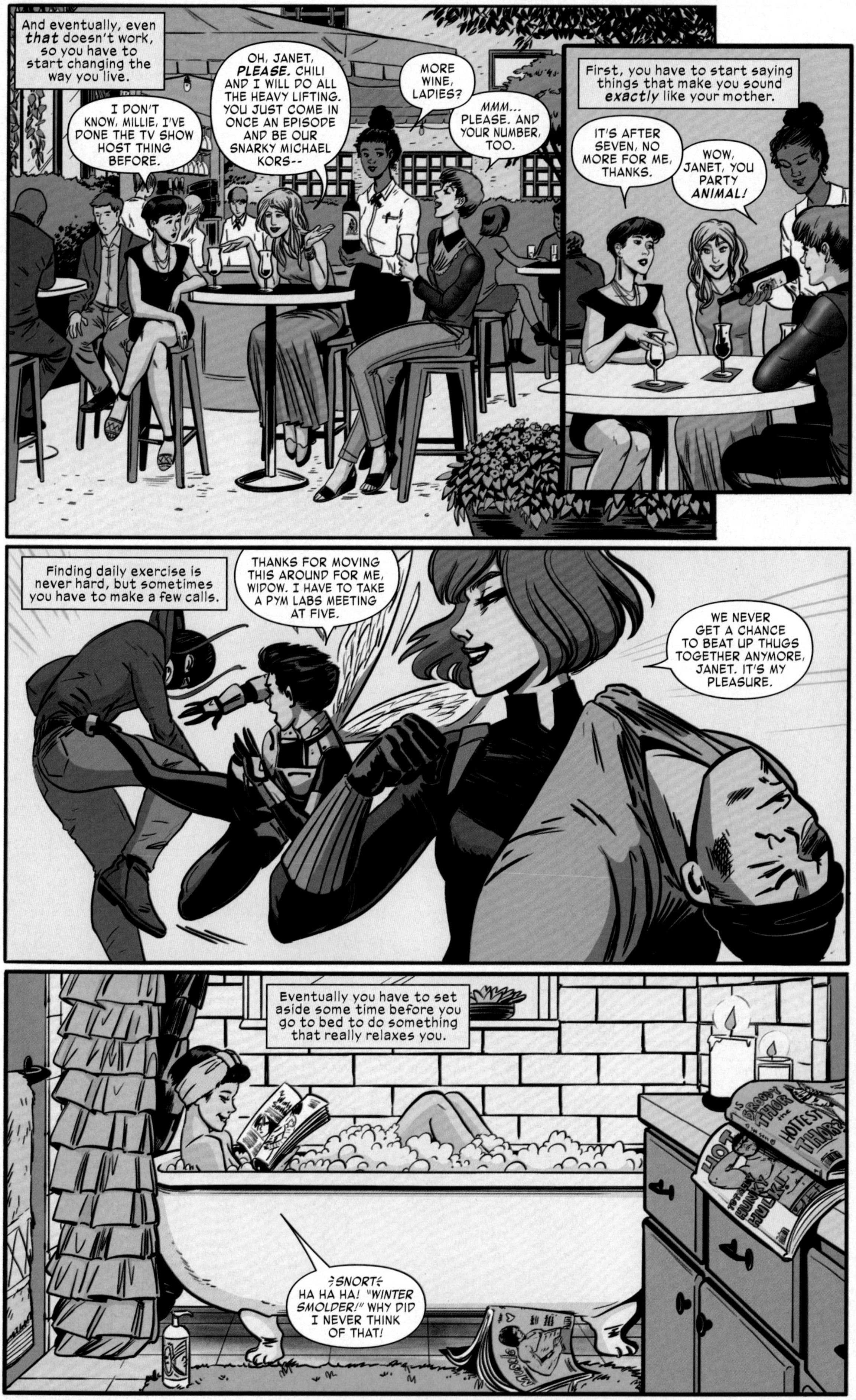

And eventually, even *that* doesn't work, so you have to start changing the way you live.
I DON'T KNOW, MILLIE, I'VE DONE THE TV SHOW HOST THING BEFORE.
OH, JANET, *PLEASE.* CHILI AND I WILL DO ALL THE HEAVY LIFTING. YOU JUST COME IN ONCE AN EPISODE AND BE OUR SNARKY MICHAEL KORS--
MORE WINE, LADIES?
MMM... PLEASE. AND YOUR NUMBER, TOO.
First, you have to start saying things that make you sound *exactly* like your mother.
IT'S AFTER SEVEN, NO MORE FOR ME, THANKS.
WOW, JANET, YOU PARTY *ANIMAL!*
Finding daily exercise is never hard, but sometimes you have to make a few calls.
THANKS FOR MOVING THIS AROUND FOR ME, WIDOW. I HAVE TO TAKE A PYM LABS MEETING AT FIVE.
WE NEVER GET A CHANCE TO BEAT UP THUGS TOGETHER ANYMORE, JANET. IT'S MY PLEASURE.
Eventually you have to set aside some time before you go to bed to do something that really relaxes you.
SNORT
HA HA HA! *"WINTER SMOLDER!"* WHY DID I NEVER THINK OF THAT!

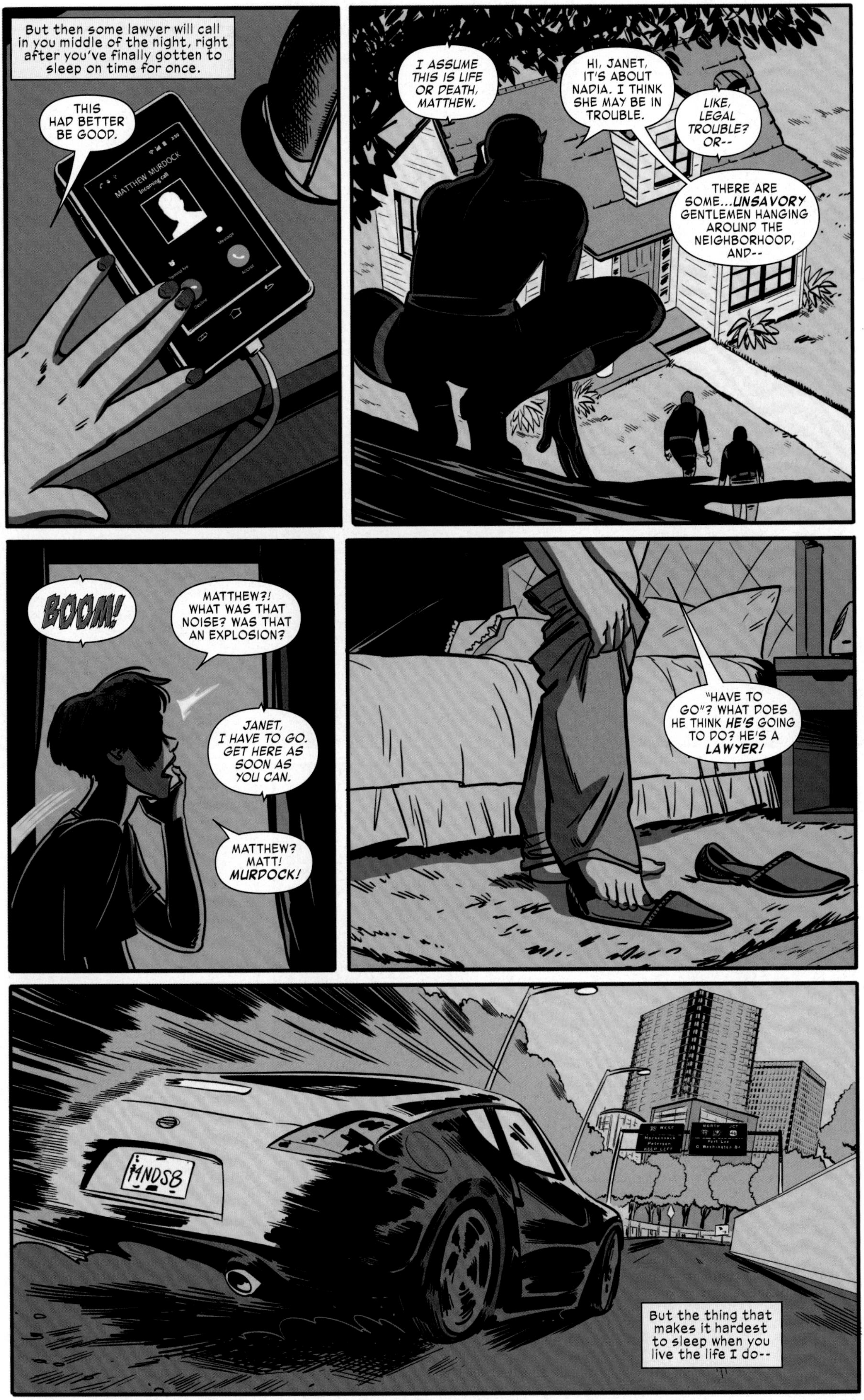
But then some lawyer will call in you middle of the night, right after you've finally gotten to sleep on time for once.
THIS HAD BETTER BE GOOD.
MATTHEW MURDOCK
Incoming call
I ASSUME THIS IS LIFE OR DEATH, MATTHEW.
HI, JANET, IT'S ABOUT NADIA. I THINK SHE MAY BE IN TROUBLE.
LIKE, LEGAL TROUBLE? OR--
THERE ARE SOME...UNSAVORY GENTLEMEN HANGING AROUND THE NEIGHBORHOOD, AND--
BOOM!
MATTHEW?! WHAT WAS THAT NOISE? WAS THAT AN EXPLOSION?
JANET, I HAVE TO GO. GET HERE AS SOON AS YOU CAN.
MATTHEW? MATT! MURDOCK!
"HAVE TO GO"? WHAT DOES HE THINK HE'S GOING TO DO? HE'S A LAWYER!
But the thing that makes it hardest to sleep when you live the life I do--

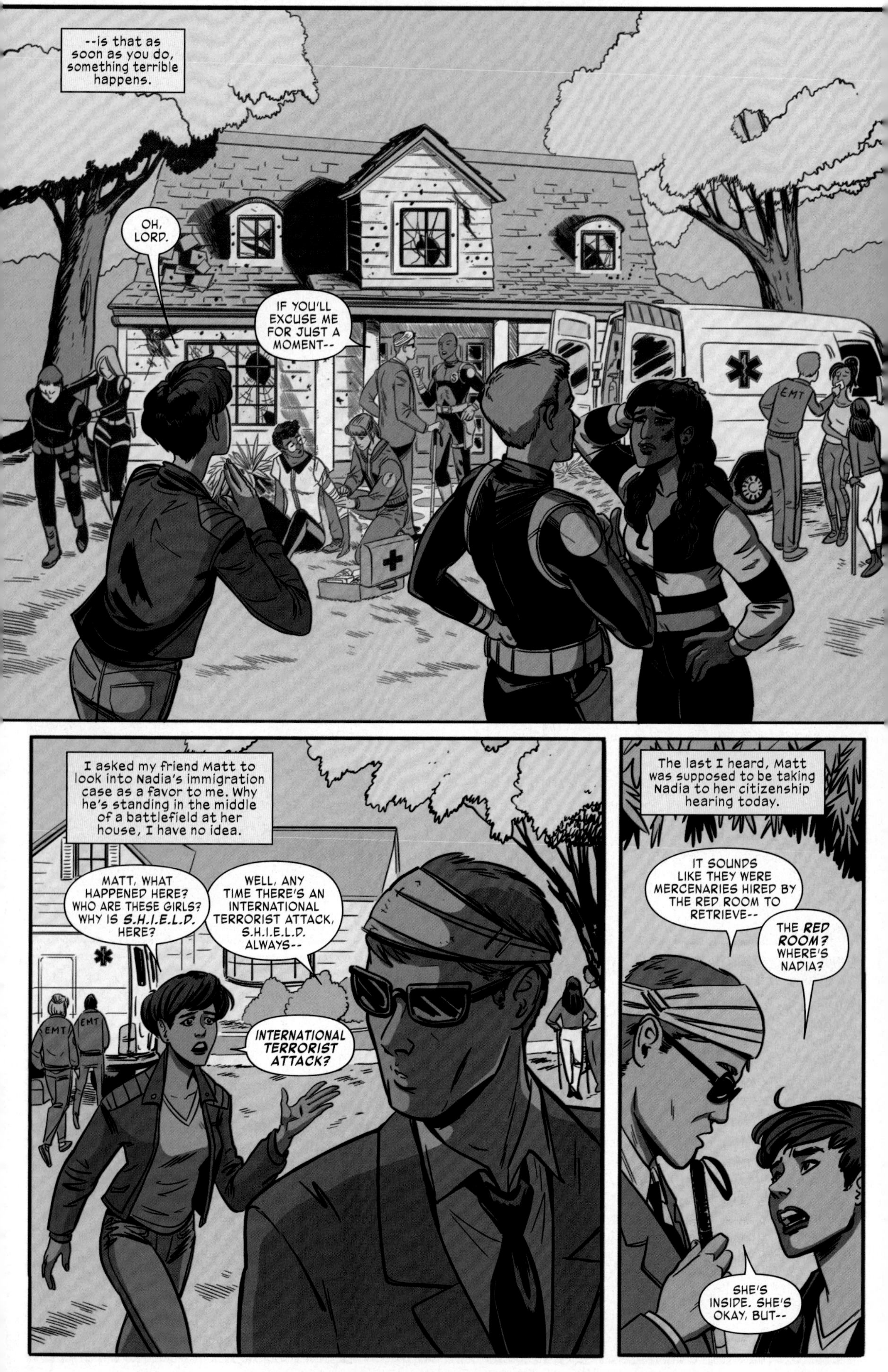
--is that as soon as you do, something terrible happens.
OH, LORD.
IF YOU'LL EXCUSE ME FOR JUST A MOMENT--
EMT
I asked my friend Matt to look into Nadia's immigration case as a favor to me. Why he's standing in the middle of a battlefield at her house, I have no idea.
MATT, WHAT HAPPENED HERE? WHO ARE THESE GIRLS? WHY IS S.H.I.E.L.D. HERE?
WELL, ANY TIME THERE'S AN INTERNATIONAL TERRORIST ATTACK, S.H.I.E.L.D. ALWAYS--
INTERNATIONAL TERRORIST ATTACK?
EMT
EMT
The last I heard, Matt was supposed to be taking Nadia to her citizenship hearing today.
IT SOUNDS LIKE THEY WERE MERCENARIES HIRED BY THE RED ROOM TO RETRIEVE--
THE RED ROOM? WHERE'S NADIA?
SHE'S INSIDE. SHE'S OKAY, BUT--

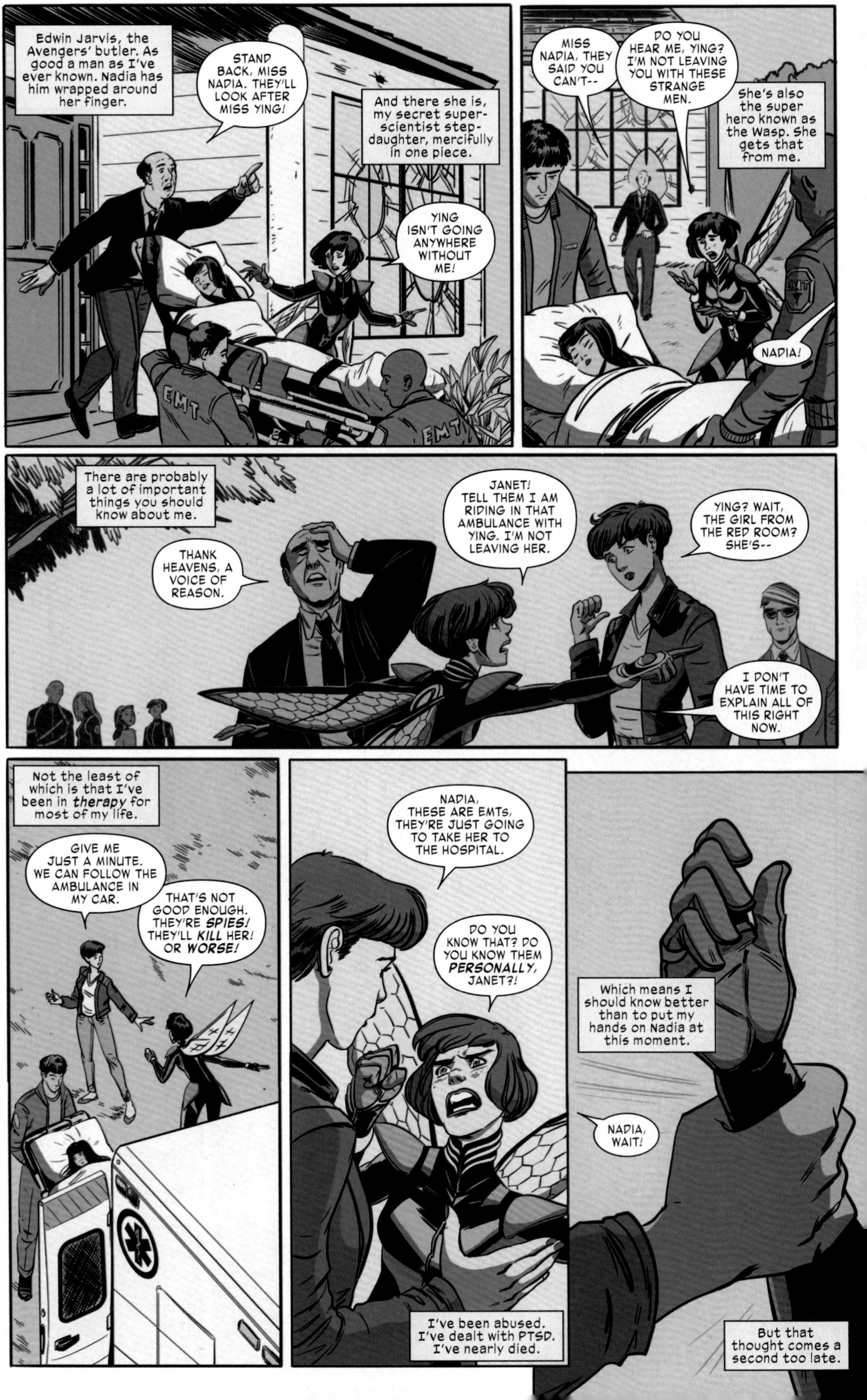
Edwin Jarvis, the Avengers' butler. As good a man as I've ever known. Nadia has him wrapped around her finger.
STAND BACK, MISS NADIA. THEY'LL LOOK AFTER MISS YING!
And there she is, my secret super-scientist step-daughter, mercifully in one piece.
YING ISN'T GOING ANYWHERE WITHOUT ME!
EMT
MISS NADIA, THEY SAID YOU CAN'T--
DO YOU HEAR ME, YING? I'M NOT LEAVING YOU WITH THESE STRANGE MEN.
She's also the super hero known as the Wasp. She gets that from me.
NADIA!
There are probably a lot of important things you should know about me.
THANK HEAVENS, A VOICE OF REASON.
JANET! TELL THEM I AM RIDING IN THAT AMBULANCE WITH YING. I'M NOT LEAVING HER.
YING? WAIT, THE GIRL FROM THE RED ROOM? SHE'S--
I DON'T HAVE TIME TO EXPLAIN ALL OF THIS RIGHT NOW.
Not the least of which is that I've been in *therapy* for most of my life.
GIVE ME JUST A MINUTE. WE CAN FOLLOW THE AMBULANCE IN MY CAR.
THAT'S NOT GOOD ENOUGH. THEY'RE ***SPIES!*** THEY'LL ***KILL*** HER! OR ***WORSE!***
NADIA, THESE ARE EMTS, THEY'RE JUST GOING TO TAKE HER TO THE HOSPITAL.
DO YOU KNOW THAT? DO YOU KNOW THEM ***PERSONALLY,*** JANET?!
I've been abused. I've dealt with PTSD. I've nearly died.
Which means I should know better than to put my hands on Nadia at this moment.
NADIA, WAIT!
But that thought comes a second too late.

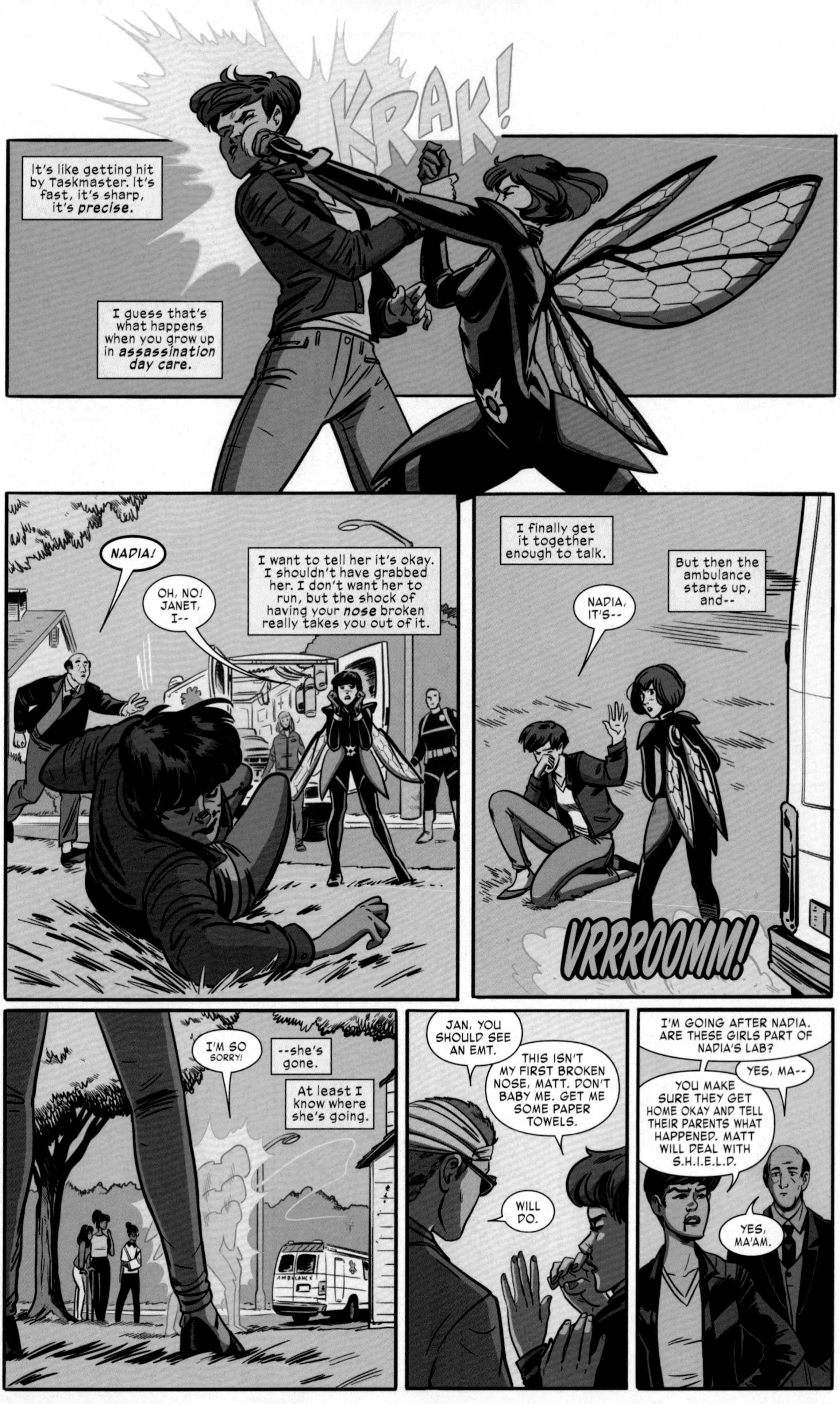
KRAK!
It's like getting hit by Taskmaster. It's fast, it's sharp, it's *precise.*
I guess that's what happens when you grow up in ***assassination day care.***
NADIA!
OH, NO! JANET, I--
I want to tell her it's okay. I shouldn't have grabbed her. I don't want her to run, but the shock of having your *nose* broken really takes you out of it.
I finally get it together enough to talk.
NADIA, IT'S--
But then the ambulance starts up, and--
VRRROOMM!
I'M SO SORRY!
--she's gone.
At least I know where she's going.
AMBULANCE
JAN, YOU SHOULD SEE AN EMT.
THIS ISN'T MY FIRST BROKEN NOSE, MATT. DON'T BABY ME. GET ME SOME PAPER TOWELS.
WILL DO.
I'M GOING AFTER NADIA. ARE THESE GIRLS PART OF NADIA'S LAB?
YES, MA--
YOU MAKE SURE THEY GET HOME OKAY AND TELL THEIR PARENTS WHAT HAPPENED. MATT WILL DEAL WITH S.H.I.E.L.D.
YES, MA'AM.

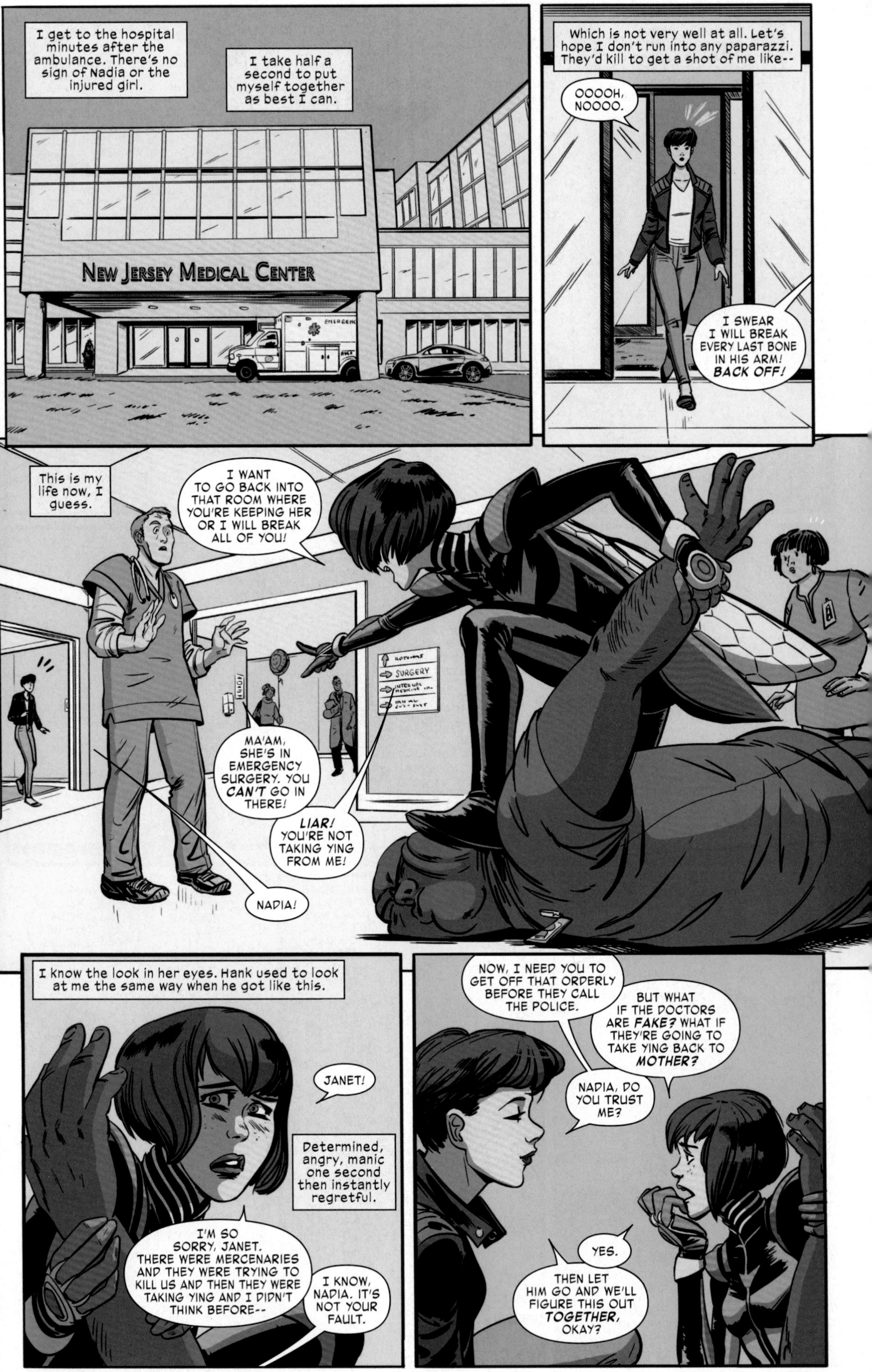

I get to the hospital minutes after the ambulance. There's no sign of Nadia or the injured girl.
I take half a second to put myself together as best I can.
NEW JERSEY MEDICAL CENTER
Which is not very well at all. Let's hope I don't run into any paparazzi. They'd kill to get a shot of me like--
OOOOH, NOOOO.
I SWEAR I WILL BREAK EVERY LAST BONE IN HIS ARM! BACK OFF!
This is my life now, I guess.
I WANT TO GO BACK INTO THAT ROOM WHERE YOU'RE KEEPING HER OR I WILL BREAK ALL OF YOU!
SURGERY
MA'AM, SHE'S IN EMERGENCY SURGERY. YOU CAN'T GO IN THERE!
LIAR! YOU'RE NOT TAKING YING FROM ME!
NADIA!
I know the look in her eyes. Hank used to look at me the same way when he got like this.
JANET!
Determined, angry, manic one second then instantly regretful.
I'M SO SORRY, JANET. THERE WERE MERCENARIES AND THEY WERE TRYING TO KILL US AND THEN THEY WERE TAKING YING AND I DIDN'T THINK BEFORE--
I KNOW, NADIA. IT'S NOT YOUR FAULT.
NOW, I NEED YOU TO GET OFF THAT ORDERLY BEFORE THEY CALL THE POLICE.
BUT WHAT IF THE DOCTORS ARE FAKE? WHAT IF THEY'RE GOING TO TAKE YING BACK TO MOTHER?
NADIA, DO YOU TRUST ME?
YES.
THEN LET HIM GO AND WE'LL FIGURE THIS OUT TOGETHER, OKAY?

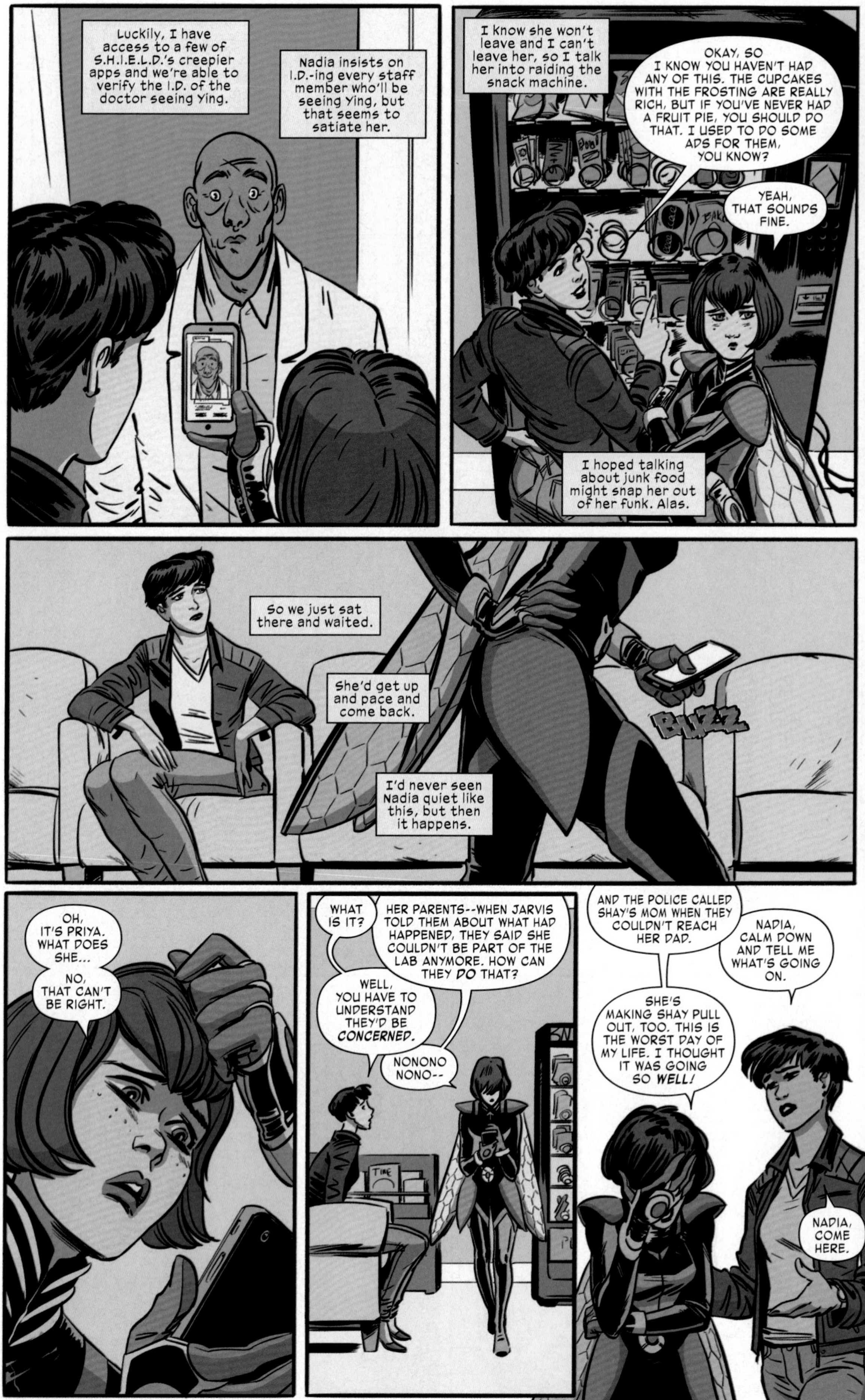
Luckily, I have access to a few of S.H.I.E.L.D.'s creepier apps and we're able to verify the I.D. of the doctor seeing Ying.
Nadia insists on I.D.-ing every staff member who'll be seeing Ying, but that seems to satiate her.
I know she won't leave and I can't leave her, so I talk her into raiding the snack machine.
OKAY, SO I KNOW YOU HAVEN'T HAD ANY OF THIS. THE CUPCAKES WITH THE FROSTING ARE REALLY RICH, BUT IF YOU'VE NEVER HAD A FRUIT PIE, YOU SHOULD DO THAT. I USED TO DO SOME ADS FOR THEM, YOU KNOW?
YEAH, THAT SOUNDS FINE.
I hoped talking about junk food might snap her out of her funk. Alas.
So we just sat there and waited.
She'd get up and pace and come back.
I'd never seen Nadia quiet like this, but then it happens.
BUZZ
OH, IT'S PRIYA. WHAT DOES SHE...
NO, THAT CAN'T BE RIGHT.
WHAT IS IT?
HER PARENTS--WHEN JARVIS TOLD THEM ABOUT WHAT HAD HAPPENED, THEY SAID SHE COULDN'T BE PART OF THE LAB ANYMORE. HOW CAN THEY *DO* THAT?
WELL, YOU HAVE TO UNDERSTAND THEY'D BE *CONCERNED.*
NONONO NONO--
AND THE POLICE CALLED SHAY'S MOM WHEN THEY COULDN'T REACH HER DAD.
NADIA, CALM DOWN AND TELL ME WHAT'S GOING ON.
SHE'S MAKING SHAY PULL OUT, TOO. THIS IS THE WORST DAY OF MY LIFE. I THOUGHT IT WAS GOING SO **WELL!**
NADIA, COME HERE.

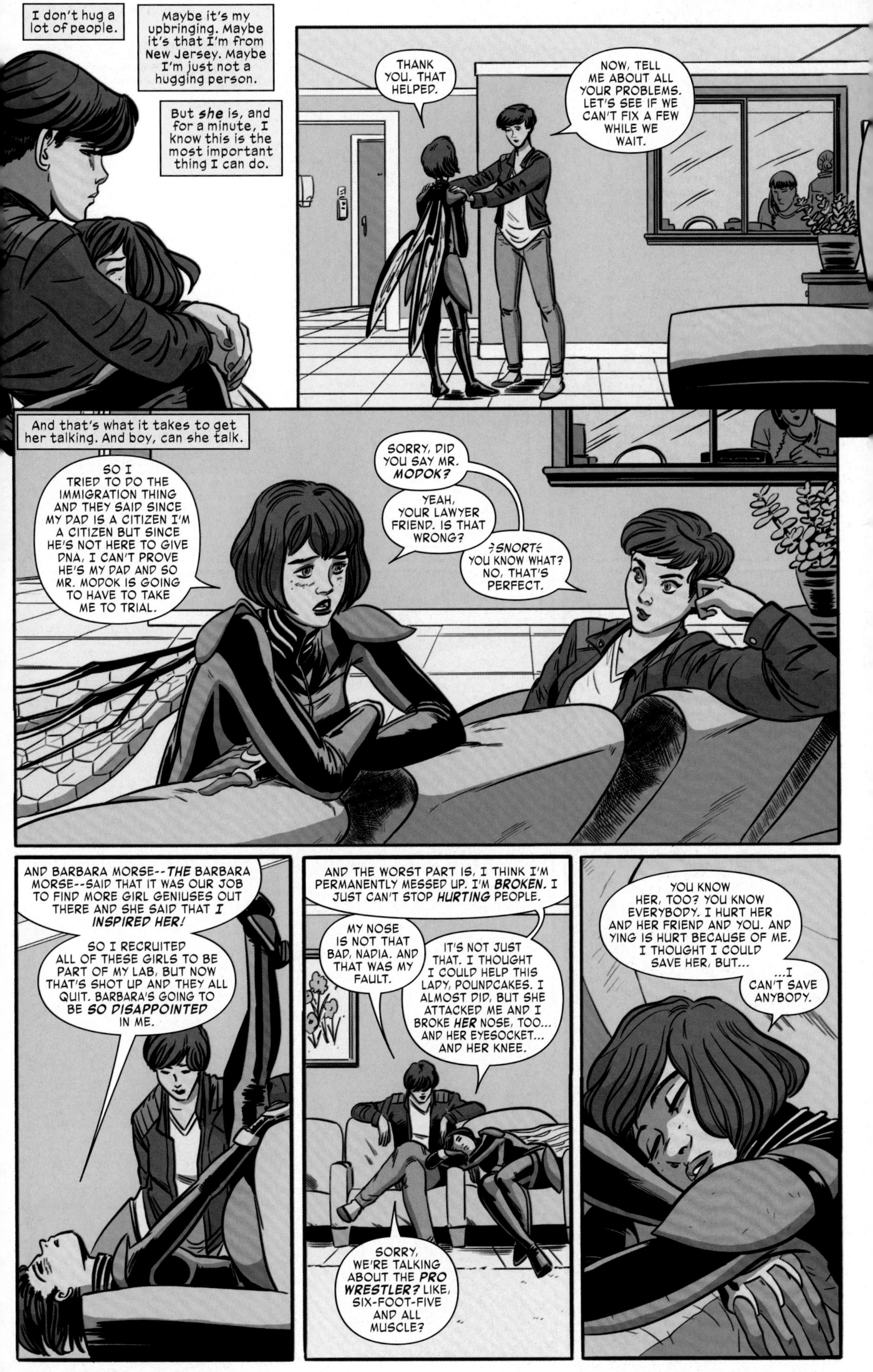

I don't hug a lot of people.
Maybe it's my upbringing. Maybe it's that I'm from New Jersey. Maybe I'm just not a hugging person.
But she is, and for a minute, I know this is the most important thing I can do.
THANK YOU. THAT HELPED.
NOW, TELL ME ABOUT ALL YOUR PROBLEMS. LET'S SEE IF WE CAN'T FIX A FEW WHILE WE WAIT.
And that's what it takes to get her talking. And boy, can she talk.
SO I TRIED TO DO THE IMMIGRATION THING AND THEY SAID SINCE MY DAD IS A CITIZEN I'M A CITIZEN BUT SINCE HE'S NOT HERE TO GIVE DNA, I CAN'T PROVE HE'S MY DAD AND SO MR. MODOK IS GOING TO HAVE TO TAKE ME TO TRIAL.
SORRY, DID YOU SAY MR. MODOK?
YEAH, YOUR LAWYER FRIEND. IS THAT WRONG?
SNORT YOU KNOW WHAT? NO, THAT'S PERFECT.
AND BARBARA MORSE--THE BARBARA MORSE--SAID THAT IT WAS OUR JOB TO FIND MORE GIRL GENIUSES OUT THERE AND SHE SAID THAT I INSPIRED HER!
SO I RECRUITED ALL OF THESE GIRLS TO BE PART OF MY LAB, BUT NOW THAT'S SHOT UP AND THEY ALL QUIT. BARBARA'S GOING TO BE SO DISAPPOINTED IN ME.
AND THE WORST PART IS, I THINK I'M PERMANENTLY MESSED UP. I'M BROKEN. I JUST CAN'T STOP HURTING PEOPLE.
MY NOSE IS NOT THAT BAD, NADIA. AND THAT WAS MY FAULT.
IT'S NOT JUST THAT. I THOUGHT I COULD HELP THIS LADY, POUNDCAKES. I ALMOST DID, BUT SHE ATTACKED ME AND I BROKE HER NOSE, TOO... AND HER EYESOCKET... AND HER KNEE.
SORRY, WE'RE TALKING ABOUT THE PRO WRESTLER? LIKE, SIX-FOOT-FIVE AND ALL MUSCLE?
YOU KNOW HER, TOO? YOU KNOW EVERYBODY. I HURT HER AND HER FRIEND AND YOU. AND YING IS HURT BECAUSE OF ME. I THOUGHT I COULD SAVE HER, BUT...
...I CAN'T SAVE ANYBODY.

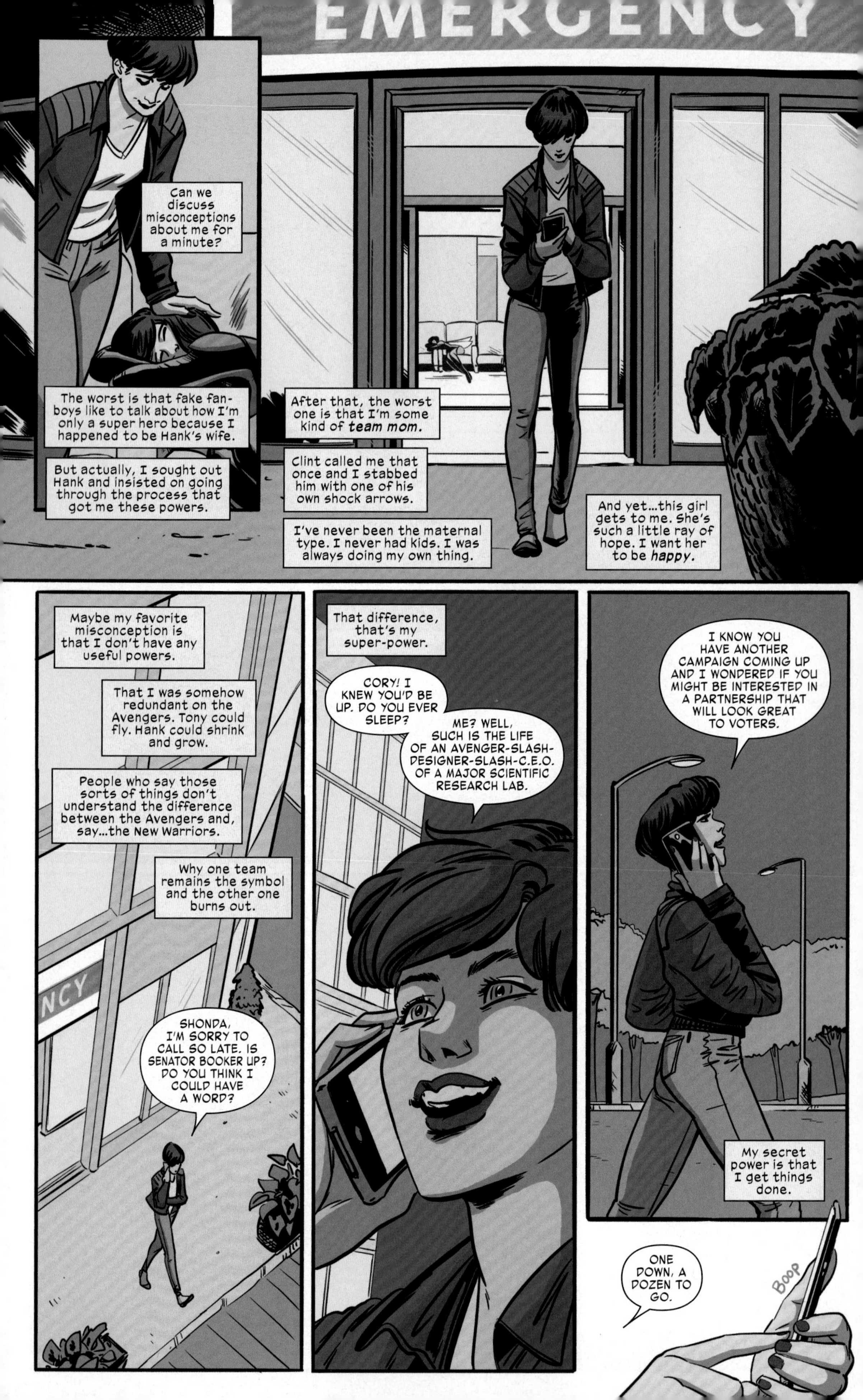
EMERGENCY
Can we discuss misconceptions about me for a minute?
The worst is that fake fanboys like to talk about how I'm only a super hero because I happened to be Hank's wife.
But actually, I sought out Hank and insisted on going through the process that got me these powers.
After that, the worst one is that I'm some kind of *team mom.*
Clint called me that once and I stabbed him with one of his own shock arrows.
I've never been the maternal type. I never had kids. I was always doing my own thing.
And yet...this girl gets to me. She's such a little ray of hope. I want her to be *happy.*
Maybe my favorite misconception is that I don't have any useful powers.
That I was somehow redundant on the Avengers. Tony could fly. Hank could shrink and grow.
People who say those sorts of things don't understand the difference between the Avengers and, say...the New Warriors.
Why one team remains the symbol and the other one burns out.
NCY
SHONDA, I'M SORRY TO CALL SO LATE. IS SENATOR BOOKER UP? DO YOU THINK I COULD HAVE A WORD?
That difference, that's my super-power.
CORY! I KNEW YOU'D BE UP. DO YOU EVER SLEEP?
ME? WELL, SUCH IS THE LIFE OF AN AVENGER-SLASH-DESIGNER-SLASH-C.E.O. OF A MAJOR SCIENTIFIC RESEARCH LAB.
I KNOW YOU HAVE ANOTHER CAMPAIGN COMING UP AND I WONDERED IF YOU MIGHT BE INTERESTED IN A PARTNERSHIP THAT WILL LOOK GREAT TO VOTERS.
My secret power is that I get things done.
ONE DOWN, A DOZEN TO GO.
BOOP

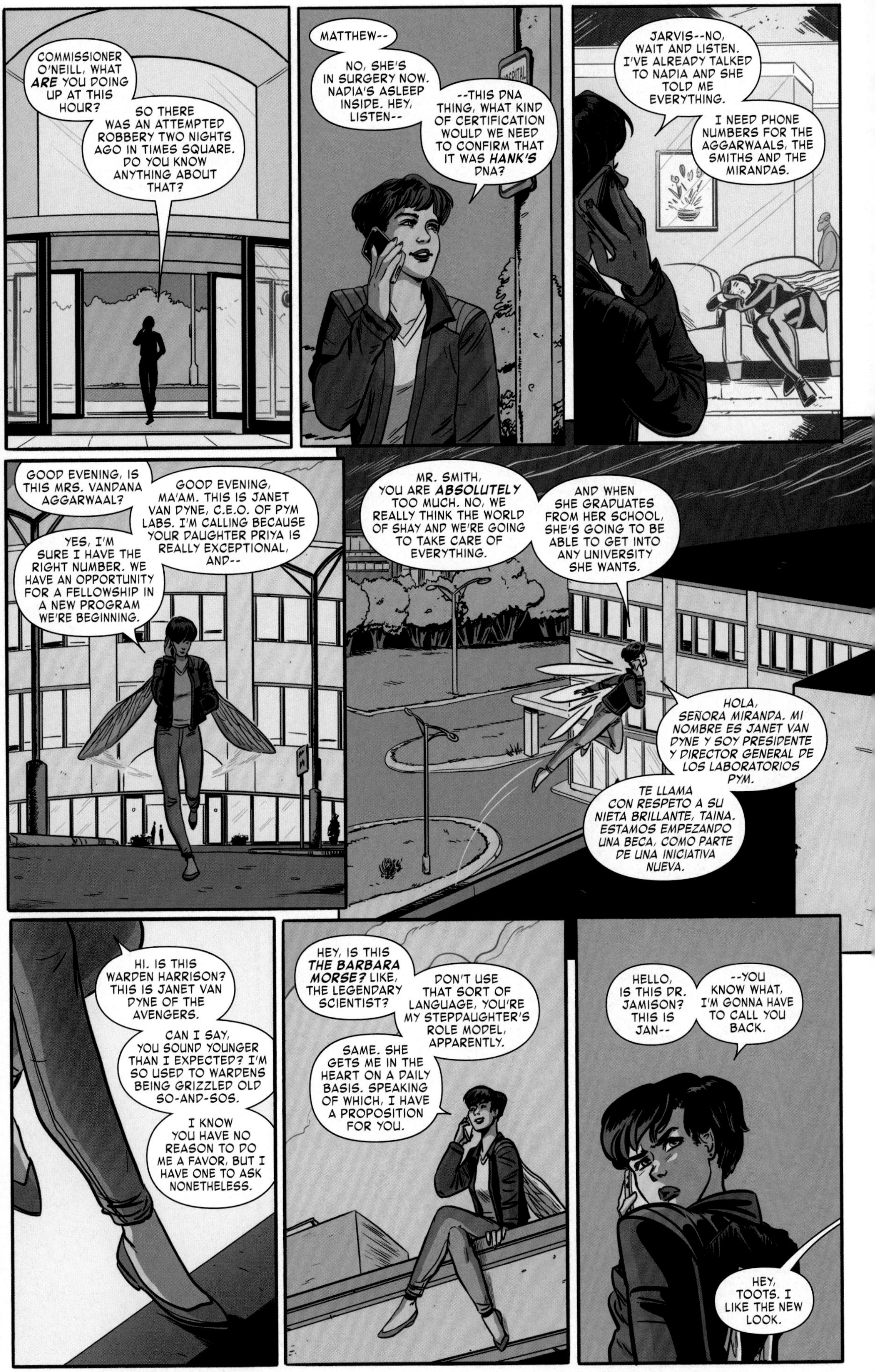
COMMISSIONER O'NEILL, WHAT ARE YOU DOING UP AT THIS HOUR?
SO THERE WAS AN ATTEMPTED ROBBERY TWO NIGHTS AGO IN TIMES SQUARE. DO YOU KNOW ANYTHING ABOUT THAT?
MATTHEW--
NO, SHE'S IN SURGERY NOW. NADIA'S ASLEEP INSIDE. HEY, LISTEN--
--THIS DNA THING, WHAT KIND OF CERTIFICATION WOULD WE NEED TO CONFIRM THAT IT WAS HANK'S DNA?
JARVIS--NO, WAIT AND LISTEN. I'VE ALREADY TALKED TO NADIA AND SHE TOLD ME EVERYTHING.
I NEED PHONE NUMBERS FOR THE AGGARWAALS, THE SMITHS AND THE MIRANDAS.
GOOD EVENING, IS THIS MRS. VANDANA AGGARWAAL?
GOOD EVENING, MA'AM. THIS IS JANET VAN DYNE, C.E.O. OF PYM LABS. I'M CALLING BECAUSE YOUR DAUGHTER PRIYA IS REALLY EXCEPTIONAL, AND--
YES, I'M SURE I HAVE THE RIGHT NUMBER. WE HAVE AN OPPORTUNITY FOR A FELLOWSHIP IN A NEW PROGRAM WE'RE BEGINNING.
MR. SMITH, YOU ARE ABSOLUTELY TOO MUCH. NO, WE REALLY THINK THE WORLD OF SHAY AND WE'RE GOING TO TAKE CARE OF EVERYTHING.
AND WHEN SHE GRADUATES FROM HER SCHOOL, SHE'S GOING TO BE ABLE TO GET INTO ANY UNIVERSITY SHE WANTS.
HOLA, SEÑORA MIRANDA. MI NOMBRE ES JANET VAN DYNE Y SOY PRESIDENTE Y DIRECTOR GENERAL DE LOS LABORATORIOS PYM.
TE LLAMA CON RESPETO A SU NIETA BRILLANTE, TAINA. ESTAMOS EMPEZANDO UNA BECA, COMO PARTE DE UNA INICIATIVA NUEVA.
HI. IS THIS WARDEN HARRISON? THIS IS JANET VAN DYNE OF THE AVENGERS.
CAN I SAY, YOU SOUND YOUNGER THAN I EXPECTED? I'M SO USED TO WARDENS BEING GRIZZLED OLD SO-AND-SOS.
I KNOW YOU HAVE NO REASON TO DO ME A FAVOR, BUT I HAVE ONE TO ASK NONETHELESS.
HEY, IS THIS THE BARBARA MORSE? LIKE, THE LEGENDARY SCIENTIST?
DON'T USE THAT SORT OF LANGUAGE, YOU'RE MY STEPDAUGHTER'S ROLE MODEL, APPARENTLY.
SAME. SHE GETS ME IN THE HEART ON A DAILY BASIS. SPEAKING OF WHICH, I HAVE A PROPOSITION FOR YOU.
HELLO, IS THIS DR. JAMISON? THIS IS JAN--
--YOU KNOW WHAT, I'M GONNA HAVE TO CALL YOU BACK.
HEY, TOOTS. I LIKE THE NEW LOOK.

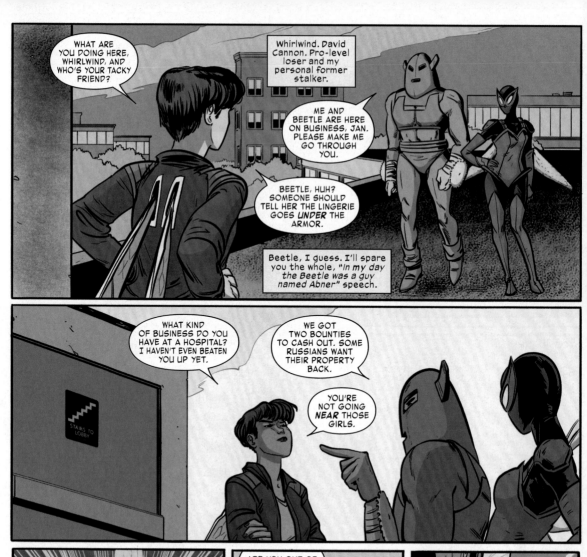

WHAT ARE YOU DOING HERE, WHIRLWIND, AND WHO'S YOUR TACKY FRIEND?

Whirlwind. David Cannon. Pro-level loser and my personal former stalker.

ME AND BEETLE ARE HERE ON BUSINESS, JAN. PLEASE MAKE ME GO THROUGH YOU.

BEETLE, HUH? SOMEONE SHOULD TELL HER THE LINGERIE GOES *UNDER* THE ARMOR.

Beetle, I guess. I'll spare you the whole, "In my day the Beetle was a guy named Abner" speech.

WHAT KIND OF BUSINESS DO YOU HAVE AT A HOSPITAL? I HAVEN'T EVEN BEATEN YOU UP YET.

WE GOT TWO BOUNTIES TO CASH OUT. SOME RUSSIANS WANT THEIR PROPERTY BACK.

YOU'RE NOT GOING *NEAR* THOSE GIRLS.

YEAH? AND WHO'S GONNA--

BOOOOORING!

ARE YOU OUT OF YOUR MIND?! YOU ALMOST TOOK MY HEAD OFF!

I GUESS THAT'S IT FOR THE WASP, EH? I ALWAYS THOUGHT IT WOULD BE A BIGGER DEAL WHEN I KILLED AN AVENGER.

YOU MOUTHY BROAD! YOU *DIDN'T* KILL HER!

IF I DIDN'T KILL HER, THEN WHY IS THERE ONLY A PILE OF ASH BETWEEN US AND THE DOORWAY?

SHE SHRUNK DOWN! ANY SECOND NOW SHE'S GONNA--

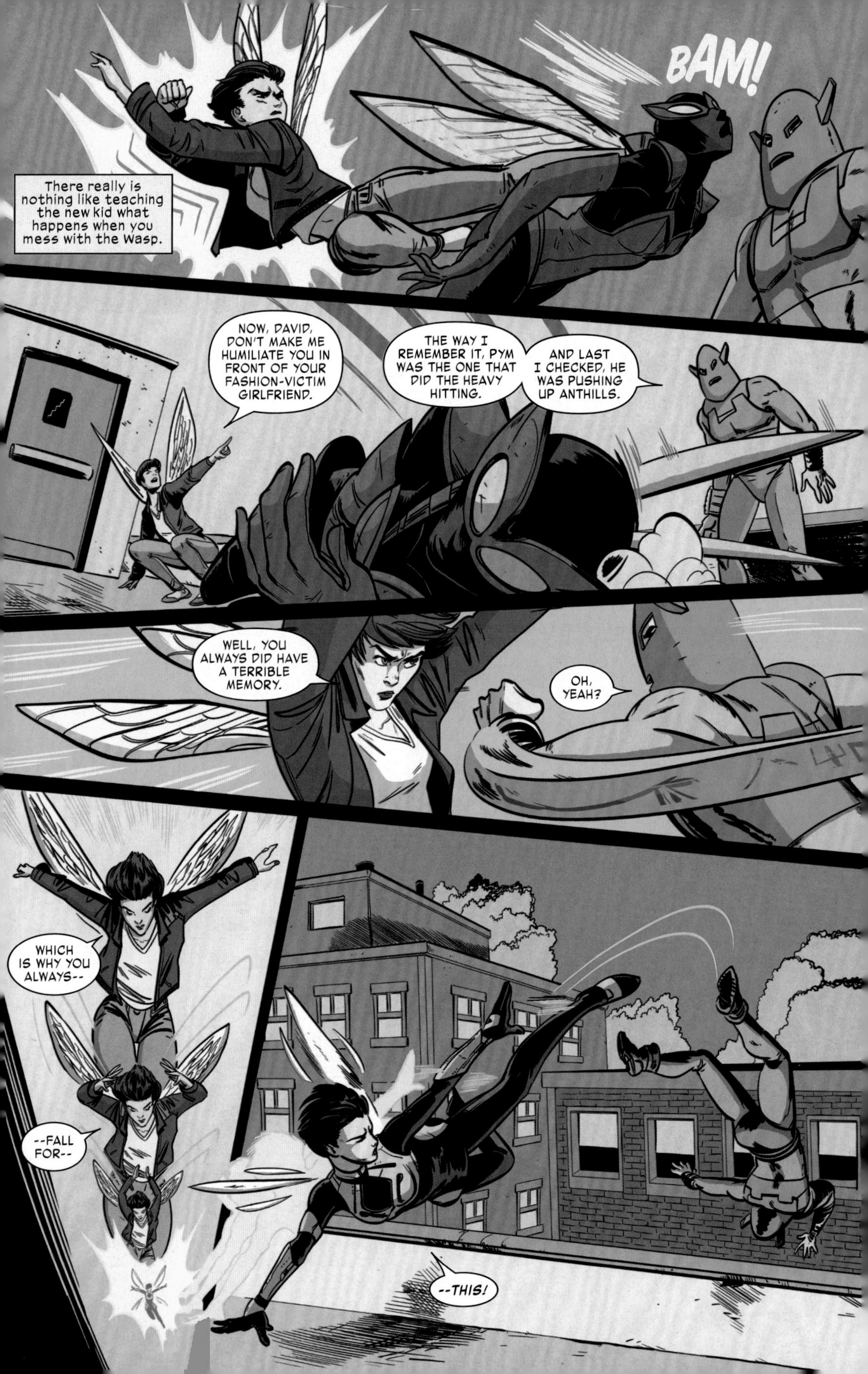
BAM!
There really is nothing like teaching the new kid what happens when you mess with the Wasp.
NOW, DAVID, DON'T MAKE ME HUMILIATE YOU IN FRONT OF YOUR FASHION-VICTIM GIRLFRIEND.
THE WAY I REMEMBER IT, PYM WAS THE ONE THAT DID THE HEAVY HITTING.
AND LAST I CHECKED, HE WAS PUSHING UP ANTHILLS.
WELL, YOU ALWAYS DID HAVE A TERRIBLE MEMORY.
OH, YEAH?
WHICH IS WHY YOU ALWAYS--
--FALL FOR--
--THIS!

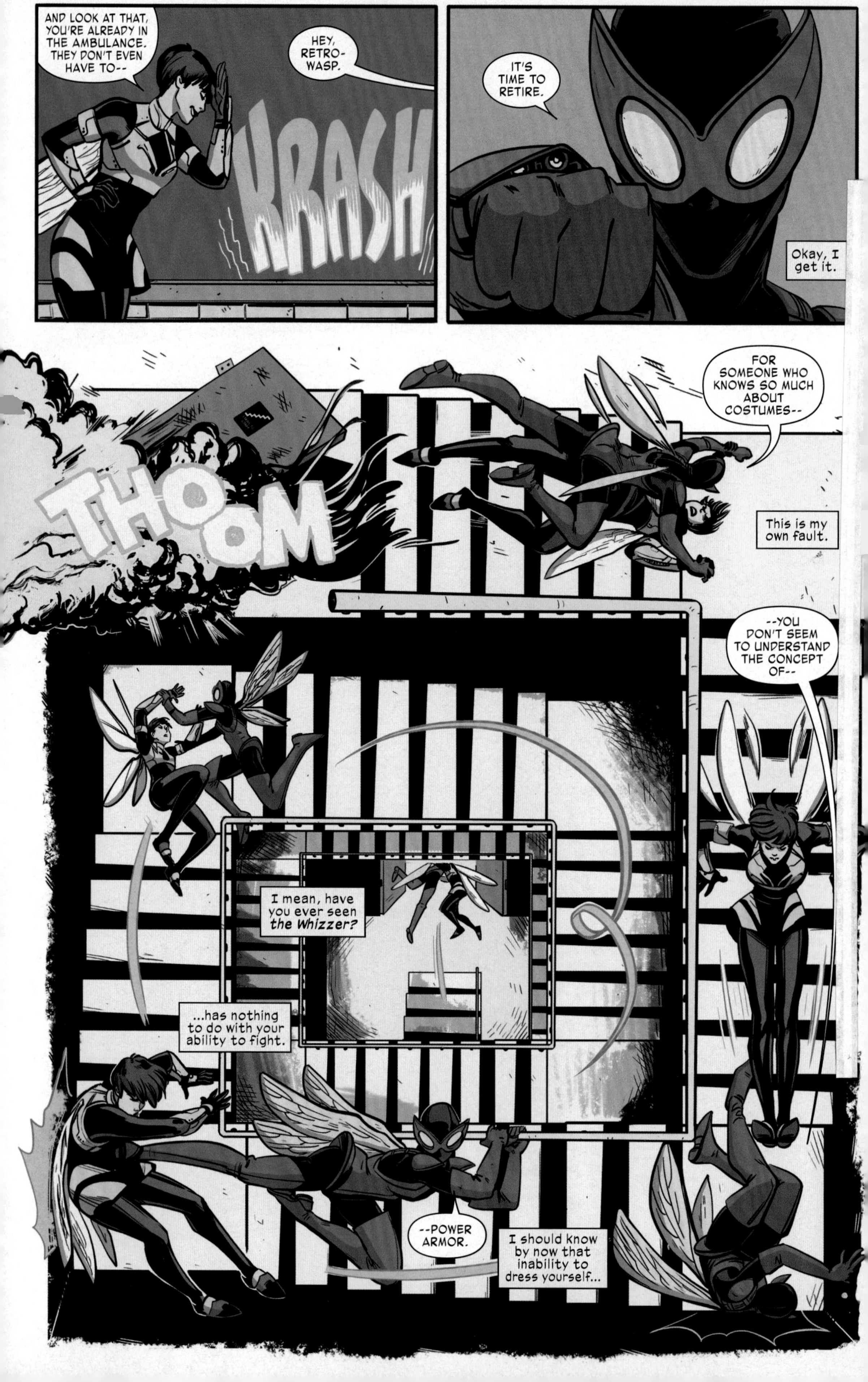

AND LOOK AT THAT, YOU'RE ALREADY IN THE AMBULANCE. THEY DON'T EVEN HAVE TO--
HEY, RETRO-WASP.
KRASH
IT'S TIME TO RETIRE.
Okay, I get it.
THOOM
FOR SOMEONE WHO KNOWS SO MUCH ABOUT COSTUMES--
This is my own fault.
--YOU DON'T SEEM TO UNDERSTAND THE CONCEPT OF--
I mean, have you ever seen the Whizzer?
...has nothing to do with your ability to fight.
--POWER ARMOR.
I should know by now that inability to dress yourself...

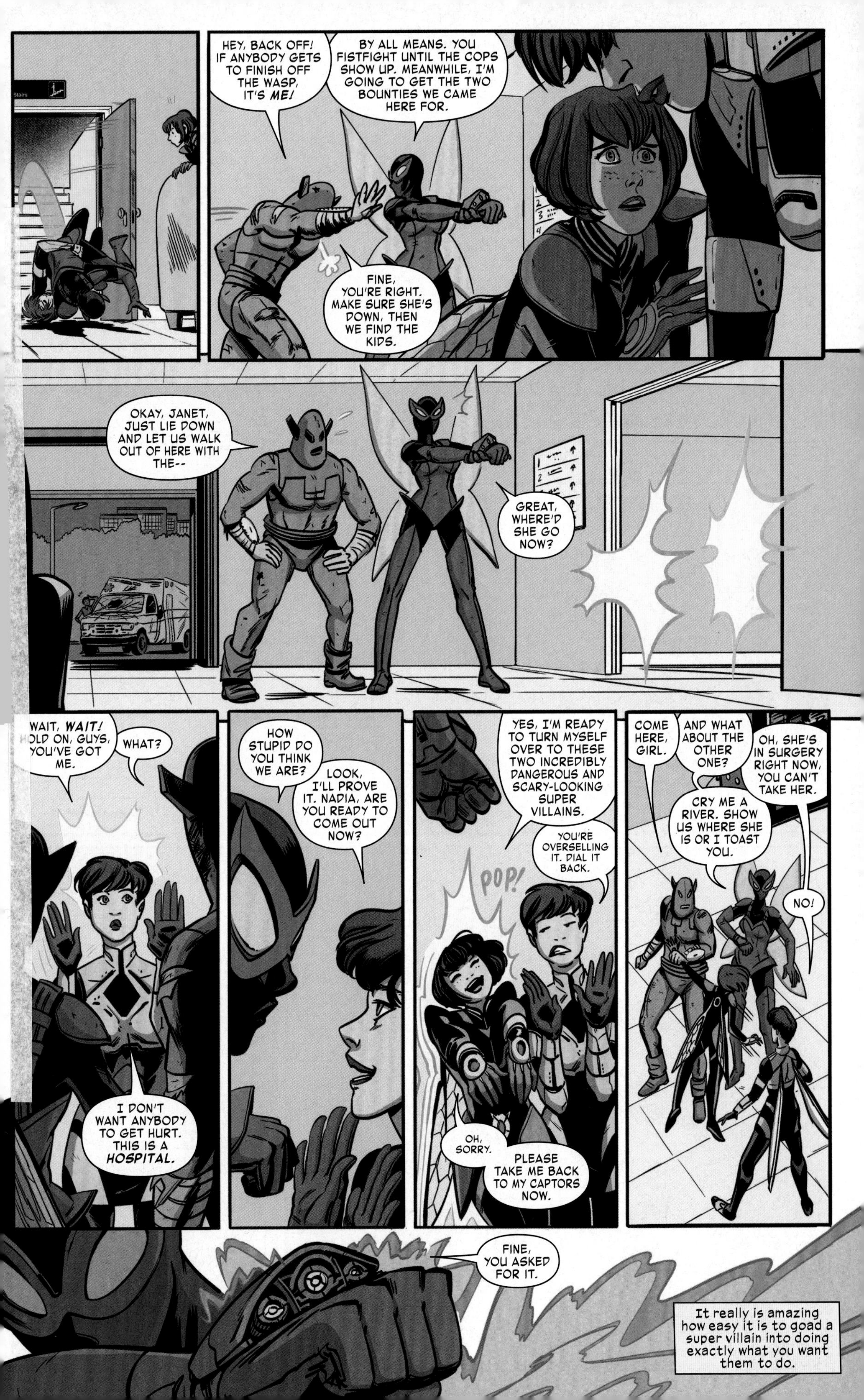
Stairs
HEY, BACK OFF! IF ANYBODY GETS TO FINISH OFF THE WASP, IT'S ME!
BY ALL MEANS. YOU FISTFIGHT UNTIL THE COPS SHOW UP. MEANWHILE, I'M GOING TO GET THE TWO BOUNTIES WE CAME HERE FOR.
FINE, YOU'RE RIGHT. MAKE SURE SHE'S DOWN, THEN WE FIND THE KIDS.
OKAY, JANET, JUST LIE DOWN AND LET US WALK OUT OF HERE WITH THE--
GREAT, WHERE'D SHE GO NOW?
WAIT, WAIT! HOLD ON, GUYS, YOU'VE GOT ME.
WHAT?
I DON'T WANT ANYBODY TO GET HURT. THIS IS A HOSPITAL.
HOW STUPID DO YOU THINK WE ARE?
LOOK, I'LL PROVE IT. NADIA, ARE YOU READY TO COME OUT NOW?
YES, I'M READY TO TURN MYSELF OVER TO THESE TWO INCREDIBLY DANGEROUS AND SCARY-LOOKING SUPER VILLAINS.
YOU'RE OVERSELLING IT. DIAL IT BACK.
POP!
OH, SORRY.
PLEASE TAKE ME BACK TO MY CAPTORS NOW.
COME HERE, GIRL.
AND WHAT ABOUT THE OTHER ONE?
OH, SHE'S IN SURGERY RIGHT NOW, YOU CAN'T TAKE HER.
CRY ME A RIVER. SHOW US WHERE SHE IS OR I TOAST YOU.
NO!
FINE, YOU ASKED FOR IT.
It really is amazing how easy it is to goad a super villain into doing exactly what you want them to do.

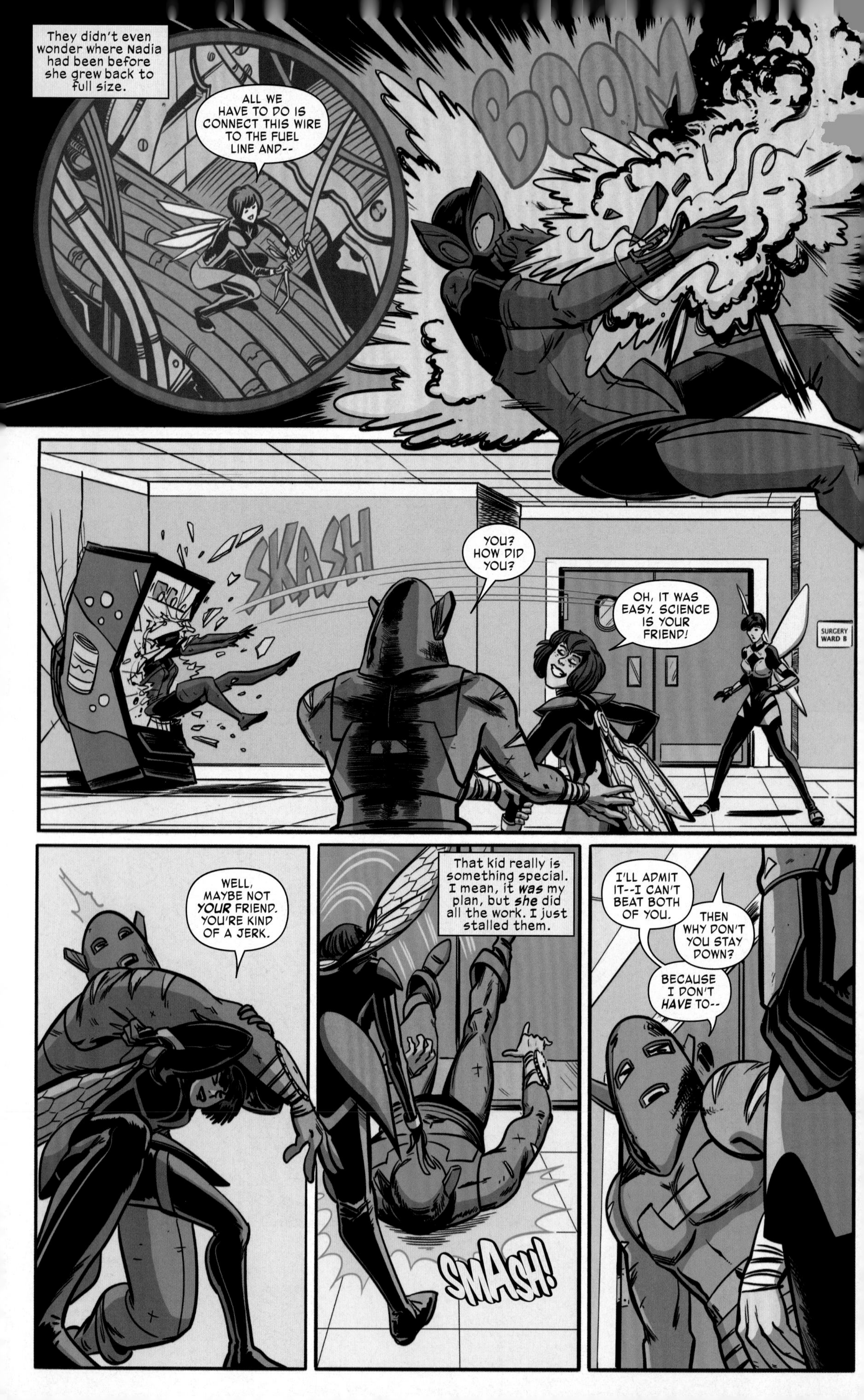

They didn't even wonder where Nadia had been before she grew back to full size.
ALL WE HAVE TO DO IS CONNECT THIS WIRE TO THE FUEL LINE AND--
BOOM
SKASH
YOU? HOW DID YOU?
OH, IT WAS EASY. SCIENCE IS YOUR FRIEND!
SURGERY WARD B
WELL, MAYBE NOT YOUR FRIEND. YOU'RE KIND OF A JERK.
That kid really is something special. I mean, it was my plan, but she did all the work. I just stalled them.
SMASH!
I'LL ADMIT IT--I CAN'T BEAT BOTH OF YOU.
THEN WHY DON'T YOU STAY DOWN?
BECAUSE I DON'T HAVE TO--

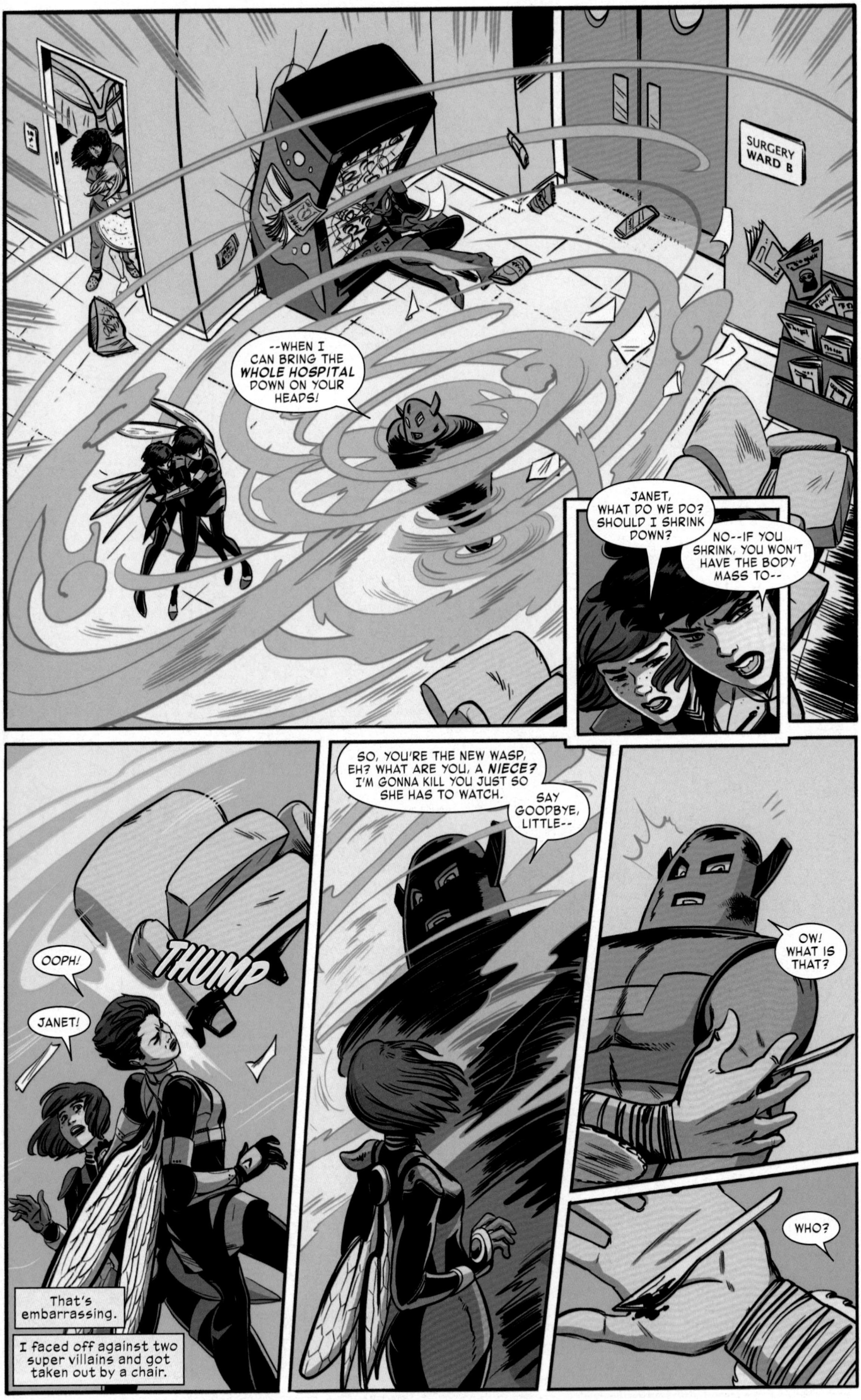
SURGERY
WARD B
--WHEN I CAN BRING THE WHOLE HOSPITAL DOWN ON YOUR HEADS!
JANET, WHAT DO WE DO? SHOULD I SHRINK DOWN?
NO--IF YOU SHRINK, YOU WON'T HAVE THE BODY MASS TO--
OOPH!
THUMP
JANET!
That's embarrassing.
I faced off against two super villains and got taken out by a chair.
SO, YOU'RE THE NEW WASP, EH? WHAT ARE YOU, A NIECE? I'M GONNA KILL YOU JUST SO SHE HAS TO WATCH.
SAY GOODBYE, LITTLE--
OW! WHAT IS THAT?
WHO?

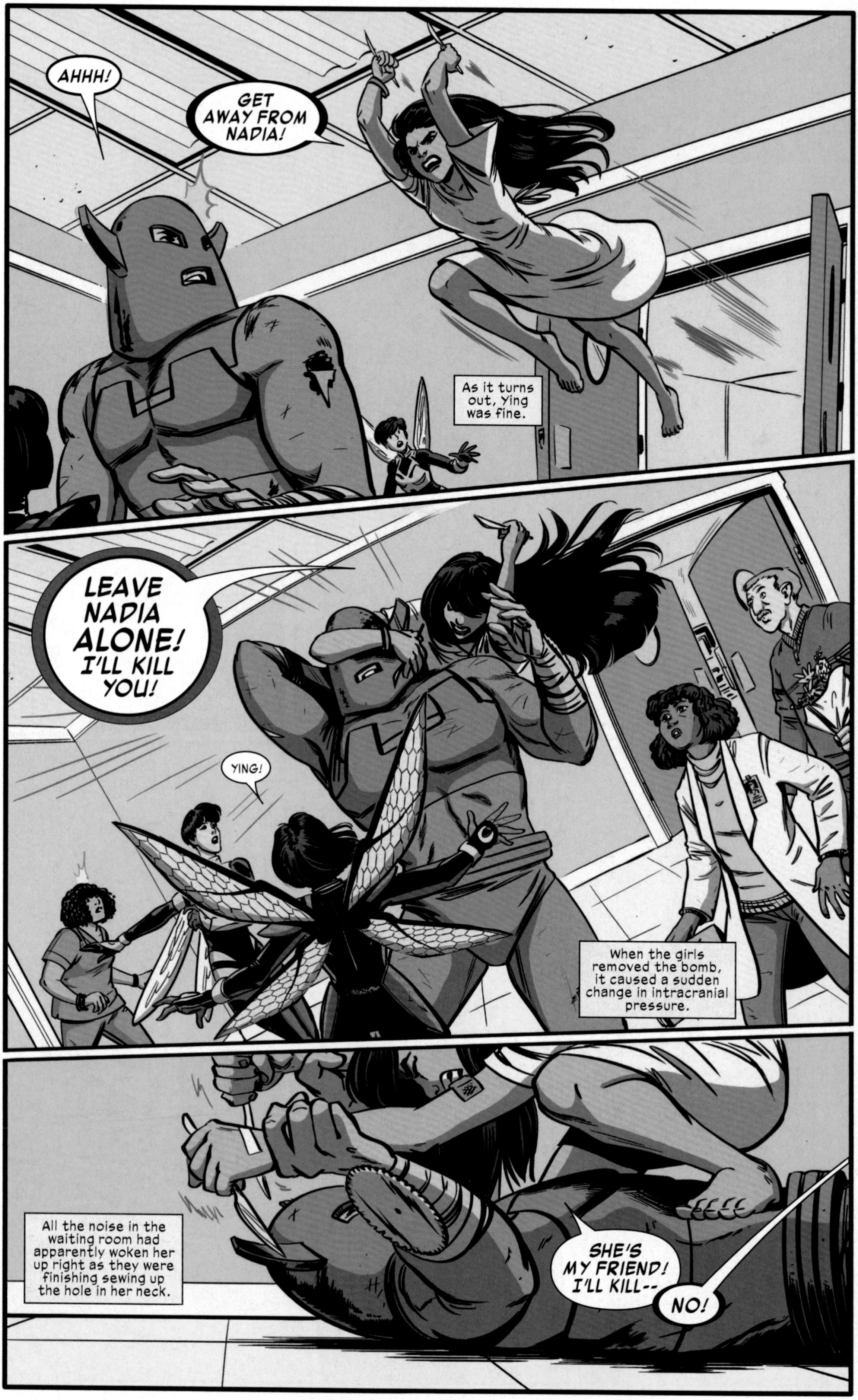
AHHH!
GET AWAY FROM NADIA!
As it turns out, Ying was fine.
LEAVE NADIA ALONE! I'LL KILL YOU!
YING!
When the girls removed the bomb, it caused a sudden change in intracranial pressure.
All the noise in the waiting room had apparently woken her up right as they were finishing sewing up the hole in her neck.
SHE'S MY FRIEND! I'LL KILL--
NO!

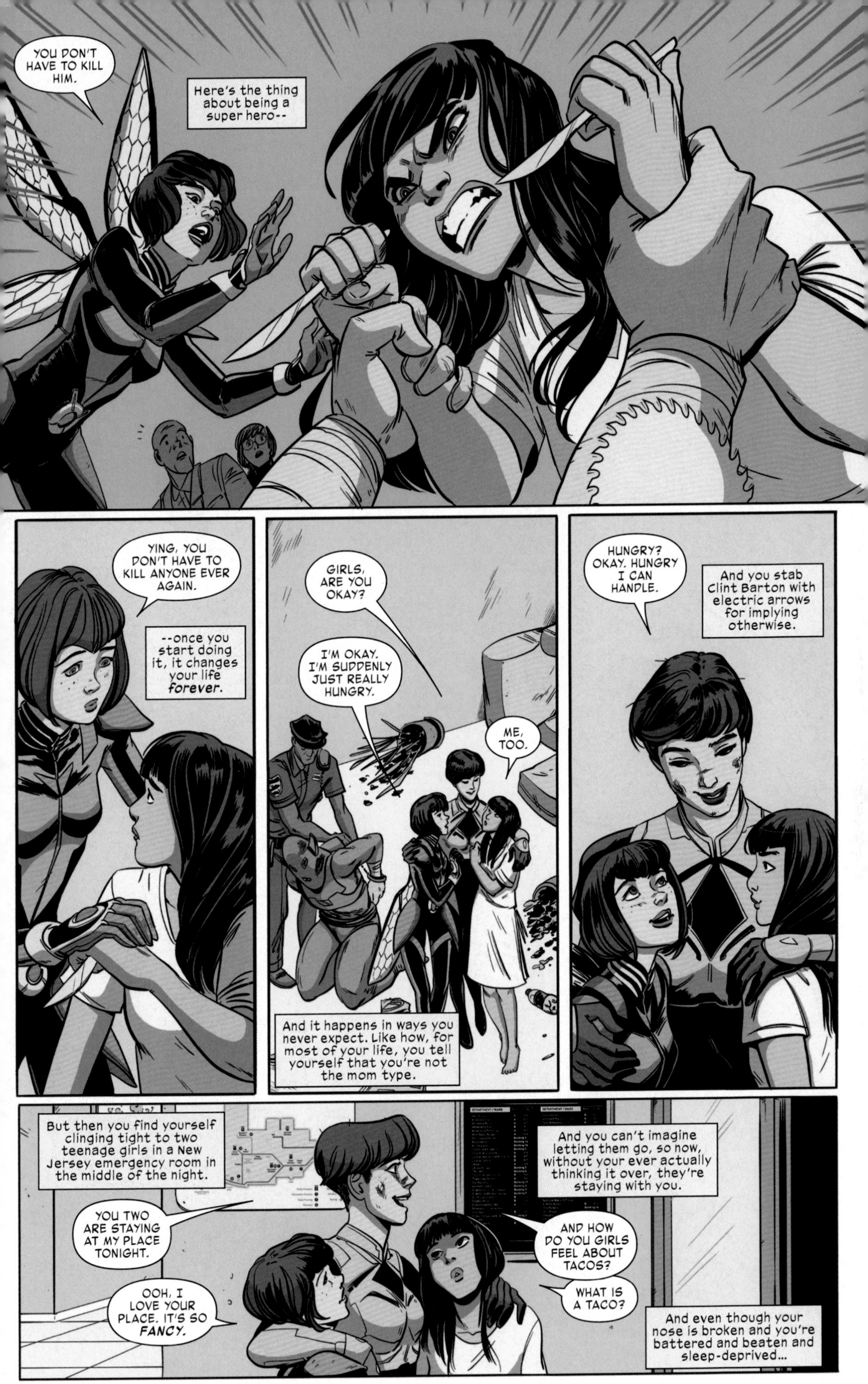
YOU DON'T HAVE TO KILL HIM.
Here's the thing about being a super hero--
YING, YOU DON'T HAVE TO KILL ANYONE EVER AGAIN.
--once you start doing it, it changes your life *forever*.
GIRLS, ARE YOU OKAY?
I'M OKAY. I'M SUDDENLY JUST REALLY HUNGRY.
ME, TOO.
And it happens in ways you never expect. Like how, for most of your life, you tell yourself that you're not the mom type.
HUNGRY? OKAY. HUNGRY I CAN HANDLE.
And you stab Clint Barton with electric arrows for implying otherwise.
But then you find yourself clinging tight to two teenage girls in a New Jersey emergency room in the middle of the night.
YOU TWO ARE STAYING AT MY PLACE TONIGHT.
OOH, I LOVE YOUR PLACE. IT'S SO *FANCY*.
And you can't imagine letting them go, so now, without your ever actually thinking it over, they're staying with you.
AND HOW DO YOU GIRLS FEEL ABOUT TACOS?
WHAT IS A TACO?
And even though your nose is broken and you're battered and beaten and sleep-deprived...

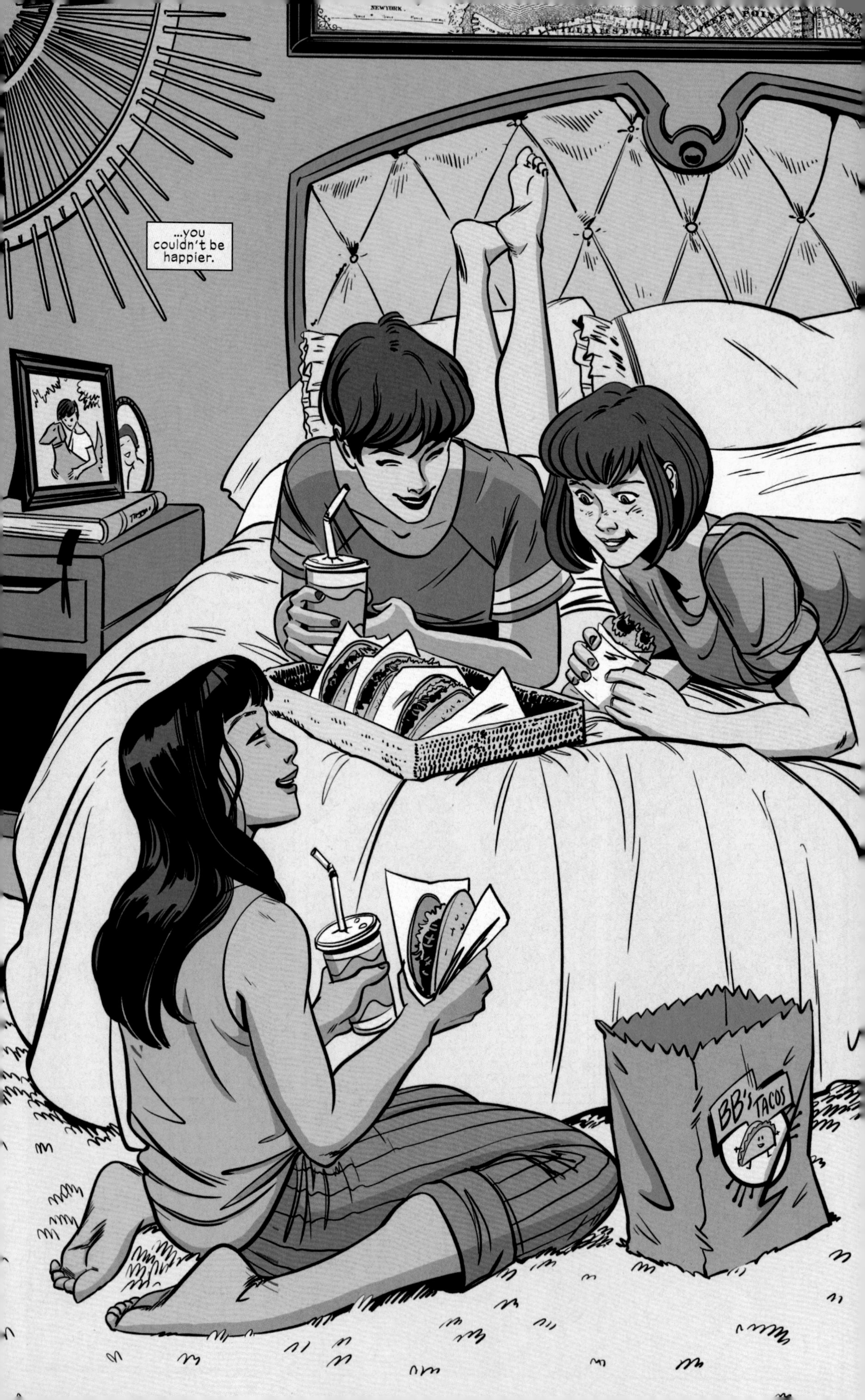
...you couldn't be happier.
BB's TACOS

8

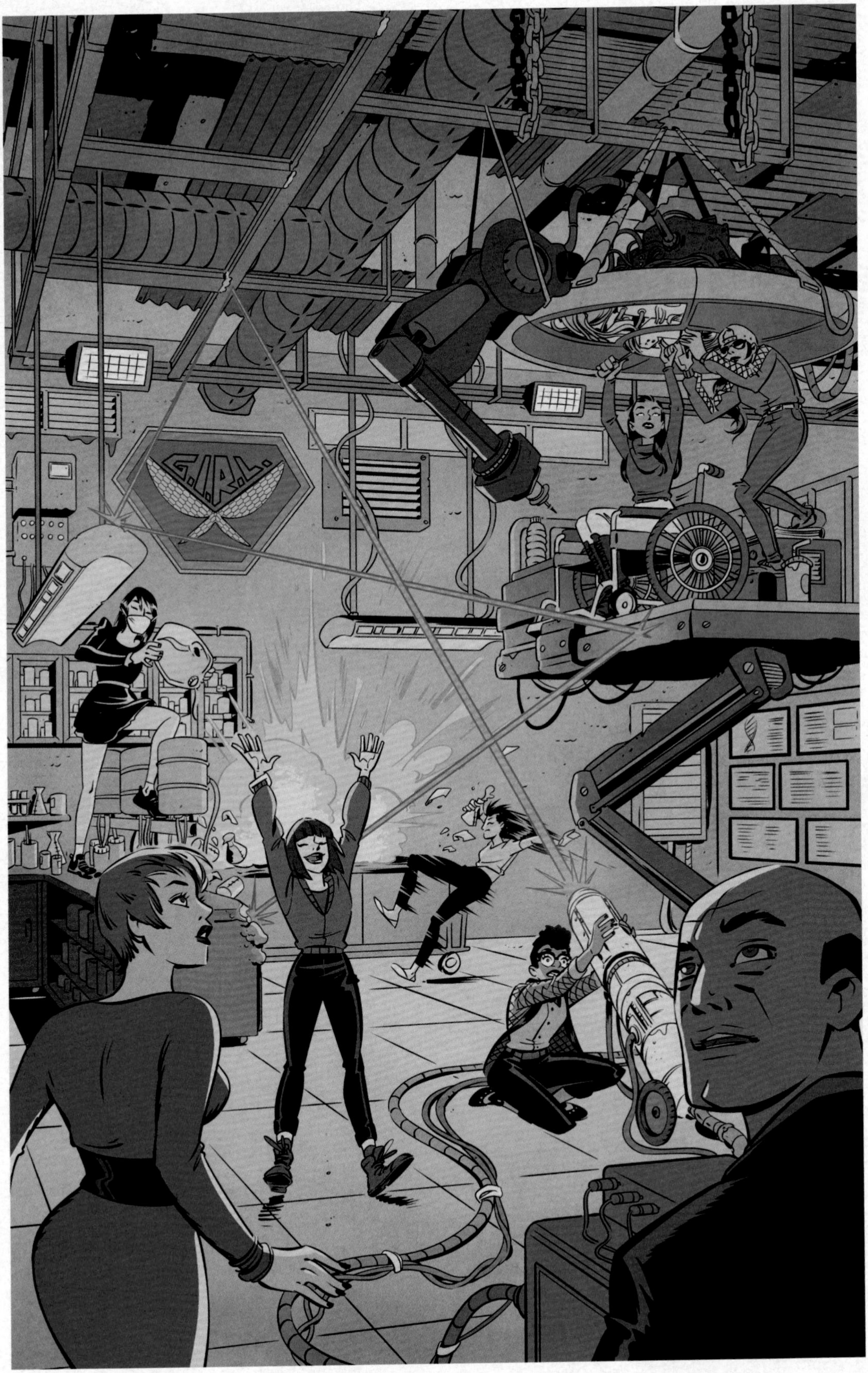
G.I.R.L.

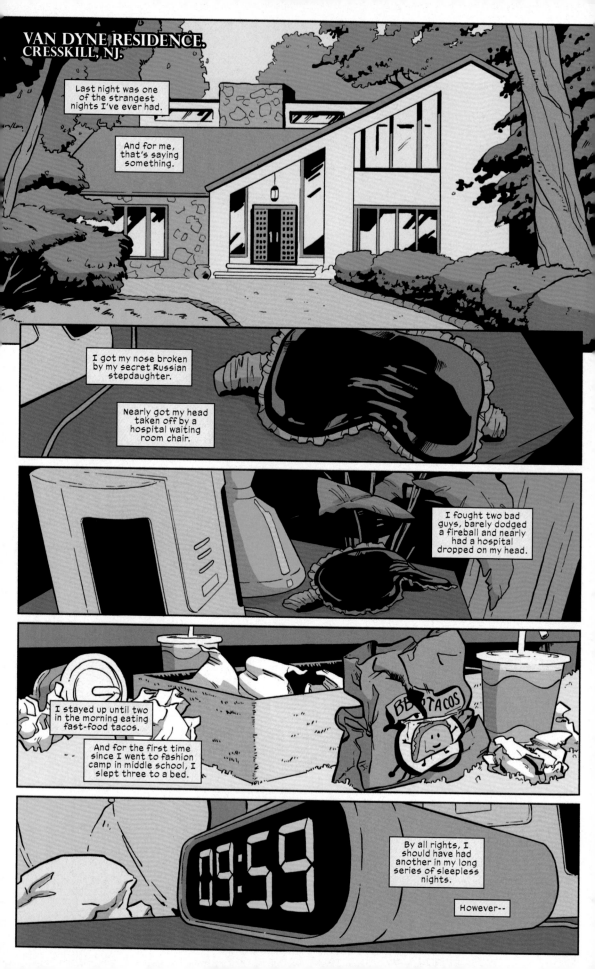

VAN DYNE RESIDENCE.
CRESSKILL, N.J.

Last night was one of the strangest nights I've ever had.

And for me, that's saying something.

I got my nose broken by my secret Russian stepdaughter.

Nearly got my head taken off by a hospital waiting room chair.

I fought two bad guys, barely dodged a fireball and nearly had a hospital dropped on my head.

I stayed up until two in the morning eating fast-food tacos.

And for the first time since I went to fashion camp in middle school, I slept three to a bed.

By all rights, I should have had another in my long series of sleepless nights.

However--

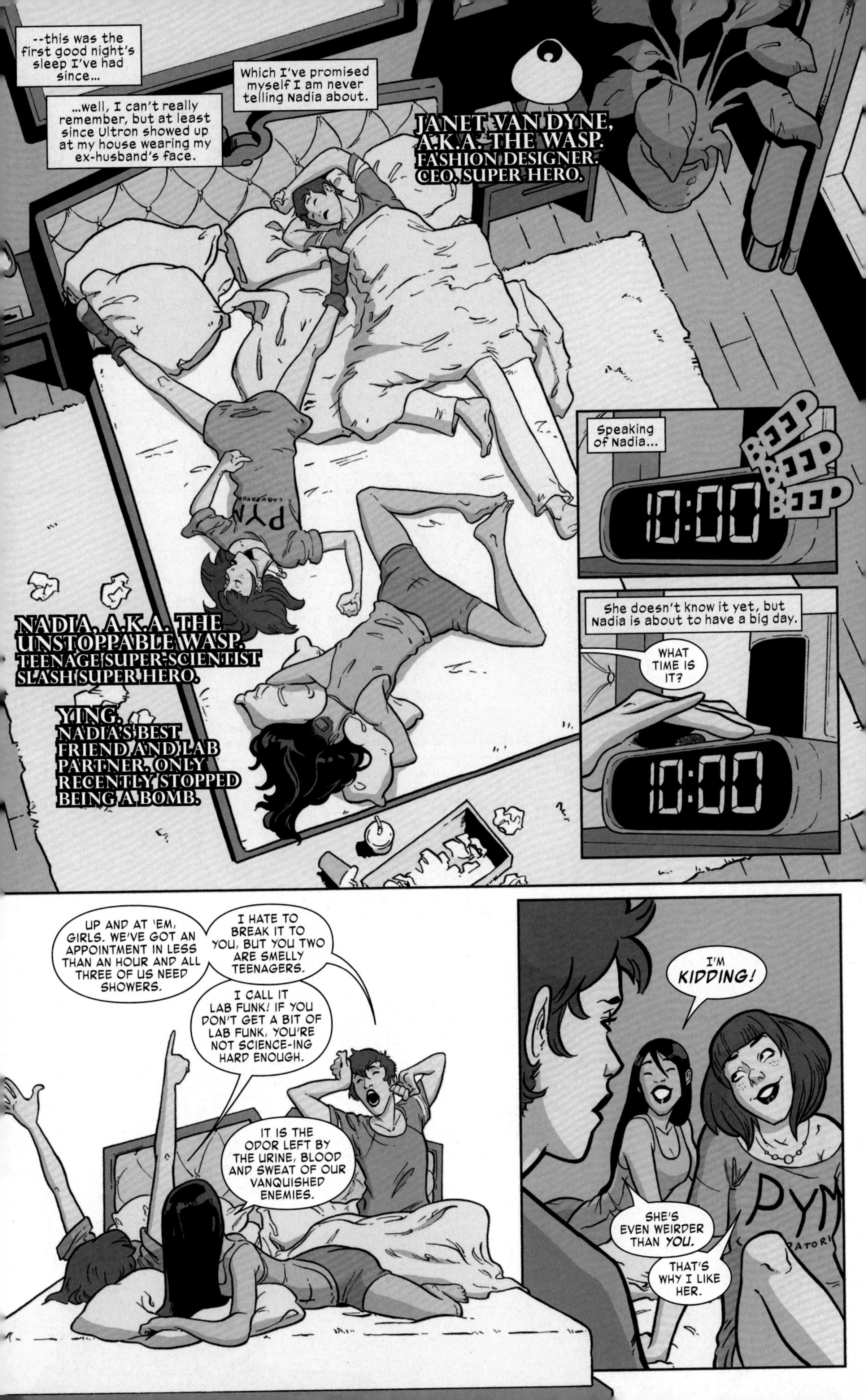
--this was the first good night's sleep I've had since...
...well, I can't really remember, but at least since Ultron showed up at my house wearing my ex-husband's face.
Which I've promised myself I am never telling Nadia about.
JANET VAN DYNE, A.K.A. THE WASP. FASHION DESIGNER. CEO. SUPER HERO.
NADIA, A.K.A. THE UNSTOPPABLE WASP. TEENAGE SUPER-SCIENTIST SLASH SUPER HERO.
YING. NADIA'S BEST FRIEND AND LAB PARTNER. ONLY RECENTLY STOPPED BEING A BOMB.
PYM
Speaking of Nadia...
BEEP
BEEP
BEEP
10:00
She doesn't know it yet, but Nadia is about to have a big day.
WHAT TIME IS IT?
10:00
UP AND AT 'EM, GIRLS. WE'VE GOT AN APPOINTMENT IN LESS THAN AN HOUR AND ALL THREE OF US NEED SHOWERS.
I HATE TO BREAK IT TO YOU, BUT YOU TWO ARE SMELLY TEENAGERS.
I CALL IT LAB FUNK! IF YOU DON'T GET A BIT OF LAB FUNK, YOU'RE NOT SCIENCE-ING HARD ENOUGH.
IT IS THE ODOR LEFT BY THE URINE, BLOOD AND SWEAT OF OUR VANQUISHED ENEMIES.
I'M KIDDING!
PYM
SHE'S EVEN WEIRDER THAN YOU.
THAT'S WHY I LIKE HER.

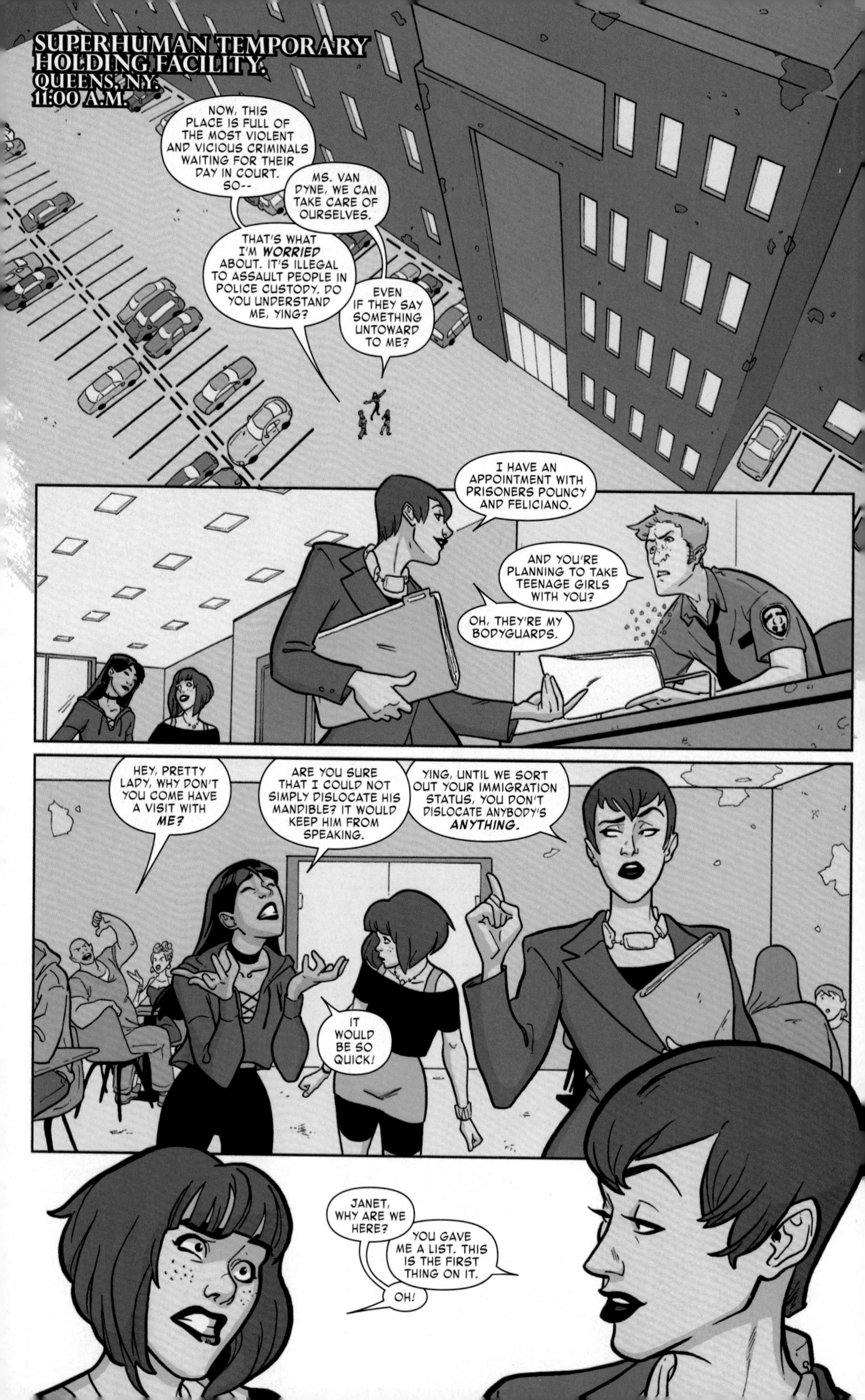
SUPERHUMAN TEMPORARY HOLDING FACILITY. QUEENS, NY. 11:00 A.M.
NOW, THIS PLACE IS FULL OF THE MOST VIOLENT AND VICIOUS CRIMINALS WAITING FOR THEIR DAY IN COURT. SO--
MS. VAN DYNE, WE CAN TAKE CARE OF OURSELVES.
THAT'S WHAT I'M WORRIED ABOUT. IT'S ILLEGAL TO ASSAULT PEOPLE IN POLICE CUSTODY. DO YOU UNDERSTAND ME, YING?
EVEN IF THEY SAY SOMETHING UNTOWARD TO ME?
I HAVE AN APPOINTMENT WITH PRISONERS POUNCY AND FELICIANO.
AND YOU'RE PLANNING TO TAKE TEENAGE GIRLS WITH YOU?
OH, THEY'RE MY BODYGUARDS.
HEY, PRETTY LADY, WHY DON'T YOU COME HAVE A VISIT WITH ME?
ARE YOU SURE THAT I COULD NOT SIMPLY DISLOCATE HIS MANDIBLE? IT WOULD KEEP HIM FROM SPEAKING.
YING, UNTIL WE SORT OUT YOUR IMMIGRATION STATUS, YOU DON'T DISLOCATE ANYBODY'S ANYTHING.
IT WOULD BE SO QUICK!
JANET, WHY ARE WE HERE?
YOU GAVE ME A LIST. THIS IS THE FIRST THING ON IT.
OH!

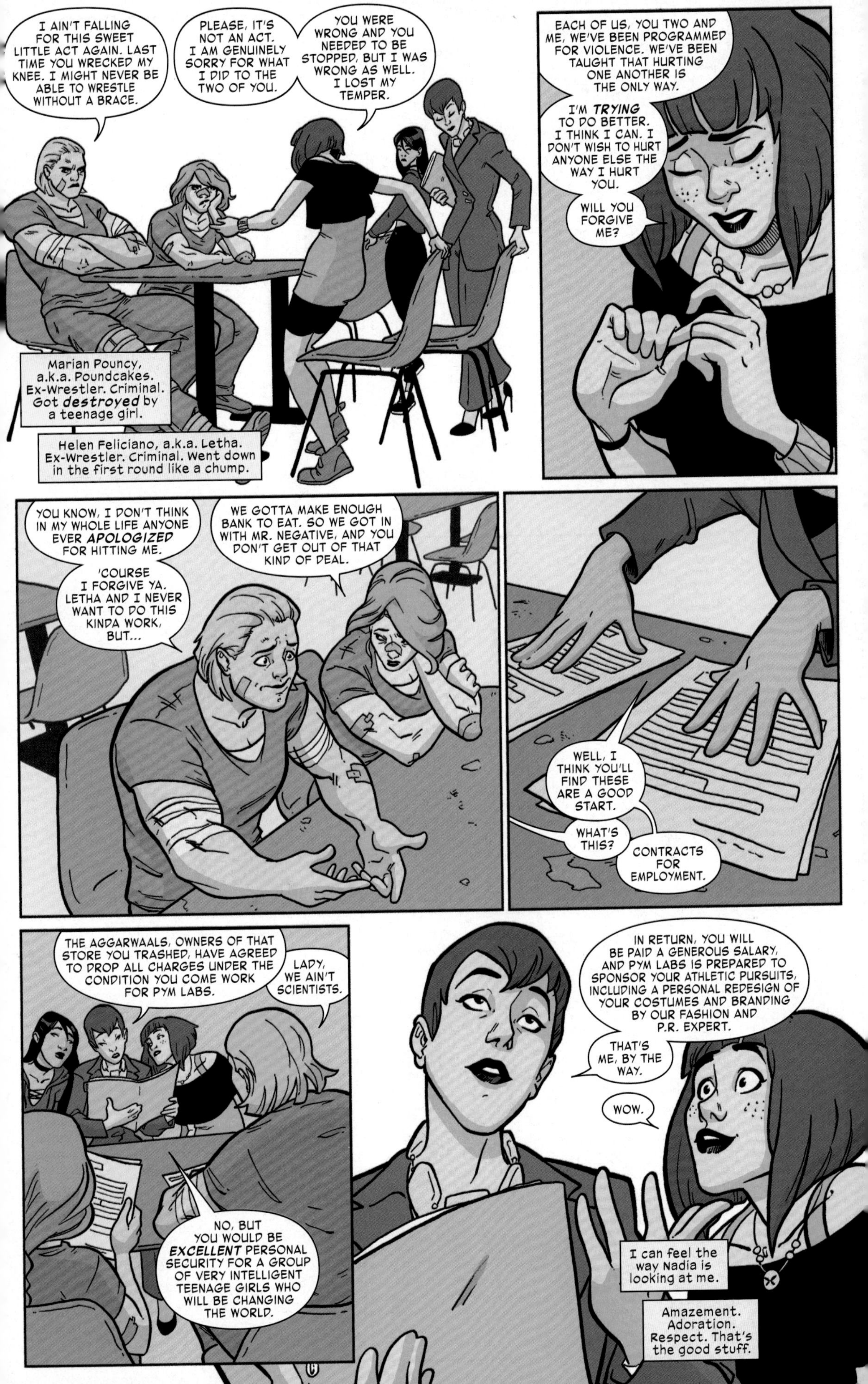
I AIN'T FALLING FOR THIS SWEET LITTLE ACT AGAIN. LAST TIME YOU WRECKED MY KNEE. I MIGHT NEVER BE ABLE TO WRESTLE WITHOUT A BRACE.
PLEASE, IT'S NOT AN ACT. I AM GENUINELY SORRY FOR WHAT I DID TO THE TWO OF YOU.
YOU WERE WRONG AND YOU NEEDED TO BE STOPPED, BUT I WAS WRONG AS WELL. I LOST MY TEMPER.
Marian Pouncy, a.k.a. Poundcakes. Ex-Wrestler. Criminal. Got *destroyed* by a teenage girl.
Helen Feliciano, a.k.a. Letha. Ex-Wrestler. Criminal. Went down in the first round like a chump.
EACH OF US, YOU TWO AND ME, WE'VE BEEN PROGRAMMED FOR VIOLENCE. WE'VE BEEN TAUGHT THAT HURTING ONE ANOTHER IS THE ONLY WAY.
I'M ***TRYING*** TO DO BETTER. I THINK I CAN. I DON'T WISH TO HURT ANYONE ELSE THE WAY I HURT YOU.
WILL YOU FORGIVE ME?
YOU KNOW, I DON'T THINK IN MY WHOLE LIFE ANYONE EVER ***APOLOGIZED*** FOR HITTING ME.
'COURSE I FORGIVE YA. LETHA AND I NEVER WANT TO DO THIS KINDA WORK, BUT...
WE GOTTA MAKE ENOUGH BANK TO EAT. SO WE GOT IN WITH MR. NEGATIVE, AND YOU DON'T GET OUT OF THAT KIND OF DEAL.
WELL, I THINK YOU'LL FIND THESE ARE A GOOD START.
WHAT'S THIS?
CONTRACTS FOR EMPLOYMENT.
THE AGGARWAALS, OWNERS OF THAT STORE YOU TRASHED, HAVE AGREED TO DROP ALL CHARGES UNDER THE CONDITION YOU COME WORK FOR PYM LABS.
LADY, WE AIN'T SCIENTISTS.
NO, BUT YOU WOULD BE ***EXCELLENT*** PERSONAL SECURITY FOR A GROUP OF VERY INTELLIGENT TEENAGE GIRLS WHO WILL BE CHANGING THE WORLD.
IN RETURN, YOU WILL BE PAID A GENEROUS SALARY, AND PYM LABS IS PREPARED TO SPONSOR YOUR ATHLETIC PURSUITS, INCLUDING A PERSONAL REDESIGN OF YOUR COSTUMES AND BRANDING BY OUR FASHION AND P.R. EXPERT.
THAT'S ME, BY THE WAY.
WOW.
I can feel the way Nadia is looking at me.
Amazement. Adoration. Respect. That's the good stuff.

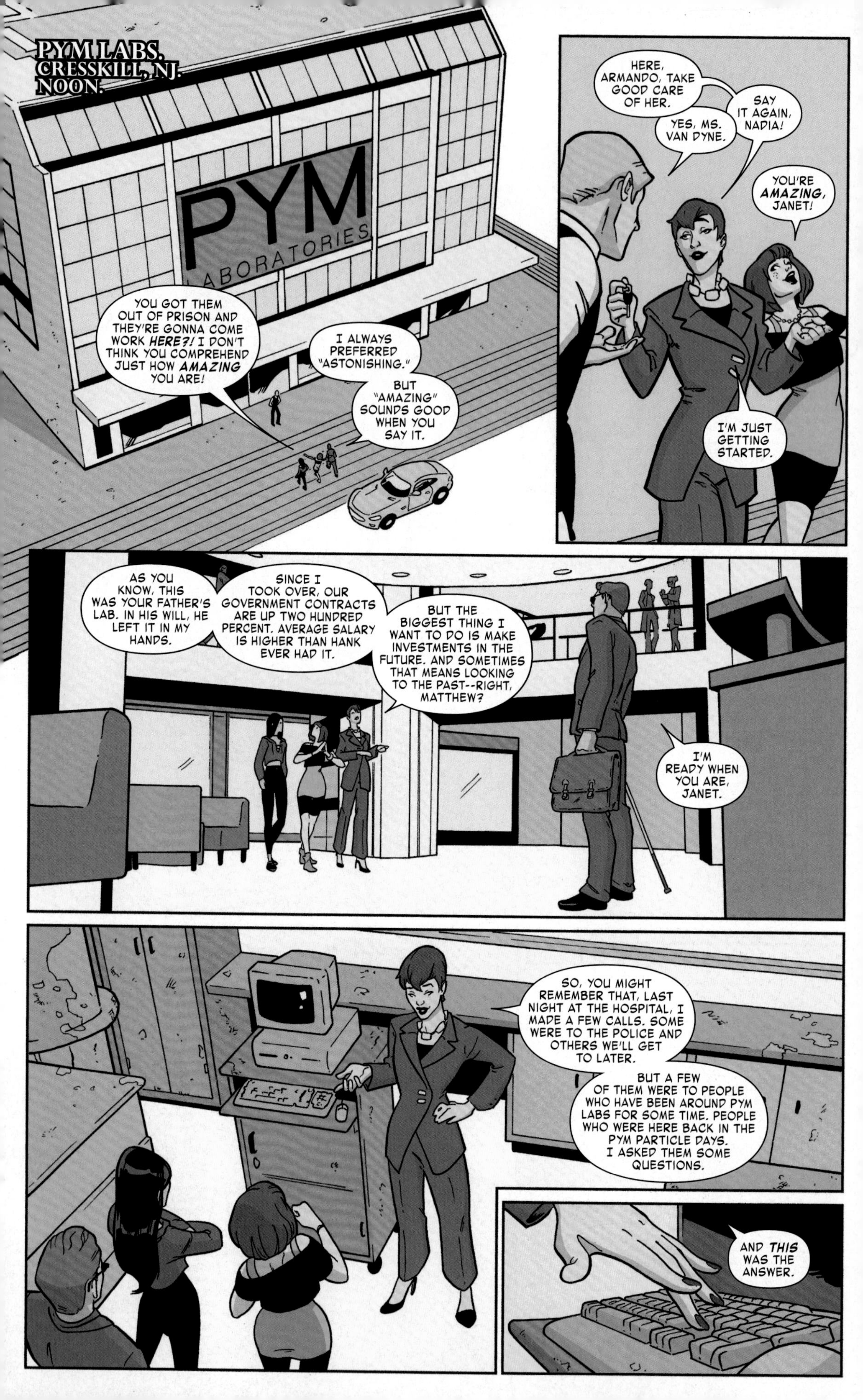
PYM LABS. CRESSKILL, NJ. NOON.
PYM LABORATORIES
YOU GOT THEM OUT OF PRISON AND THEY'RE GONNA COME WORK HERE?! I DON'T THINK YOU COMPREHEND JUST HOW AMAZING YOU ARE!
I ALWAYS PREFERRED "ASTONISHING."
BUT "AMAZING" SOUNDS GOOD WHEN YOU SAY IT.
HERE, ARMANDO, TAKE GOOD CARE OF HER.
YES, MS. VAN DYNE.
SAY IT AGAIN, NADIA!
YOU'RE AMAZING, JANET!
I'M JUST GETTING STARTED.
AS YOU KNOW, THIS WAS YOUR FATHER'S LAB. IN HIS WILL, HE LEFT IT IN MY HANDS.
SINCE I TOOK OVER, OUR GOVERNMENT CONTRACTS ARE UP TWO HUNDRED PERCENT. AVERAGE SALARY IS HIGHER THAN HANK EVER HAD IT.
BUT THE BIGGEST THING I WANT TO DO IS MAKE INVESTMENTS IN THE FUTURE. AND SOMETIMES THAT MEANS LOOKING TO THE PAST--RIGHT, MATTHEW?
I'M READY WHEN YOU ARE, JANET.
SO, YOU MIGHT REMEMBER THAT, LAST NIGHT AT THE HOSPITAL, I MADE A FEW CALLS. SOME WERE TO THE POLICE AND OTHERS WE'LL GET TO LATER.
BUT A FEW OF THEM WERE TO PEOPLE WHO HAVE BEEN AROUND PYM LABS FOR SOME TIME. PEOPLE WHO WERE HERE BACK IN THE PYM PARTICLE DAYS. I ASKED THEM SOME QUESTIONS.
AND THIS WAS THE ANSWER.

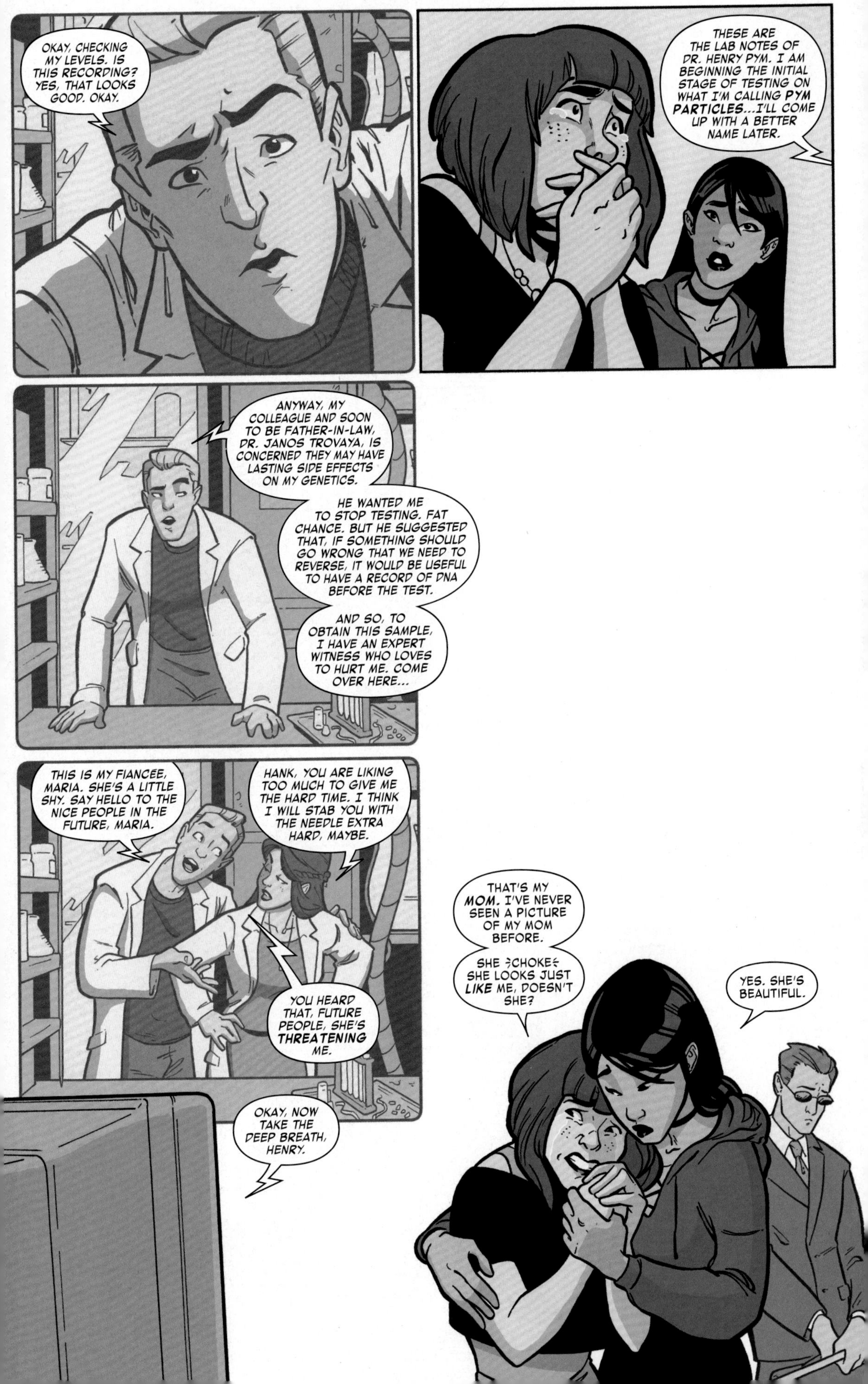
OKAY, CHECKING MY LEVELS. IS THIS RECORDING? YES, THAT LOOKS GOOD. OKAY.
THESE ARE THE LAB NOTES OF DR. HENRY PYM. I AM BEGINNING THE INITIAL STAGE OF TESTING ON WHAT I'M CALLING **PYM PARTICLES**...I'LL COME UP WITH A BETTER NAME LATER.
ANYWAY, MY COLLEAGUE AND SOON TO BE FATHER-IN-LAW, DR. JANOS TROVAYA, IS CONCERNED THEY MAY HAVE LASTING SIDE EFFECTS ON MY GENETICS.
HE WANTED ME TO STOP TESTING. FAT CHANCE. BUT HE SUGGESTED THAT, IF SOMETHING SHOULD GO WRONG THAT WE NEED TO REVERSE, IT WOULD BE USEFUL TO HAVE A RECORD OF DNA BEFORE THE TEST.
AND SO, TO OBTAIN THIS SAMPLE, I HAVE AN EXPERT WITNESS WHO LOVES TO HURT ME. COME OVER HERE...
THIS IS MY FIANCEE, MARIA. SHE'S A LITTLE SHY. SAY HELLO TO THE NICE PEOPLE IN THE FUTURE, MARIA.
HANK, YOU ARE LIKING TOO MUCH TO GIVE ME THE HARD TIME. I THINK I WILL STAB YOU WITH THE NEEDLE EXTRA HARD, MAYBE.
YOU HEARD THAT, FUTURE PEOPLE, SHE'S **THREATENING** ME.
OKAY, NOW TAKE THE DEEP BREATH, HENRY.
THAT'S MY **MOM**. I'VE NEVER SEEN A PICTURE OF MY MOM BEFORE.
SHE ≶CHOKE≶ SHE LOOKS JUST **LIKE** ME, DOESN'T SHE?
YES. SHE'S BEAUTIFUL.

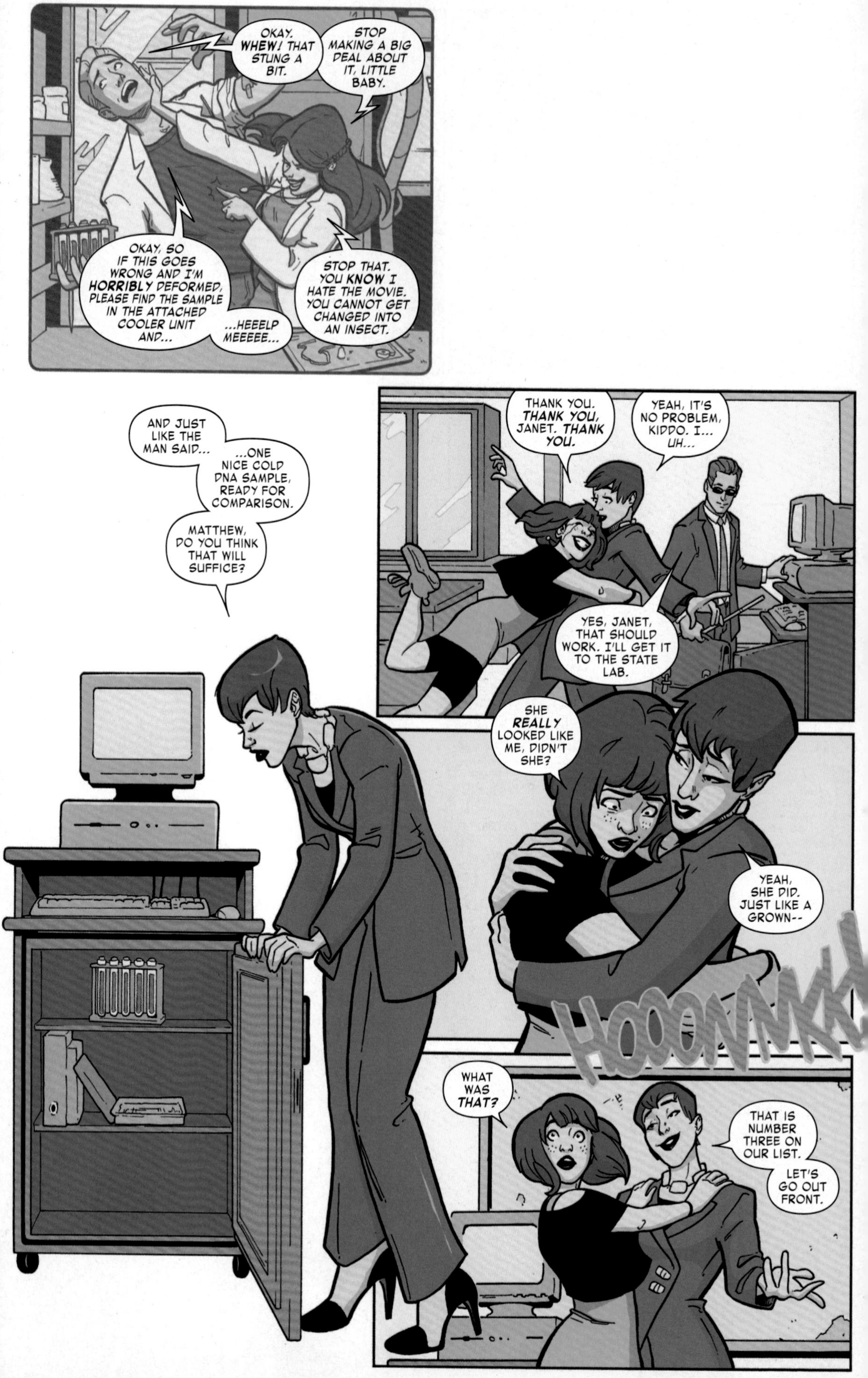
OKAY. WHEW! THAT STUNG A BIT.
STOP MAKING A BIG DEAL ABOUT IT, LITTLE BABY.
OKAY, SO IF THIS GOES WRONG AND I'M HORRIBLY DEFORMED, PLEASE FIND THE SAMPLE IN THE ATTACHED COOLER UNIT AND...
...HEEELP MEEEEE...
STOP THAT. YOU KNOW I HATE THE MOVIE. YOU CANNOT GET CHANGED INTO AN INSECT.
AND JUST LIKE THE MAN SAID...
...ONE NICE COLD DNA SAMPLE, READY FOR COMPARISON.
MATTHEW, DO YOU THINK THAT WILL SUFFICE?
THANK YOU. THANK YOU, JANET. THANK YOU.
YEAH, IT'S NO PROBLEM, KIDDO. I... UH...
YES, JANET, THAT SHOULD WORK. I'LL GET IT TO THE STATE LAB.
SHE REALLY LOOKED LIKE ME, DIDN'T SHE?
YEAH, SHE DID. JUST LIKE A GROWN--
HOOONNK!
WHAT WAS THAT?
THAT IS NUMBER THREE ON OUR LIST.
LET'S GO OUT FRONT.

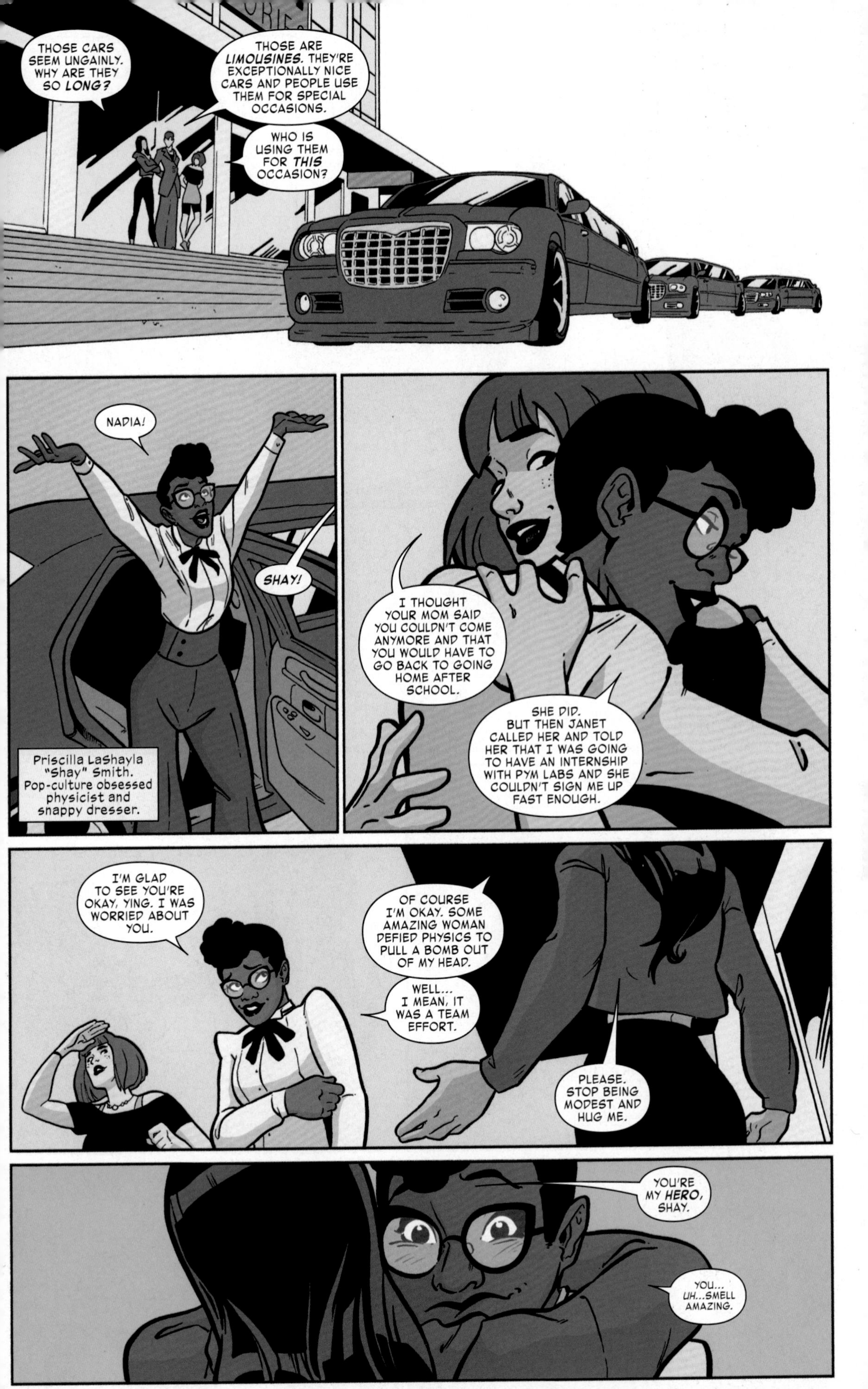
THOSE CARS SEEM UNGAINLY. WHY ARE THEY SO LONG?
THOSE ARE LIMOUSINES. THEY'RE EXCEPTIONALLY NICE CARS AND PEOPLE USE THEM FOR SPECIAL OCCASIONS.
WHO IS USING THEM FOR THIS OCCASION?
NADIA!
SHAY!
Priscilla LaShayla "Shay" Smith. Pop-culture obsessed physicist and snappy dresser.
I THOUGHT YOUR MOM SAID YOU COULDN'T COME ANYMORE AND THAT YOU WOULD HAVE TO GO BACK TO GOING HOME AFTER SCHOOL.
SHE DID. BUT THEN JANET CALLED HER AND TOLD HER THAT I WAS GOING TO HAVE AN INTERNSHIP WITH PYM LABS AND SHE COULDN'T SIGN ME UP FAST ENOUGH.
I'M GLAD TO SEE YOU'RE OKAY, YING. I WAS WORRIED ABOUT YOU.
OF COURSE I'M OKAY. SOME AMAZING WOMAN DEFIED PHYSICS TO PULL A BOMB OUT OF MY HEAD.
WELL... I MEAN, IT WAS A TEAM EFFORT.
PLEASE. STOP BEING MODEST AND HUG ME.
YOU'RE MY HERO, SHAY.
YOU... UH...SMELL AMAZING.

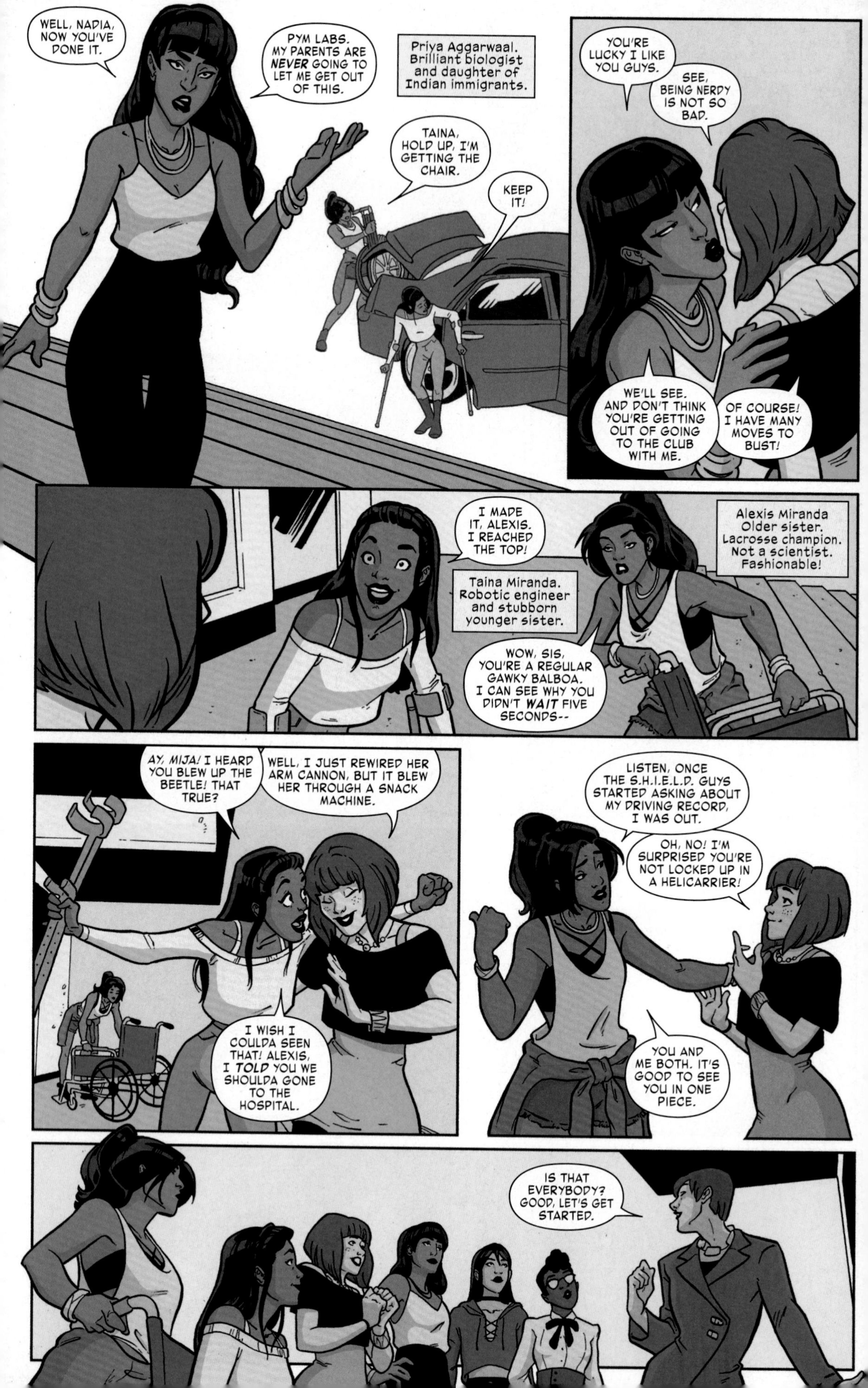
WELL, NADIA, NOW YOU'VE DONE IT.
PYM LABS. MY PARENTS ARE NEVER GOING TO LET ME GET OUT OF THIS.
Priya Aggarwaal. Brilliant biologist and daughter of Indian immigrants.
TAINA, HOLD UP, I'M GETTING THE CHAIR.
KEEP IT!
YOU'RE LUCKY I LIKE YOU GUYS.
SEE, BEING NERDY IS NOT SO BAD.
WE'LL SEE. AND DON'T THINK YOU'RE GETTING OUT OF GOING TO THE CLUB WITH ME.
OF COURSE! I HAVE MANY MOVES TO BUST!
I MADE IT, ALEXIS. I REACHED THE TOP!
Taina Miranda. Robotic engineer and stubborn younger sister.
Alexis Miranda Older sister. Lacrosse champion. Not a scientist. Fashionable!
WOW, SIS, YOU'RE A REGULAR GAWKY BALBOA. I CAN SEE WHY YOU DIDN'T WAIT FIVE SECONDS--
AY, MIJA! I HEARD YOU BLEW UP THE BEETLE! THAT TRUE?
WELL, I JUST REWIRED HER ARM CANNON, BUT IT BLEW HER THROUGH A SNACK MACHINE.
I WISH I COULDA SEEN THAT! ALEXIS, I TOLD YOU WE SHOULDA GONE TO THE HOSPITAL.
LISTEN, ONCE THE S.H.I.E.L.D. GUYS STARTED ASKING ABOUT MY DRIVING RECORD, I WAS OUT.
OH, NO! I'M SURPRISED YOU'RE NOT LOCKED UP IN A HELICARRIER!
YOU AND ME BOTH. IT'S GOOD TO SEE YOU IN ONE PIECE.
IS THAT EVERYBODY? GOOD, LET'S GET STARTED.

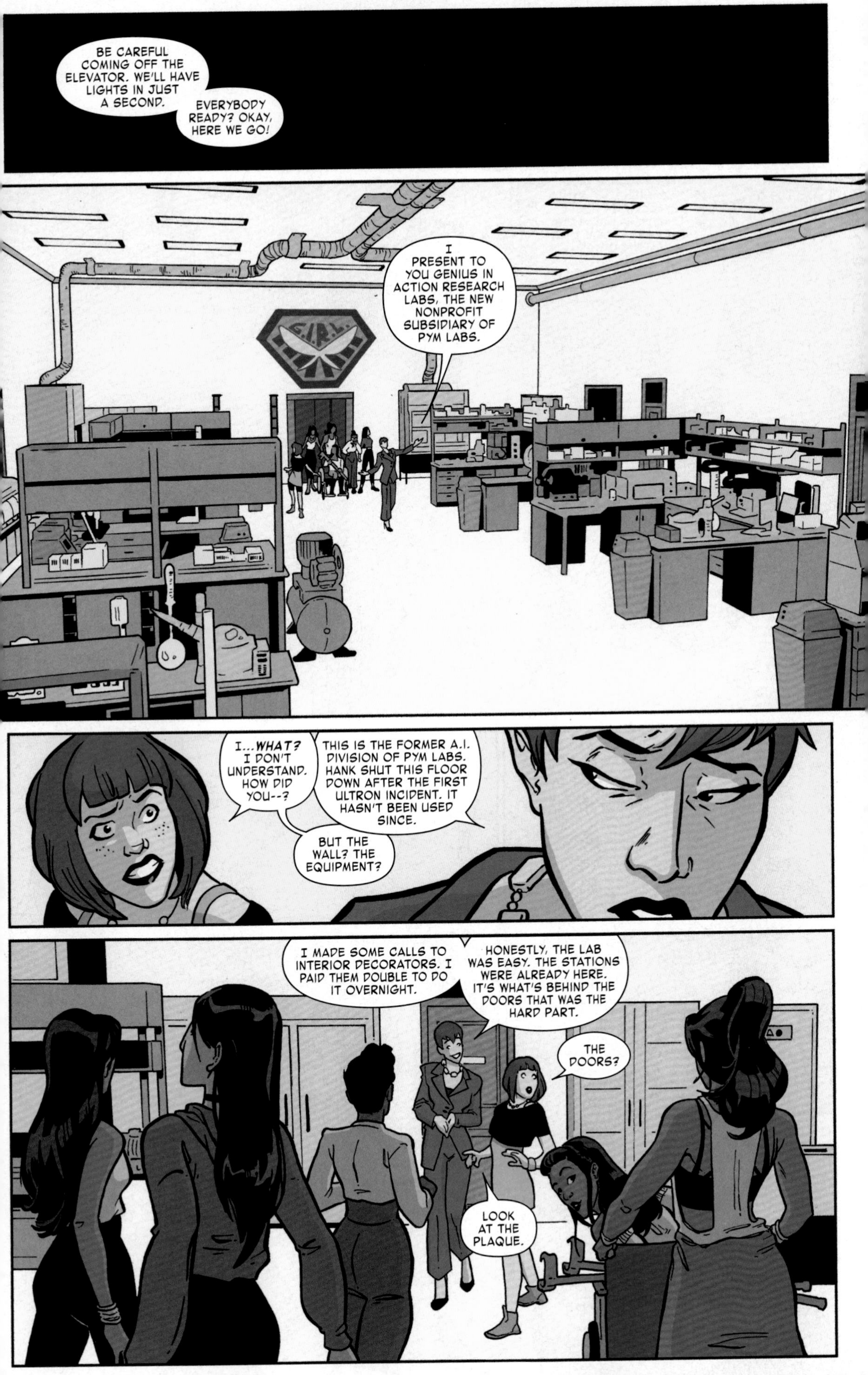
BE CAREFUL COMING OFF THE ELEVATOR. WE'LL HAVE LIGHTS IN JUST A SECOND.
EVERYBODY READY? OKAY, HERE WE GO!
I PRESENT TO YOU GENIUS IN ACTION RESEARCH LABS, THE NEW NONPROFIT SUBSIDIARY OF PYM LABS.
G.I.R.L.
I...*WHAT?* I DON'T UNDERSTAND. HOW DID YOU--?
THIS IS THE FORMER A.I. DIVISION OF PYM LABS. HANK SHUT THIS FLOOR DOWN AFTER THE FIRST ULTRON INCIDENT. IT HASN'T BEEN USED SINCE.
BUT THE WALL? THE EQUIPMENT?
I MADE SOME CALLS TO INTERIOR DECORATORS. I PAID THEM DOUBLE TO DO IT OVERNIGHT.
HONESTLY, THE LAB WAS EASY. THE STATIONS WERE ALREADY HERE. IT'S WHAT'S BEHIND THE DOORS THAT WAS THE HARD PART.
THE DOORS?
LOOK AT THE PLAQUE.

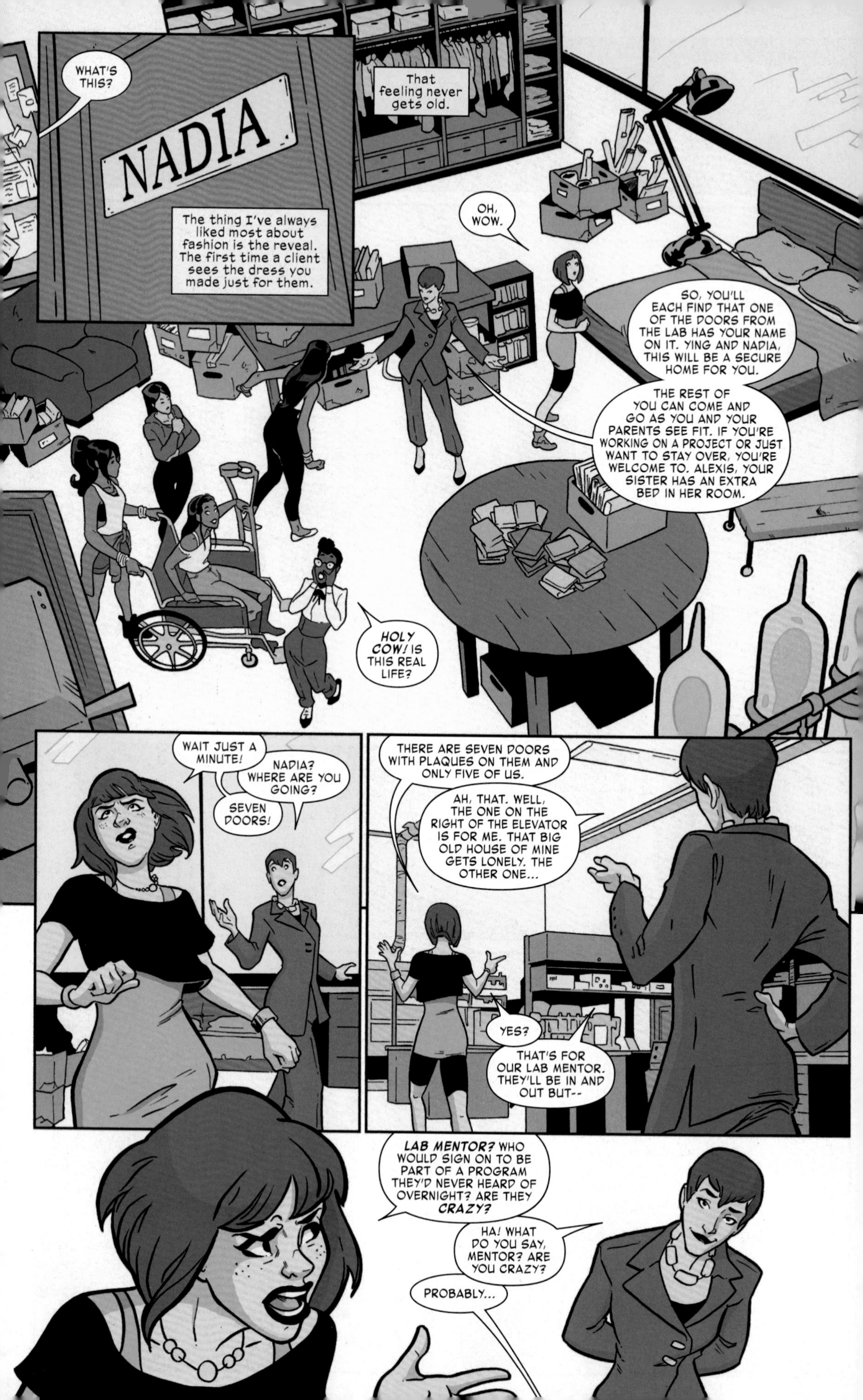
WHAT'S THIS?
NADIA
The thing I've always liked most about fashion is the reveal. The first time a client sees the dress you made just for them.
That feeling never gets old.
OH, WOW.
SO, YOU'LL EACH FIND THAT ONE OF THE DOORS FROM THE LAB HAS YOUR NAME ON IT. YING AND NADIA, THIS WILL BE A SECURE HOME FOR YOU.
THE REST OF YOU CAN COME AND GO AS YOU AND YOUR PARENTS SEE FIT. IF YOU'RE WORKING ON A PROJECT OR JUST WANT TO STAY OVER, YOU'RE WELCOME TO. ALEXIS, YOUR SISTER HAS AN EXTRA BED IN HER ROOM.
HOLY COW! IS THIS REAL LIFE?
WAIT JUST A MINUTE!
NADIA? WHERE ARE YOU GOING?
SEVEN DOORS!
THERE ARE SEVEN DOORS WITH PLAQUES ON THEM AND ONLY FIVE OF US.
AH, THAT. WELL, THE ONE ON THE RIGHT OF THE ELEVATOR IS FOR ME. THAT BIG OLD HOUSE OF MINE GETS LONELY. THE OTHER ONE...
YES?
THAT'S FOR OUR LAB MENTOR. THEY'LL BE IN AND OUT BUT--
LAB MENTOR? WHO WOULD SIGN ON TO BE PART OF A PROGRAM THEY'D NEVER HEARD OF OVERNIGHT? ARE THEY CRAZY?
HA! WHAT DO YOU SAY, MENTOR? ARE YOU CRAZY?
PROBABLY...

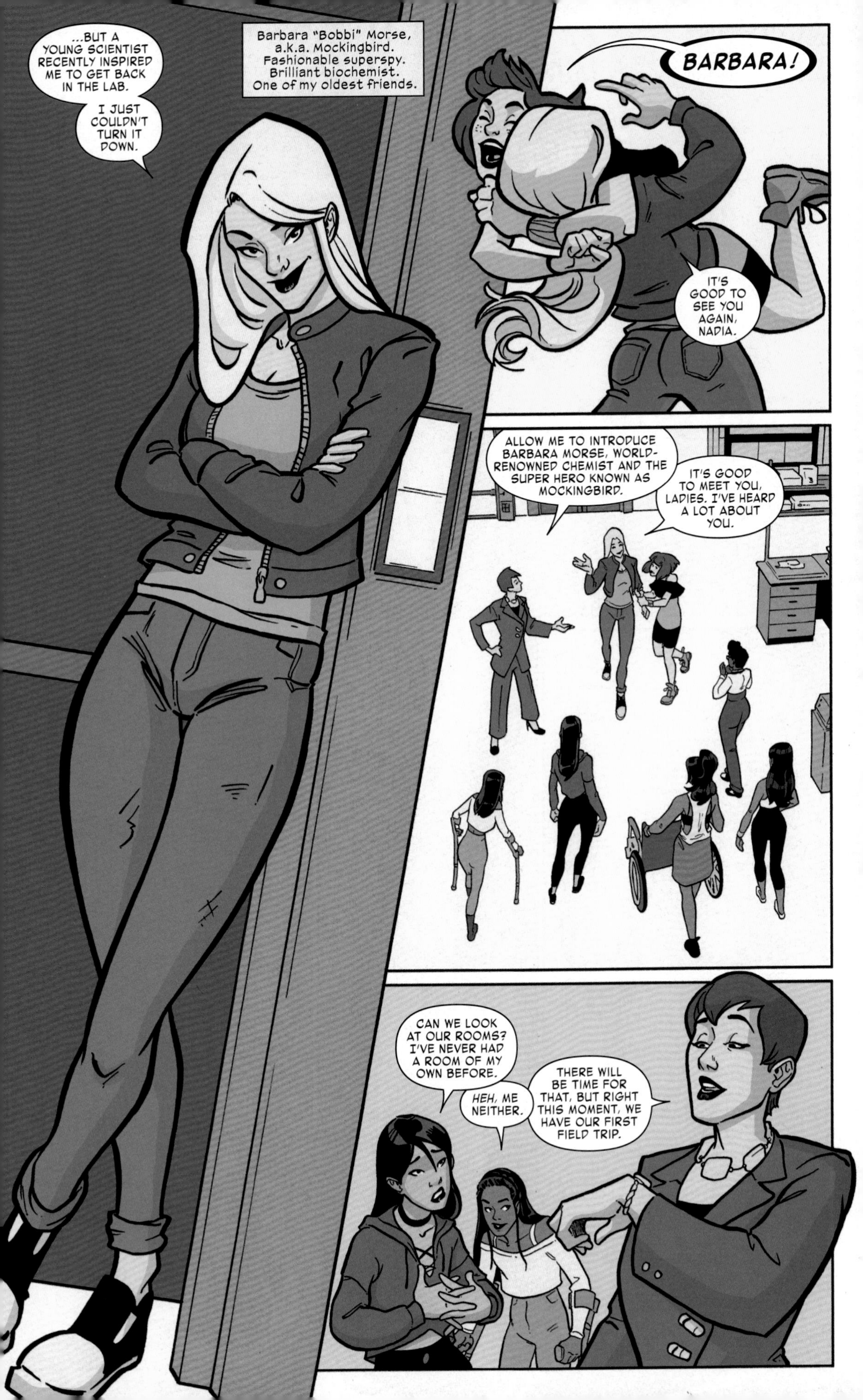
...BUT A YOUNG SCIENTIST RECENTLY INSPIRED ME TO GET BACK IN THE LAB.
I JUST COULDN'T TURN IT DOWN.
Barbara "Bobbi" Morse, a.k.a. Mockingbird. Fashionable superspy. Brilliant biochemist. One of my oldest friends.
BARBARA!
IT'S GOOD TO SEE YOU AGAIN, NADIA.
ALLOW ME TO INTRODUCE BARBARA MORSE, WORLD-RENOWNED CHEMIST AND THE SUPER HERO KNOWN AS MOCKINGBIRD.
IT'S GOOD TO MEET YOU, LADIES. I'VE HEARD A LOT ABOUT YOU.
CAN WE LOOK AT OUR ROOMS? I'VE NEVER HAD A ROOM OF MY OWN BEFORE.
HEH, ME NEITHER.
THERE WILL BE TIME FOR THAT, BUT RIGHT THIS MOMENT, WE HAVE OUR FIRST FIELD TRIP.

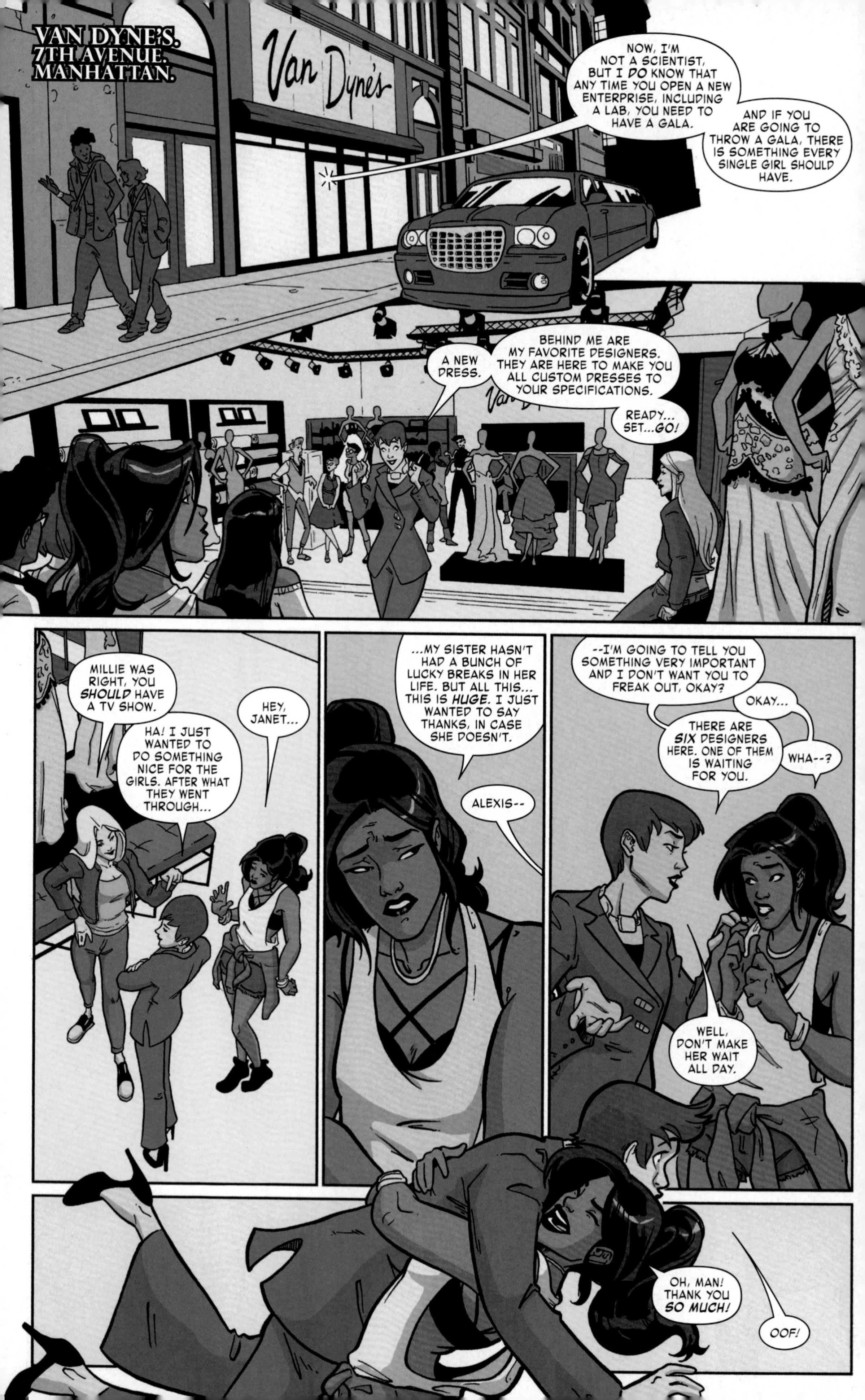
VAN DYNE'S. 7TH AVENUE. MANHATTAN.
Van Dyne's
NOW, I'M NOT A SCIENTIST, BUT I DO KNOW THAT ANY TIME YOU OPEN A NEW ENTERPRISE, INCLUDING A LAB, YOU NEED TO HAVE A GALA.
AND IF YOU ARE GOING TO THROW A GALA, THERE IS SOMETHING EVERY SINGLE GIRL SHOULD HAVE.
A NEW DRESS.
BEHIND ME ARE MY FAVORITE DESIGNERS. THEY ARE HERE TO MAKE YOU ALL CUSTOM DRESSES TO YOUR SPECIFICATIONS.
READY... SET...GO!
MILLIE WAS RIGHT, YOU SHOULD HAVE A TV SHOW.
HA! I JUST WANTED TO DO SOMETHING NICE FOR THE GIRLS. AFTER WHAT THEY WENT THROUGH...
HEY, JANET...
...MY SISTER HASN'T HAD A BUNCH OF LUCKY BREAKS IN HER LIFE. BUT ALL THIS... THIS IS HUGE. I JUST WANTED TO SAY THANKS, IN CASE SHE DOESN'T.
ALEXIS--
--I'M GOING TO TELL YOU SOMETHING VERY IMPORTANT AND I DON'T WANT YOU TO FREAK OUT, OKAY?
OKAY...
THERE ARE SIX DESIGNERS HERE. ONE OF THEM IS WAITING FOR YOU.
WHA--?
WELL, DON'T MAKE HER WAIT ALL DAY.
OH, MAN! THANK YOU SO MUCH!
OOF!

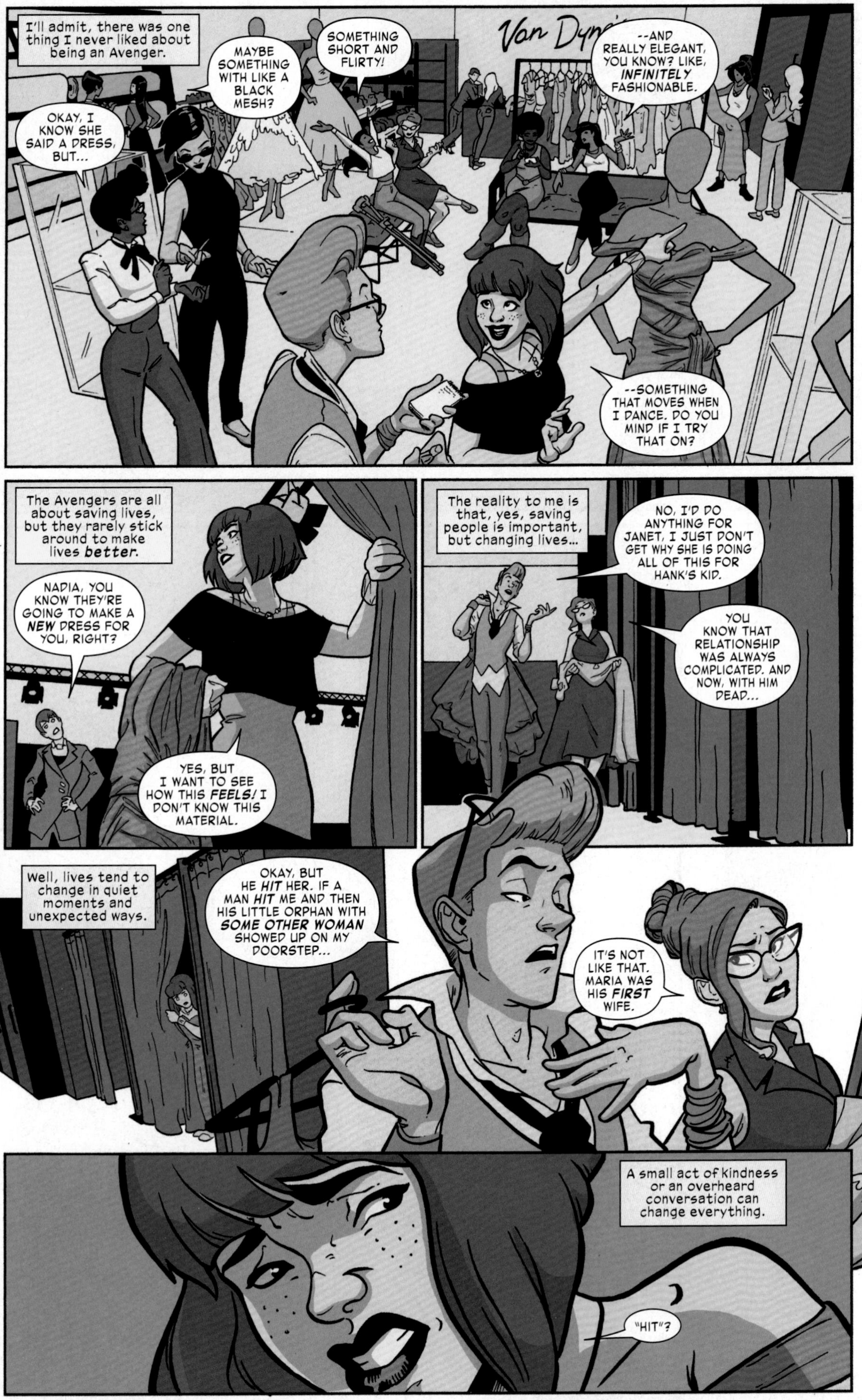

I'll admit, there was one thing I never liked about being an Avenger.
MAYBE SOMETHING WITH LIKE A BLACK MESH?
SOMETHING SHORT AND FLIRTY!
Van Dyne's
--AND REALLY ELEGANT, YOU KNOW? LIKE, INFINITELY FASHIONABLE.
OKAY, I KNOW SHE SAID A DRESS, BUT...
--SOMETHING THAT MOVES WHEN I DANCE. DO YOU MIND IF I TRY THAT ON?
The Avengers are all about saving lives, but they rarely stick around to make lives better.
NADIA, YOU KNOW THEY'RE GOING TO MAKE A NEW DRESS FOR YOU, RIGHT?
YES, BUT I WANT TO SEE HOW THIS FEELS! I DON'T KNOW THIS MATERIAL.
The reality to me is that, yes, saving people is important, but changing lives...
NO, I'D DO ANYTHING FOR JANET. I JUST DON'T GET WHY SHE IS DOING ALL OF THIS FOR HANK'S KID.
YOU KNOW THAT RELATIONSHIP WAS ALWAYS COMPLICATED. AND NOW, WITH HIM DEAD...
Well, lives tend to change in quiet moments and unexpected ways.
OKAY, BUT HE HIT HER. IF A MAN HIT ME AND THEN HIS LITTLE ORPHAN WITH SOME OTHER WOMAN SHOWED UP ON MY DOORSTEP...
IT'S NOT LIKE THAT. MARIA WAS HIS FIRST WIFE.
A small act of kindness or an overheard conversation can change everything.
"HIT"?

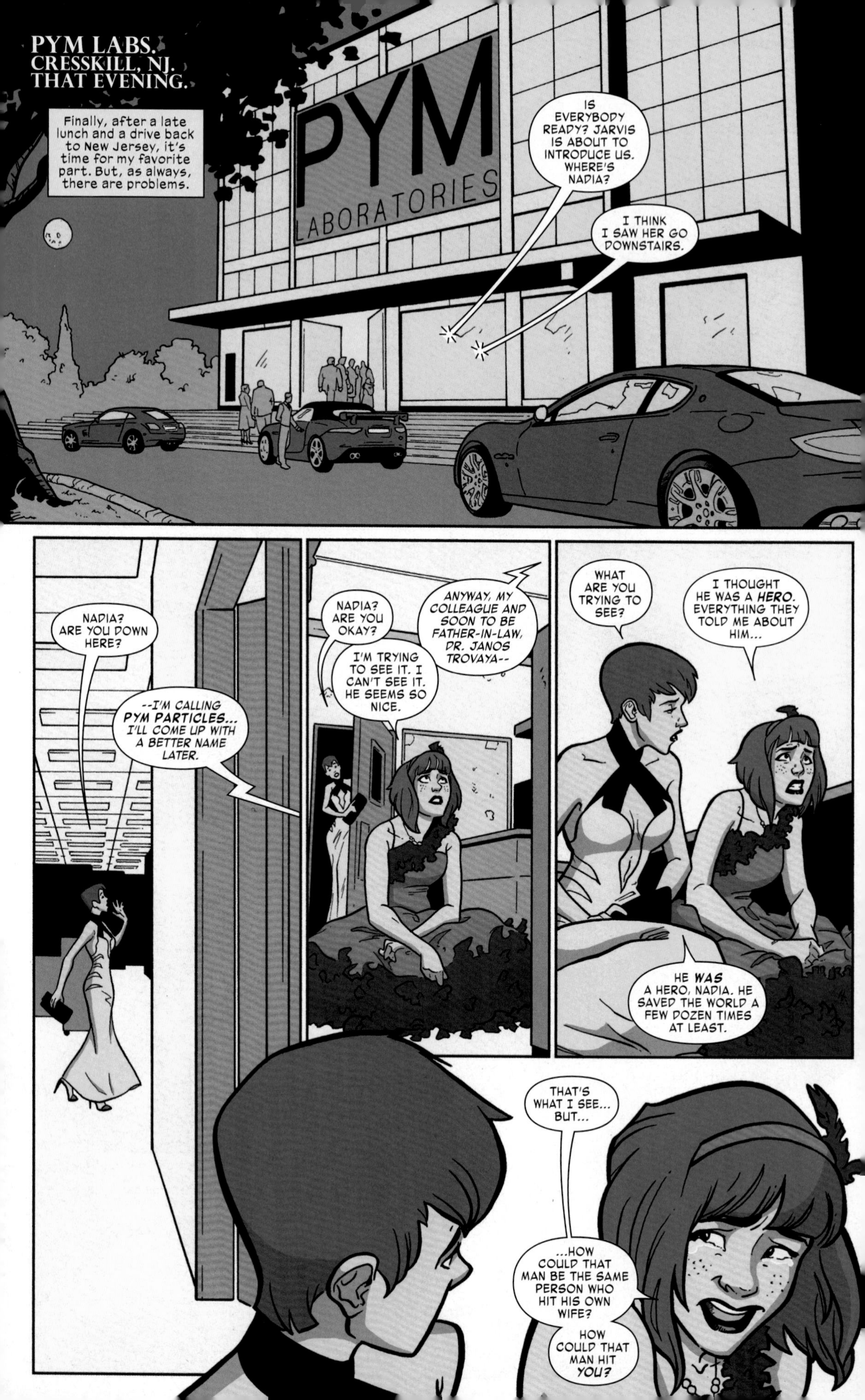
PYM LABS. CRESSKILL, NJ. THAT EVENING.
Finally, after a late lunch and a drive back to New Jersey, it's time for my favorite part. But, as always, there are problems.
PYM LABORATORIES
IS EVERYBODY READY? JARVIS IS ABOUT TO INTRODUCE US. WHERE'S NADIA?
I THINK I SAW HER GO DOWNSTAIRS.
NADIA? ARE YOU DOWN HERE?
--I'M CALLING PYM PARTICLES... I'LL COME UP WITH A BETTER NAME LATER.
NADIA? ARE YOU OKAY?
ANYWAY, MY COLLEAGUE AND SOON TO BE FATHER-IN-LAW, DR. JANOS TROVAYA--
I'M TRYING TO SEE IT. I CAN'T SEE IT. HE SEEMS SO NICE.
WHAT ARE YOU TRYING TO SEE?
I THOUGHT HE WAS A HERO. EVERYTHING THEY TOLD ME ABOUT HIM...
HE WAS A HERO, NADIA. HE SAVED THE WORLD A FEW DOZEN TIMES AT LEAST.
THAT'S WHAT I SEE... BUT...
...HOW COULD THAT MAN BE THE SAME PERSON WHO HIT HIS OWN WIFE?
HOW COULD THAT MAN HIT YOU?

WHO TOLD YOU?

I SAW IT ON THE INTERNET. I DON'T KNOW HOW I DIDN'T FIND OUT BEFORE. IT'S EVERYWHERE.

WHY DIDN'T *YOU* TELL ME HE WAS EVIL?

FIRST, LET'S GET ONE THING STRAIGHT. HANK PYM WAS *NOT* AN EVIL MAN.

HE DID AN EVIL THING AND HE HAD TO LIVE WITH THAT. THERE IS *NO* EXCUSE TO TREAT A PERSON YOU CARE ABOUT THE WAY HE TREATED ME.

HOW COULD YOU *FORGIVE* HIM FOR THAT?

WELL, HONESTLY I DON'T KNOW IF "FORGIVE" IS THE RIGHT WORD. I ACCEPTED WHAT HAPPENED AND MOVED ON.

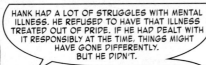

HANK HAD A LOT OF STRUGGLES WITH MENTAL ILLNESS. HE REFUSED TO HAVE THAT ILLNESS TREATED OUT OF PRIDE. IF HE HAD DEALT WITH IT RESPONSIBLY AT THE TIME, THINGS MIGHT HAVE GONE DIFFERENTLY. BUT HE DIDN'T.

I HELD ON TO THAT ANGER FOR A *LONG* TIME. IT TOOK ME A WHILE TO REALIZE WHAT *YOU* ALREADY KNEW WHEN I MET YOU.

YOU CAN'T LET THE THINGS THAT OTHER PEOPLE DO TO YOU DEFINE YOU. YOU HAVE TO TAKE CONTROL OF YOUR OWN LIFE.

WHAT'S THAT?

I REALIZED I COULDN'T LET HANK DEFINE MY LIFE. I DIDN'T LEAVE HIM BECAUSE HE WAS ILL, I LEFT BECAUSE HE PUT HIS OWN PRIDE ABOVE MY SAFETY AND THAT'S UNACCEPTABLE.

I'VE BEEN WORSHIPING HIM FOR *YEARS*, YOU KNOW? I THOUGHT HE WAS THE GREATEST PERSON IN THE WORLD.

NOBODY IS GOING TO LIVE UP TO THAT--NOT YOUR FATHER, NOT ME, NOT BOBBI MORSE. IT'S HOW YOU *DEAL* WITH IT THAT COUNTS.

YOU DON'T HAVE TO KEEP BEING SO NICE TO ME. JUST BECAUSE THIS STUFF WAS HIS DOESN'T MEAN IT SHOULD BE MINE.

OH, NADIA. IS THAT WHAT YOU THINK? THAT I'M DOING THIS BECAUSE OF HANK?

WHY ELSE? YOU'RE NOT RELATED TO ME. YOU DON'T HAVE TO DO ANY OF THIS.

LOOK, I'LL ADMIT THAT I SEE HANK IN YOU SOMETIMES AND I WANT TO HELP THAT PIECE, BUT THAT ISN'T IT.

I LOVE YA, KID. YOU MAKE THE WORLD A BETTER PLACE JUST BY WALKING THROUGH IT. YOU CARE ABOUT EVERYTHING AND EVERYBODY. I SEE YOU AND I THINK--

--I WANT TO BE MORE LIKE HER. SHE'S GOT IT ALL FIGURED OUT.

I LOVE YOU TOO, JANET.

YOU KNOW I DON'T REALLY HAVE IT FIGURED OUT THOUGH, RIGHT?

YEAH, KID. ME NEITHER. LET'S GO DANCE.

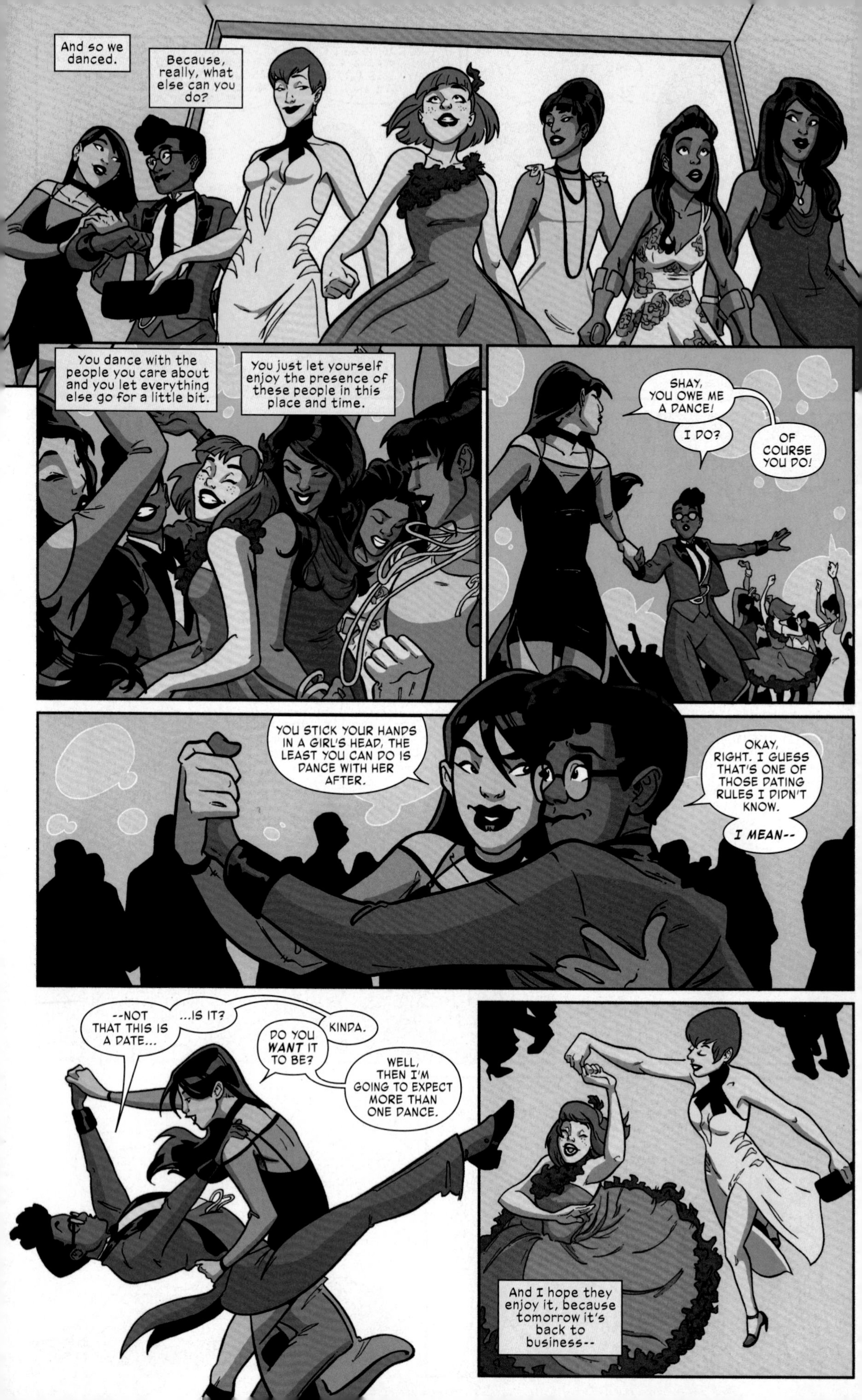
And so we danced.
Because, really, what else can you do?
You dance with the people you care about and you let everything else go for a little bit.
You just let yourself enjoy the presence of these people in this place and time.
SHAY, YOU OWE ME A DANCE!
I DO?
OF COURSE YOU DO!
YOU STICK YOUR HANDS IN A GIRL'S HEAD, THE LEAST YOU CAN DO IS DANCE WITH HER AFTER.
OKAY, RIGHT. I GUESS THAT'S ONE OF THOSE DATING RULES I DIDN'T KNOW.
I MEAN--
--NOT THAT THIS IS A DATE...
...IS IT?
KINDA.
DO YOU WANT IT TO BE?
WELL, THEN I'M GOING TO EXPECT MORE THAN ONE DANCE.
And I hope they enjoy it, because tomorrow it's back to business--

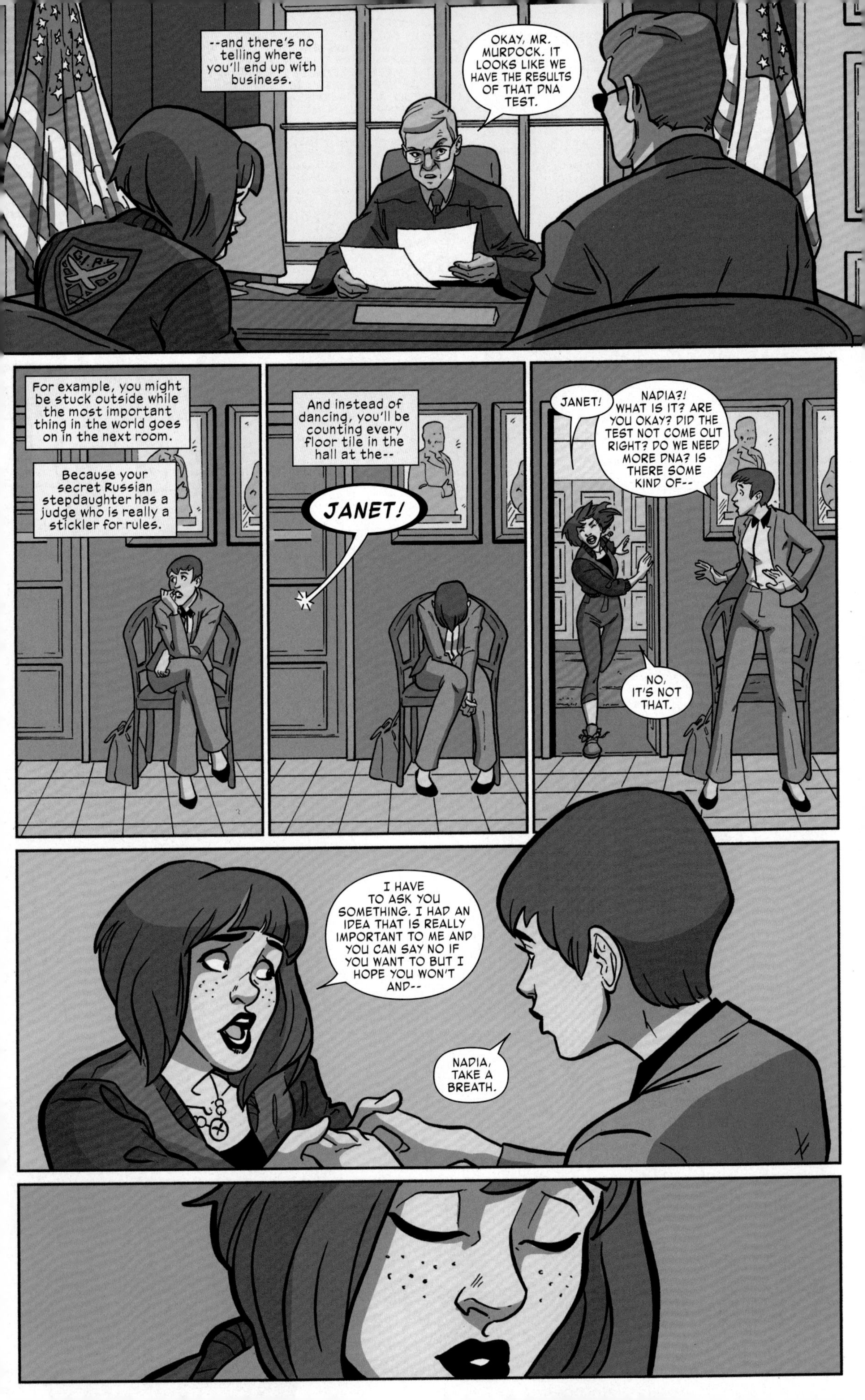
--and there's no telling where you'll end up with business.
OKAY, MR. MURDOCK. IT LOOKS LIKE WE HAVE THE RESULTS OF THAT DNA TEST.
For example, you might be stuck outside while the most important thing in the world goes on in the next room.
Because your secret Russian stepdaughter has a judge who is really a stickler for rules.
And instead of dancing, you'll be counting every floor tile in the hall at the--
JANET!
JANET!
NADIA?! WHAT IS IT? ARE YOU OKAY? DID THE TEST NOT COME OUT RIGHT? DO WE NEED MORE DNA? IS THERE SOME KIND OF--
NO, IT'S NOT THAT.
I HAVE TO ASK YOU SOMETHING. I HAD AN IDEA THAT IS REALLY IMPORTANT TO ME AND YOU CAN SAY NO IF YOU WANT TO BUT I HOPE YOU WON'T AND--
NADIA, TAKE A BREATH.

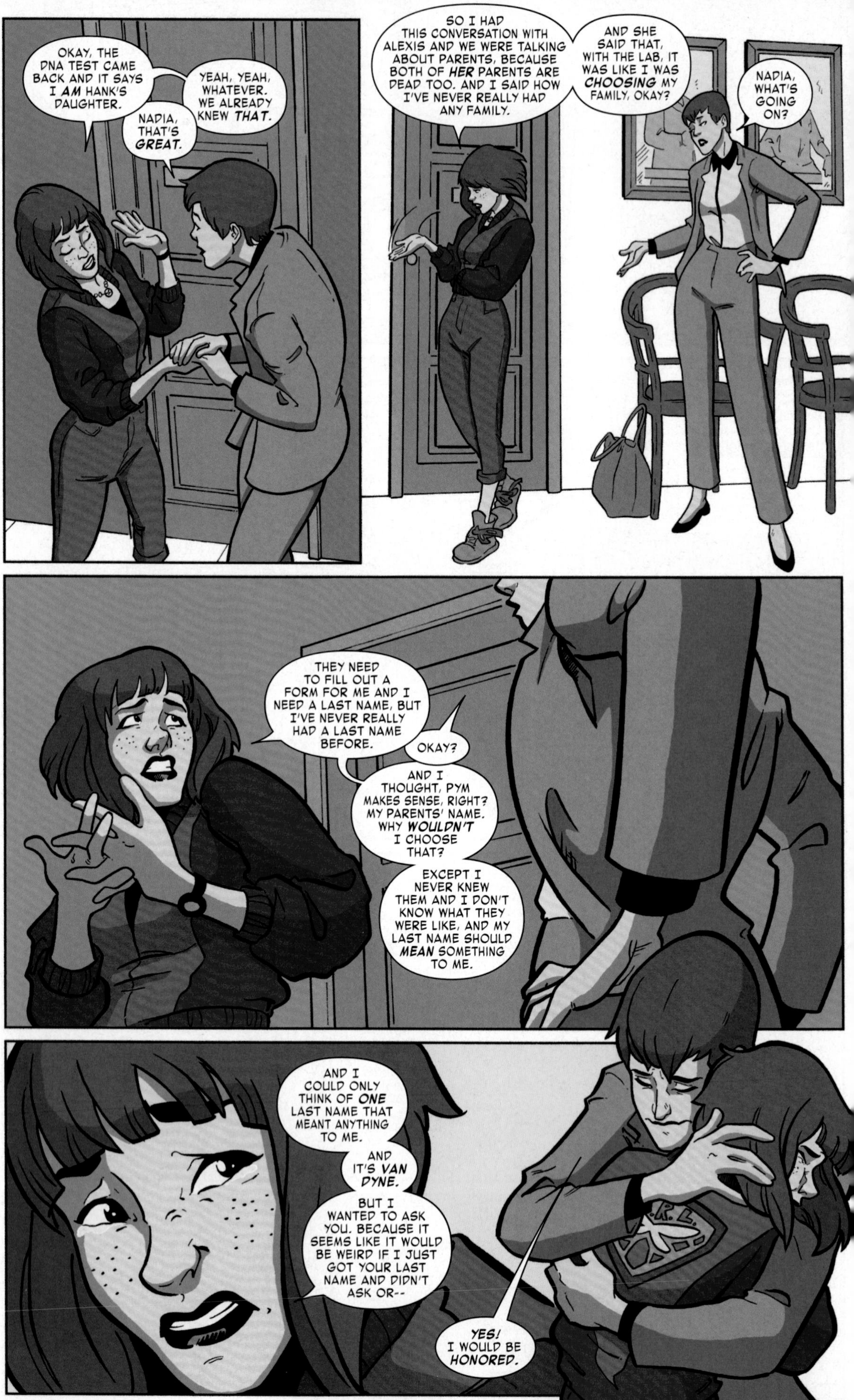
OKAY, THE DNA TEST CAME BACK AND IT SAYS I AM HANK'S DAUGHTER.
YEAH, YEAH, WHATEVER. WE ALREADY KNEW THAT.
NADIA, THAT'S GREAT.
SO I HAD THIS CONVERSATION WITH ALEXIS AND WE WERE TALKING ABOUT PARENTS, BECAUSE BOTH OF HER PARENTS ARE DEAD TOO. AND I SAID HOW I'VE NEVER REALLY HAD ANY FAMILY.
AND SHE SAID THAT, WITH THE LAB, IT WAS LIKE I WAS CHOOSING MY FAMILY, OKAY?
NADIA, WHAT'S GOING ON?
THEY NEED TO FILL OUT A FORM FOR ME AND I NEED A LAST NAME, BUT I'VE NEVER REALLY HAD A LAST NAME BEFORE.
OKAY?
AND I THOUGHT, PYM MAKES SENSE, RIGHT? MY PARENTS' NAME. WHY WOULDN'T I CHOOSE THAT?
EXCEPT I NEVER KNEW THEM AND I DON'T KNOW WHAT THEY WERE LIKE, AND MY LAST NAME SHOULD MEAN SOMETHING TO ME.
AND I COULD ONLY THINK OF ONE LAST NAME THAT MEANT ANYTHING TO ME.
AND IT'S VAN DYNE.
BUT I WANTED TO ASK YOU. BECAUSE IT SEEMS LIKE IT WOULD BE WEIRD IF I JUST GOT YOUR LAST NAME AND DIDN'T ASK OR--
YES! I WOULD BE HONORED.

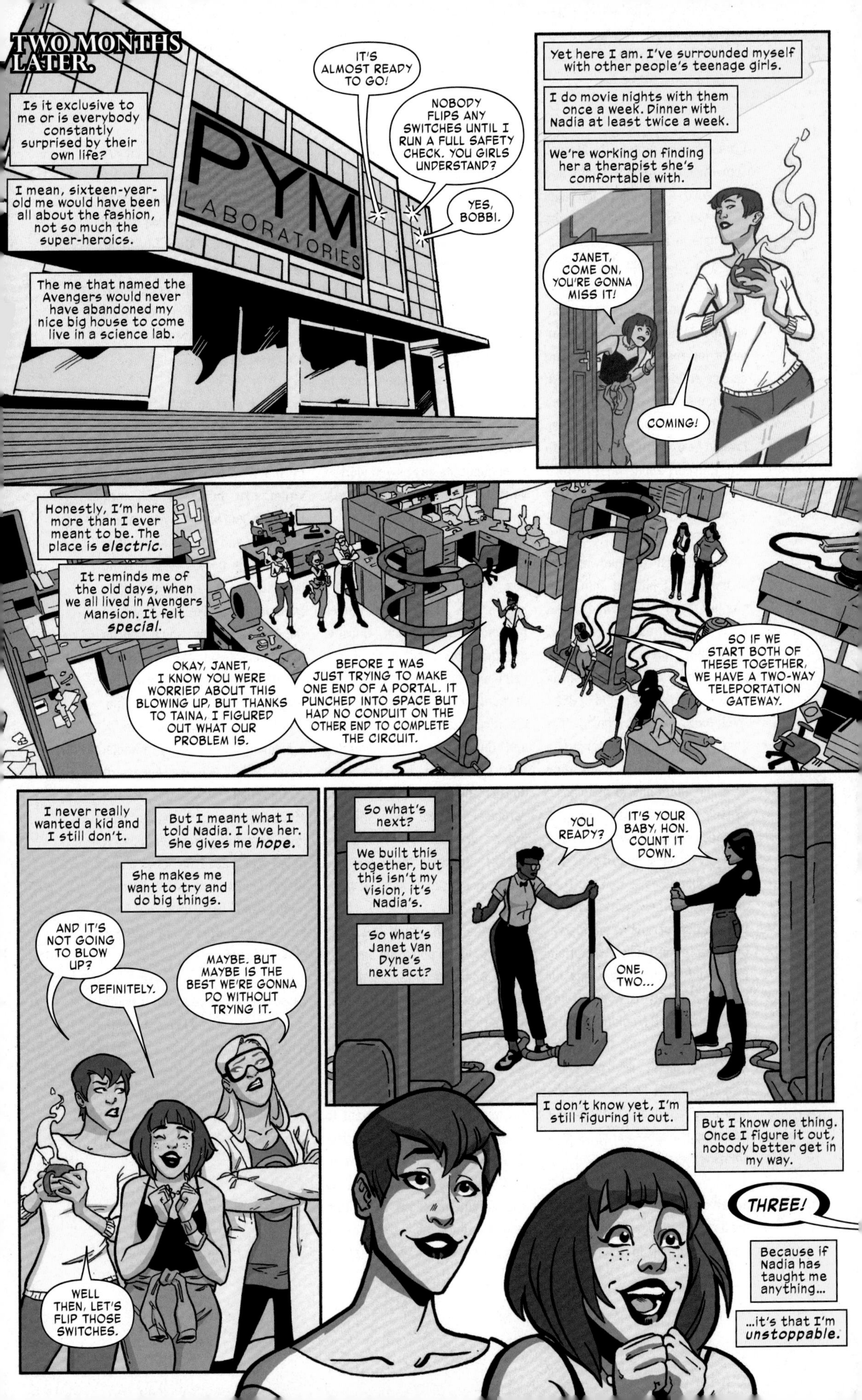
TWO MONTHS LATER.
Is it exclusive to me or is everybody constantly surprised by their own life?
I mean, sixteen-year-old me would have been all about the fashion, not so much the super-heroics.
The me that named the Avengers would never have abandoned my nice big house to come live in a science lab.
PYM LABORATORIES
IT'S ALMOST READY TO GO!
NOBODY FLIPS ANY SWITCHES UNTIL I RUN A FULL SAFETY CHECK. YOU GIRLS UNDERSTAND?
YES, BOBBI.
Yet here I am. I've surrounded myself with other people's teenage girls.
I do movie nights with them once a week. Dinner with Nadia at least twice a week.
We're working on finding her a therapist she's comfortable with.
JANET, COME ON, YOU'RE GONNA MISS IT!
COMING!
Honestly, I'm here more than I ever meant to be. The place is *electric*.
It reminds me of the old days, when we all lived in Avengers Mansion. It felt *special*.
OKAY, JANET, I KNOW YOU WERE WORRIED ABOUT THIS BLOWING UP, BUT THANKS TO TAINA, I FIGURED OUT WHAT OUR PROBLEM IS.
BEFORE I WAS JUST TRYING TO MAKE ONE END OF A PORTAL. IT PUNCHED INTO SPACE BUT HAD NO CONDUIT ON THE OTHER END TO COMPLETE THE CIRCUIT.
SO IF WE START BOTH OF THESE TOGETHER, WE HAVE A TWO-WAY TELEPORTATION GATEWAY.
I never really wanted a kid and I still don't.
But I meant what I told Nadia. I love her. She gives me *hope*.
She makes me want to try and do big things.
AND IT'S NOT GOING TO BLOW UP?
DEFINITELY.
MAYBE. BUT MAYBE IS THE BEST WE'RE GONNA DO WITHOUT TRYING IT.
WELL THEN, LET'S FLIP THOSE SWITCHES.
So what's next?
We built this together, but this isn't my vision, it's Nadia's.
So what's Janet Van Dyne's next act?
YOU READY?
IT'S YOUR BABY, HON. COUNT IT DOWN.
ONE, TWO...
I don't know yet, I'm still figuring it out.
But I know one thing. Once I figure it out, nobody better get in my way.
THREE!
Because if Nadia has taught me anything...
...it's that I'm *unstoppable*.

I am eternally grateful to Marvel, Tom Brevoort, Alanna Smith and Mark Waid. A year and a half ago, Nadia Van Dyne appeared for the first time in our Marvel Universe. I picked up a Free Comic Book Day book, read her story with my daughter, thought she was a cool addition to the Marvel U and then spent the rest of the day signing comics at Ultimate Comics here in Durham, North Carolina. I had no idea that only a month or two later, I would be exchanging emails with Tom Brevoort about what I would do were I given the opportunity to write a solo series about Nadia.

What you just finished reading is the story I pitched Tom after chatting with Mark Waid about what made Nadia special. At that point, Nadia had a grand total of three appearances--all in Mark's ALL-NEW, ALL-DIFFERENT AVENGERS. I was given the amazing privilege of taking a character with little more than an origin and a link to the classic Marvel Universe and shaping a story around her. There have been very few times in the last year that Tom or Alanna have said no. They didn't say no when I started writing the wordiest scripts in the Marvel Universe full of Nadia's fangirling (shout-out to Joe Caramagna for making it all fit). They didn't say no when I pulled Mockingbird and Ms. Marvel into the first issue. And they didn't say no when Elsa and I came to them with the idea of filling what should be our letters pages with interviews with amazing female scientists.

Speaking of Elsa Charretier, I could not have asked for a more amazing creative partner in making this book what it is. While everybody gives her props on her art, Elsa is responsible for so much more of this book. She worked with me to come up with the idea of doing interviews. She drew the amazing cross section of that giant robot's joints in issue #1 that gave birth to "Nadia's Awesome Science Facts," and when I wrote that we needed a two-page spread of the girls working in the lab, she asked what I would think about setting it as a montage that moved throughout the day as you worked your way across the page. I cannot say enough about her talent.

Megan Wilson's colors and Joe Caramagna's letters are inseparable from what makes this book the original, unusual and beautiful piece of art it is. I can't express how grateful I am to them for making the incredibly ambitious art and letters that Elsa and I threw at them into something truly spectacular. And the same goes for the astonishingly talented Veronica Fish, Ro Stein and Ted Brandt, who picked up where Elsa left off and made these last two issues as special as the first six.

And I can't talk about this book without talking about the amazing Preeti Chhibber, who volunteered to read scripts for me and tell me where I was screwing up. She gets a special thanks in every issue, and boy did she earn that.

But more than anyone, I want to thank the amazing lady scientists who took a few minutes off from their science adventures to answer our questions and share their passion with us. We made some fun stories about super heroes and scientists, but they're out there changing the world every day. I cannot thank them enough (especially my dear friends Rachel Silverstein and Marina Chanidou, who volunteered to be in our first issue, sight unseen). I hope it was as awesome for all of them to be in a comic as it was for me to interview them.

Finally, I want to thank you, the reader. You picked up a book for a character with three appearances in the Marvel Universe, with a writer that many of you may have not known, and you gave it your time and money month after month. This book's ending is no reflection on the fans. You are, as ever, amazing. Like Nadia said on the previous page, she'll still be found in issues of AVENGERS and/or CHAMPIONS for the foreseeable future, so be sure to keep reading. And let me say, I don't believe for a moment that the story of Nadia, Janet, Bobbi and the Agents of G.I.R.L. ends here. This is the Marvel Universe. If enough fans love something hard enough, it never stays dead for long. Share these books with your friends, family and that little girl you know who started a fire with her chemistry set.

Since Nadia left you with a quote from Carl Sagan, I'll leave you with a quote from Nadia:

"If this is the last time I see you all, don't stop inventing. Don't stop being amazing. Keep G.I.R.L. alive."

Jeremy Whitley

AGENTS of G.I.R.L.

Guhhhh! Bad feelings! Bad feelings! Shake it off! Okay, Mother is just horrible, but let's forget about her. Hi, everybody, it's Nadia again! We have a special treat for our readers this month: not only are these G.I.R.L. recruits science ladies, but they're celebrities! Guys, I'm gonna freak out. Have you heard of *MythBusters: The Search*? Well, Dr. Tracy Fanara (@inspectorplanet) and Tamara Robertson, EIT (@tlynnr85) were on it, teaching people all over the world about science, technology, engineering and math ON TV! I'm gonna go sit in a corner and take deep breaths. Tamara and Tracy, take it away!

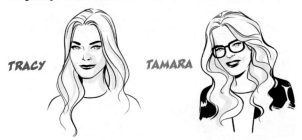

TRACY   TAMARA

WHAT KIND OF WORK DO YOU DO AND WHY?

Tracy: I am an environmental engineer PhD and manage the environmental health program at Mote Marine Laboratory. My expertise is in water and stormwater treatment, sustainable development, and hydrologic restoration of watersheds. In my current role, I research how natural and manmade toxins affect the environment and then develop sustainable designs to protect human and ecosystem health. I grew up in Buffalo, NY, and learned about the Love Canal catastrophe--this began my passion for science and the environment. I saw how everything in the world is connected and that each one of us makes an impact, and I wanted mine to be a positive one. I believe that science education has the power to spark change and sustainable behaviors, which is why outreach and education are focuses of my research program.

Tamara: My specialty is chemical and biomolecular engineering, which, when combined with my knack for tinkering and fabrication, has led me to a career in process/product designs and builds. I've worked in a varied range of fields including biofuels, vaccines, additive technologies, and consumer packaging. What I love about my degree is that it's given me the flexibility to really pursue my passions within engineering! The latest passion it let me pursue was getting onto *MythBusters: The Search* as a finalist--I got to build some really amazing things, including a vacuum pack that I scaled a seven-story building with!

WHAT EXCITES YOU ABOUT YOUR WORK?

Tracy: What most excites me about my work is that I have the opportunity to help people and wildlife on a global scale for generations to come; that I can be creative and propose research and designs that have never been attempted while inspiring people to fall in love with science by showing them how it impacts their lives. In short, what excites me most is the power to make the world better place.

Tamara: The exciting thing about my work is that, every day, I know that I am working to help people. Whether I'm retrofitting a biodiesel plant to provide my alma mater, NC State, with biofuel for their farm, or helping to design and build a vaccine facility, there is never a doubt that what I'm doing is enriching the areas and people around me. Working in these fields as an engineer is even more exciting because I get to focus on efficient designs and help alleviate the cost burden to consumers while still meeting their needs. In a world

where we all are working to make ends meet and provide for our families, I think it's important to help keep costs down for necessities.

WHY ARE YOU PASSIONATE ABOUT YOUNG WOMEN GETTING INTO SCIENCE?

Tracy: I am passionate about inspiring young women to pursue science not only because of the exciting opportunities it presents and the need for great scientists as well as unique ideas, but because I want to show them that they can, that there is no stereotype to science, and STEM is for anyone with a passion for knowledge, curiosity about how the world works, and willingness to work hard.

Tamara: As a woman in science, I feel that it's vital to connect with young women and let them know that they can be anything they want to be, regardless of whether it seems like a "boy" or "girl" job. Growing up, I was really good at math and science. I struggled a lot with the realization that I wasn't really drawn to any of the "women" jobs, and was labeled a tomboy because I chose to pursue sports and building. At the time, I didn't know any engineers (let alone female ones) so I never even considered it as a potential path. It wasn't until my second year in college that I met a female mathematics professor that helped me find my way in life, and I am grateful for that. Now I want to pay that forward and teach little girls they can hold their own among the men. As the only female finalist on *MythBusters: The Search*, I think I accomplished that. :)

WHAT FEMALE SCIENTISTS (REAL AND/OR FICTIONAL) HAVE INSPIRED YOU?

Tracy: When I was younger, I was not aware of actual female scientists--pop culture didn't do a great job of presenting them. Penny was the brains behind Inspector Gadget--a blonde, young genius who didn't need credit for her work in saving the world. Dr. Brennan from *Bones*, Dr. Jo Harding from *Twister*, and "Murph" from *Interstellar* are inspiring characters --I loved to see their passion for their work drive them to success. As an adult, I see that there are many real, inspiring female scientists, one being Dr. Eugene Clark, who followed her passion for research, philanthropy, and outreach, shaping the institution that I work for now.

Tamara: I didn't know any female scientists growing up--I don't think I could name any aside from Marie Curie, who was inspiring to me as the mother of physics. I got most of my female science role models from comics and sci-fi shows instead! I was a huge fan of X-MEN and *Star Trek* growing up, and getting to see women as

scientists, leaders, and warriors helped me to feel like I could do anything! I think that's why the role of toys is so important in inspiring kids to pursue STEAM because it helps to make science and tech fun and introduces kids to these concepts at a young age--much like comics and sci-fi did with science and me.

DO YOU HAVE A FAVORITE EXAMPLE OF NONSENSICAL SCIENCE IN POPULAR CULTURE?

Tracy: Time travel--not only do you go through time, but space as well in *Back to the Future*! I have thought long and hard about possible ways to make this a reality...let's just say I haven't completely abandoned it. Time travel is number one. However, X-Men super-powers (telepathy, strength, speed) and shape-shifting (as presented in *True Blood*, although *Supernatural* is my preferred show) would come in quite handy.

Tamara: I always loved the idea of Peter Parker becoming Spider-Man--that a bite from a radioactive spider could give you super-powers. To me, it's quite neat to think of the alterations to the genome that would have to occur to give him all the amazing traits he has. I remember becoming super interested in bugs after learning about Spider-Man when I was little and thinking that perhaps they could give me super-powers too. Most of them were friendly and didn't bite, so I didn't quite get to test my hypothesis--but I did learn a lot about entomology, so that was a plus. :)

HOW LONG HAVE YOU BEEN READING COMICS AND WHAT WAS YOUR FIRST COMIC BOOK?

Tracy: I have been reading comics for as long as I could read, started with *Transformers*, but X-MEN and *Captain Planet* were my favorites (I always felt that I was different from my peers, so unique characters with good intentions drew me in).

Tamara: I started reading comics when I was a kid--I hung out mainly with the boys I knew, since they always had cooler toys and games, so I got to learn about the comic book world. X-MEN was always my favorite--there were so many strong women characters to connect with and see do amazing things! Storm was my favorite, though--I loved how she could control the weather and fly! I grew up in Hurricane Alley, so I always thought that she was out there flying around when we would have storms. I think too, as a redhead who knew that my hair color was a genetic anomaly, that the life of a "mutant" made sense to me. I got made fun of a lot for my hair, but now I wear it like a badge of honor-- the X-Men made me realize it's my own super-power (and comes with a temper like She-Hulk's!).

Now, tell me that wasn't cool! Go look online for videos of Tamara climbing a wall like Spider-Man using a vacuum! *HEART EYES EMOJI.* Anyway, see you again next month so you guys can see how we save Ying (I hope!).

Do svidaniya,
Nadia

AGENTS of G.I.R.L.

Hey, guys, it's Janet. Nadia is…having a rough time right now, so as your original Wasp, I'm stepping in to do the introduction to the letters page. Things may look dim right now, but we have two stunning and brilliant women in STEM to celebrate, so let's step it up and let them know how much we appreciate their amazing work! Please welcome nuclear engineer Mareena Robinson Snowden (@mrobinsnow) and aerospace engineer Lisa Johnson (@tehnakki)!

MEREENA

LISA

WHAT KIND OF WORK DO YOU DO AND WHY?

Mareena: As a nuclear engineer working in the nuclear security space, my research focuses on technology that could be used to verify future arms-control treaties. The U.S. and Russia have a long history of cooperation on reducing the size of their nuclear weapon arsenals, and much of this progress was based on the technical verification possibilities of the time. As a technical scientist, I believe it is important that we continue to provide the policy and political community with an understanding of what is possible in the boundaries of science and technology. Since verification of compliance to an arms-reduction treaty is often a stumbling block to the success of an agreement, scientists and engineers play a key role in shaping the boundaries of what is possible, and this is why my work is important.

Lisa: I'm an aerospace engineer with a focus in space systems, a.k.a. a rocket scientist--though I work primarily on spacecraft, not launchers. I'm currently designing small cubesats (about the size of a shoebox) that are launched as part of a constellation that tracks ships and collects weather data. I have about 30 satellites in orbit.

WHAT EXCITES YOU ABOUT YOUR WORK?

Mareena: Nuclear security is a field that exists at the intersection of policy, history, science and technology. It's this interdisciplinary nature that keeps my work interesting, because the ground is always changing beneath my feet. Whether it's new geopolitical dimensions that emerge--like what is currently happening with U.S.-Russia relations--or new technologies that expand the verification possibilities, the constantly evolving context of my work requires me to be active in my participation. It requires me to be able to think beyond common assumptions or circumstances, and foreshadow the relevancy of my technology in a future world. It is exciting to think that technology I create could have a bearing on reducing, or even eliminating, the nuclear threats we face today. These opportunities for direct impact are the things that make my work exciting.

Lisa: I love designing and building these little vehicles that are then hurled into the most INHOSPITABLE environment we know of and trying to keep them alive and happy. It's challenging, frustrating, expensive, time consuming and a whole lot of fun!

WHY ARE YOU PASSIONATE ABOUT YOUNG WOMEN GETTING INTO SCIENCE?

Mareena: One of the things I discovered as an undergrad majoring in physics was that my training was not applicable solely to scientific problems. I was also learning critical thinking skills that would be transferrable to many other complex questions outside of science. This ability to see to the relevance of my training outside of the boundaries of science gave me a confidence in my mind and my logic. This is one of the things I hope for for young women entering STEM: that they understand the value of the skills they earn, and recognize their agency in what problems they choose to apply those scientific tools and methods to.

I choose to share my experiences as a scientist and engineer because I believe images and narratives matter, and can have a direct impact on how someone perceives herself. My passion for inclusion comes from the understanding that each community has something of value to offer, and that success in these traditionally male-dominated fields does not have to come at the expense of your womanhood.

Lisa: There were so many times in my personal journey where I was told "no" by someone. No, you can't take that Algebra class, girls aren't good at math. No, you can't learn to fly, no one likes to hear women on the radio. No, you can't go to M.I.T., black girls don't get into that school. I'm lucky that I have the tenacity of a spiteful bulldozer, but so many of the young women I mentor don't, and they shouldn't have to adjust to get an opportunity to study something cool! I just want to make it easier for the next generation of girls to follow their neat space dreams.

WHAT FEMALE SCIENTISTS (REAL AND/OR FICTIONAL) HAVE INSPIRED YOU?

Mareena: Katherine Johnson of NASA--as a black woman who played a key role in the U.S. space race at the height of the Jim Crow era, her bravery and brilliance are a constant source of inspiration to me.

Lisa: Samantha Carter from *SG-1* and B'Elanna Torres from *Star Trek Voyager* were my idols. Sam with her ability to hold her own with her male superiors through competency and intelligence, and B'Elanna as the angriest engineer to ever keep a starship running showed me there was a place for me in aerospace. And as a mixed-race child, B'Elanna made me feel better about navigating the space between my two worlds. As for real people, I always looked up to the barnstormer Bessie Coleman, the first African-American to get a pilot's license. I carry a picture of her taped to the inside of my flight log.

DO YOU HAVE A FAVORITE EXAMPLE OF NONSENSICAL SCIENCE IN POPULAR CULTURE?

Mareena: I'd have to say the science of climate change denial. That is pretty nonsensical to me.

Lisa: It always cracks me up when super heroes like Supergirl or Captain Marvel "fly" to or from space. The first time I met Kelly Sue DeConnick, I had three pages of notes on how she described Captain Marvel's reentry incorrectly, including mathematical proofs. We've been friends ever since.

HOW LONG HAVE YOU BEEN READING COMICS AND WHAT WAS YOUR FIRST COMIC BOOK?

Mareena: I first started reading comics as a young child out of the Sunday newspaper, specifically *Dilbert, Garfield* and *The Boondocks*. My first comic book was probably *Teenage Mutant Ninja Turtles*.

Lisa: I've been reading manga like *Sailor Moon* since elementary school, but I started actively reading American comics in 2012 with the Kelly Sue DeConnick's CAPTAIN MARVEL run. And now, my favorite comics include MS. MARVEL, BLACK PANTHER and a lot of indie/creator-owned works by my friends.

Well, kids, that's it for this month. They're really something huh? Feel better now? What if I told you that, next month, you get a little peek inside my head? That's right, next month you get twice the Wasp for the price of one as original Avenger and fashion icon Janet Van Dyne takes the wheel of THE UNSTOPPABLE WASP! (Don't worry, Nadia will be here too!)

Kisses,
Janet!

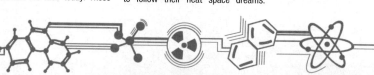

AGENTS OF G.I.R.L.

Hey reader, you're looking great today! Are you doing something new?

It's Janet again, standing in for Nadia. You know, I was tempted to do an article about hot new designers, seeing as I know more about that than scientists, but if you wanted to hear me give a two-hour thesis on Christian Siriano's shoe line, you could just check out my YouTube channel. Just real quick, have you seen the multicolor strap heel he's selling right now? I can't keep them in the closet; my other shoes get jealous.

Anyway, we have two really amazing scientists to share with you today: Erin Winick (@erinwinick) and Erika Bongen (@erika_bongen). Ladies, let them know who you are!

ERIN

ERIKA

WHAT KIND OF WORK DO YOU DO AND WHY?

Erin: I just graduated with my mechanical engineering degree from the University of Florida. I work as the CEO of my company, Sci Chic, and as a freelance science writer. At Sci Chic I use plastic and metal 3D printing to create science- and engineering-inspired jewelry. I've had my writing printed in publications ranging from Engineering.com to the *New York Times.*

Erika: In high school, I loved math and I loved science, but I loved biology best, so that's what I chose to study in college. After a few years, I really missed math, but I didn't know how to do both biology and math. Turns out they call that COMPUTATIONAL BIOLOGY! You see, computational biology is using computer science methods to answer questions in biology--and, to me, writing code is just another kind of math. Now, I'm working on my PhD in Immunology, where I'm using computer science methods, like machine learning, to figure out why women in general have stronger immune systems than men. This is a problem, because if your immune system is too strong it can cause autoimmune diseases, like lupus, and if it's too weak, you're vulnerable to infections.

WHAT EXCITES YOU ABOUT YOUR WORK?

Erin: I founded my company Sci Chic to show that science, technology, engineering and math can be fun, creative and even fashionable. I love sparking conversations about science through fashion and being able to use my mechanical engineering knowledge to encourage young girls to consider the STEM fields. I am a maker at heart and love creating new things, so this is my dream company.

Erika: Day to day, I love the process of breaking one big problem into many little problems. I'm pretty sure that solving a bug in my code gives me the same dopamine ping in my brain that video games do. So I can get pretty excited to jump back into my code to figure it out!

WHY ARE YOU PASSIONATE ABOUT YOUNG WOMEN GETTING INTO SCIENCE?

Erin: I want all girls to see science and engineering as potential careers. I do not want young girls to be discouraged from pursuing a career that could be perfect for them. I think that STEM fields are often perceived as hard and calculating, when they are actually very creative and artistic. In mechanical engineering, I got to learn how to design items on the computer and then make them. I believe that if we can get across the creativity in STEM to young girls, we can help change the current ratios of women in STEM fields.

Erika: We need you. The world needs you. In science, people's experiences change what questions they ask and how they interpret their results. By joining in, you'll help keep science from being biased. You can help us get closer to the truth. And whenever I worry about whether I'm good enough, I remind myself that I don't have to be the best. There's way too many problems out there; we need all the help we can get!

WHAT FEMALE SCIENTISTS (REAL AND/OR FICTIONAL) HAVE INSPIRED YOU?

Erin: Growing up, most of my role models in science were men, which is one reason I am particularly passionate about science communication. I want to give young girls more women to look up to in science and engineering. Now that I am older, I really admire Debbie Sterling, the founder of GoldieBlox, Ayah Bdeir, the founder of littleBits, and co-founders of the space fashion blog *STARtorialist,* Summer Ash and Emily Rice.

Erika: My mom works as a microbiologist in a hospital, so she'd always come home with these stories about how she'd identified a particularly tricky bacterium or virus from a patient sample. If I got a sore throat, she'd swab me herself and grow up the bacterial colonies in the basement, and in the morning she'd explain to me how she identified it as *Streptococcus pyogenes,* which causes strep throat! I came home from school once to find her with a microscope on the dining room table. She was identifying a tick she found on our dog, Toby, to see if it was a species that could carry Lyme disease! I love how Mom and I ended up studying two sides of the same problem: she studies how microbes cause disease while I study how the immune system fights it!

DO YOU HAVE A FAVORITE EXAMPLE OF NONSENSICAL SCIENCE IN POPULAR CULTURE?

Erin: Although I enjoyed watching it, the movie *Gravity* was full of things that just did not work scientifically. For example, the Hubble Space Telescope, International Space Station and Chinese Space Station cannot all be seen at the same time, and Sandra Bullock's hair always stayed perfectly around her head despite the zero gravity.

Erika: I love X-23 because she was cloned from Logan/Wolverine's DNA, except the Y-chromosome sequence was no good, so they just gave her two X-chromosomes. I keep wishing she was real so I could study the effects of having two identical X-chromosomes! Each female cell expresses one of its X-chromosomes and deactivates the other. This happens in the embryo, so your hand can express your mother's X-chromosome, while your elbow expresses your father's. (This is why we have calico cats! It's called X-inactivation.) But, X-23 won't have that effect because her X-chromosomes are identical. What I wouldn't give to study how that changes her biology!

HOW LONG HAVE YOU BEEN READING COMICS, AND WHAT WAS YOUR FIRST COMIC BOOK?

Erin: I actually first read graphic novels when I was in middle school. All my friends were really into manga so I figured, why not give it a shot? The first one I ever read was a *Kingdom Hearts* graphic novel.

Erika: In middle school, I got obsessed with the X-Men because of the movies, so I'd bike to the library and read everything they had about them. I especially loved Kitty Pryde. She's clever, optimistic and fiercely loyal, like I try to be!

A mechanical engineer that makes science-inspired jewelry? I think I just found Nadia's Christmas present! Well, kids, we'll be back next month with more tales of the Unstoppable Wasps. That's right, Wasps. We're in this together.

XOXO Janet

AGENTS OF G.I.R.L.

Hello again, all you beautiful, brilliant readers. Nadia here! I have some very important things to say to you this month, but before we get to that, we have one last interview to run. And it's very special, because she's the colorist of the very book you hold in your hands. Please give love to colorist extraordinaire, wonderful person and mechanical engineer: Megan Wilson! (@meganenginerd on Twitter).

MEGAN

G.I.R.L. is an absolute good. We built something here. We brought together some of the brightest and most brilliant girls in the world and we proved that when we put our heads together, we can do anything. And before I go any further, let me say that G.I.R.L. is not going anywhere. We'll keep creating, keep sciencing, and I'm told we're going to be having a movie marathon really soon. Shay says we should watch all of the *Harry Potter* movies, but Taina says I need to see *Star Wars* first. They keep arguing about something called "prequels," but I'm sure we'll sort it out.

But I do have to say that, for the moment, this is the last issue of our story. Does that mean we're going away? Never! You'll still see my adventures with the Avengers, and if you spread the word and look for our collections, you can bet the Agents of G.I.R.L. will be back in comics before you know it.

The biggest thing I want you to know is that just because you don't see our comic on the stands every month, it doesn't mean the Agents of G.I.R.L. aren't working. Now, I'm not just talking about me, Ying, Shay (aren't they cute together?), Taina, Priya, Alexis or even Bobbi and Janet. I'm talking about the agents you've met in our back pages every month. Women, real women like you and me, are making amazing discoveries and changing the world every single day. If you want to be one of them, there is a whole multiverse of science, technology, engineering and math out there waiting for you. You may not see interviews running every month, but they'll still be out there on Twitter and in the lab making the world great. And if you ever need a little encouragement, I'll be here, saving the world.

Let me leave you with a quote you probably already know, especially if you've read this series. It's from indisputable cool guy Carl Sagan: "Somewhere, something incredible is waiting to be known." So get out there and discover it, G.I.R.Ls!

Do svidaniya,
Nadia Van Dyne

WHAT KIND OF WORK DO YOU DO?

I'm a mechanical engineer and I do aerodynamics and acoustics in the wind energy industry. My current role covers aspects of turbine rotor design all the way up to the full farm and how turbines interact with each other and their surroundings. I get to do a little bit of everything: computer simulations, coding, data analysis, experiments in controlled environments, full-scale tests in the field and design work. I also color this comic!

WHAT EXCITES YOU ABOUT YOUR WORK?

A lot of things! I've always loved problem-solving and coming up with new ways to do things. I'm very curious and like to do a little bit of everything, and mechanical engineering is incredibly diverse! Even though my graduate research specialized in computational fluid mechanics, my current role has enabled me to branch out and learn things about other subfields, such as acoustics and controls. The modern incarnation of wind energy is exciting because it is relatively new compared to other energy sectors, and the technology turnover is rapid. I could go on!

WHY ARE YOU PASSIONATE ABOUT YOUNG WOMEN GETTING INTO ENGINEERING?

I want to encourage young women to pursue their interests, whatever they may be. Take chances on the things you like, because you'll figure the specifics out as you go. I certainly didn't have a clear plan of what I wanted to do and meandered my way to where I'm at, but I've gotten to be part of a lot of really cool things along the way.

WHAT FEMALE ENGINEERS (REAL OR FICTIONAL) HAVE INSPIRED YOU IN YOUR WORK?

Inspiration is usually a small and ongoing thing for me that serves as a gentle reminder to keep challenging myself! As an example, I recently saw an article about Tiera Guinn: at age 22, she's wrapping up school and is already part of a team working to build a rocket to take people to Mars! I really admired her drive and focus, and I hope to see big things from her and other up-and-comers like her in the future!

DO YOU HAVE A FAVORITE EXAMPLE OF CLEVER/UNUSUAL/NONSENSICAL USE OF SCIENCE/ENGINEERING IN COMICS?

I suppose my favorite things probably are the ones that are completely absurd, because I'll often catch myself engineering my way through it and have to laugh at how ridiculous it is to be having a mini brainstorming session. To be fair, though, I like a good challenge!

HOW LONG HAVE YOU BEEN READING COMICS? WHAT WAS YOUR FIRST COMIC BOOK?

I started reading comics in 2012, right around the time *Manhattan Projects* came out, and I think that was the first book I picked up and stuck with.

Isn't she amazing? She does all that AND colors the best comic book in the world! How many people do you know who can say that? (Here's a hint: The answer is zero, because she colored every issue of this book!) Okay, I said I had some important things to say, so...deep breath and let's jump into it.

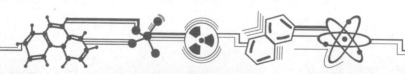

CHARACTER DESIGNS BY ELSA CHARRETIER

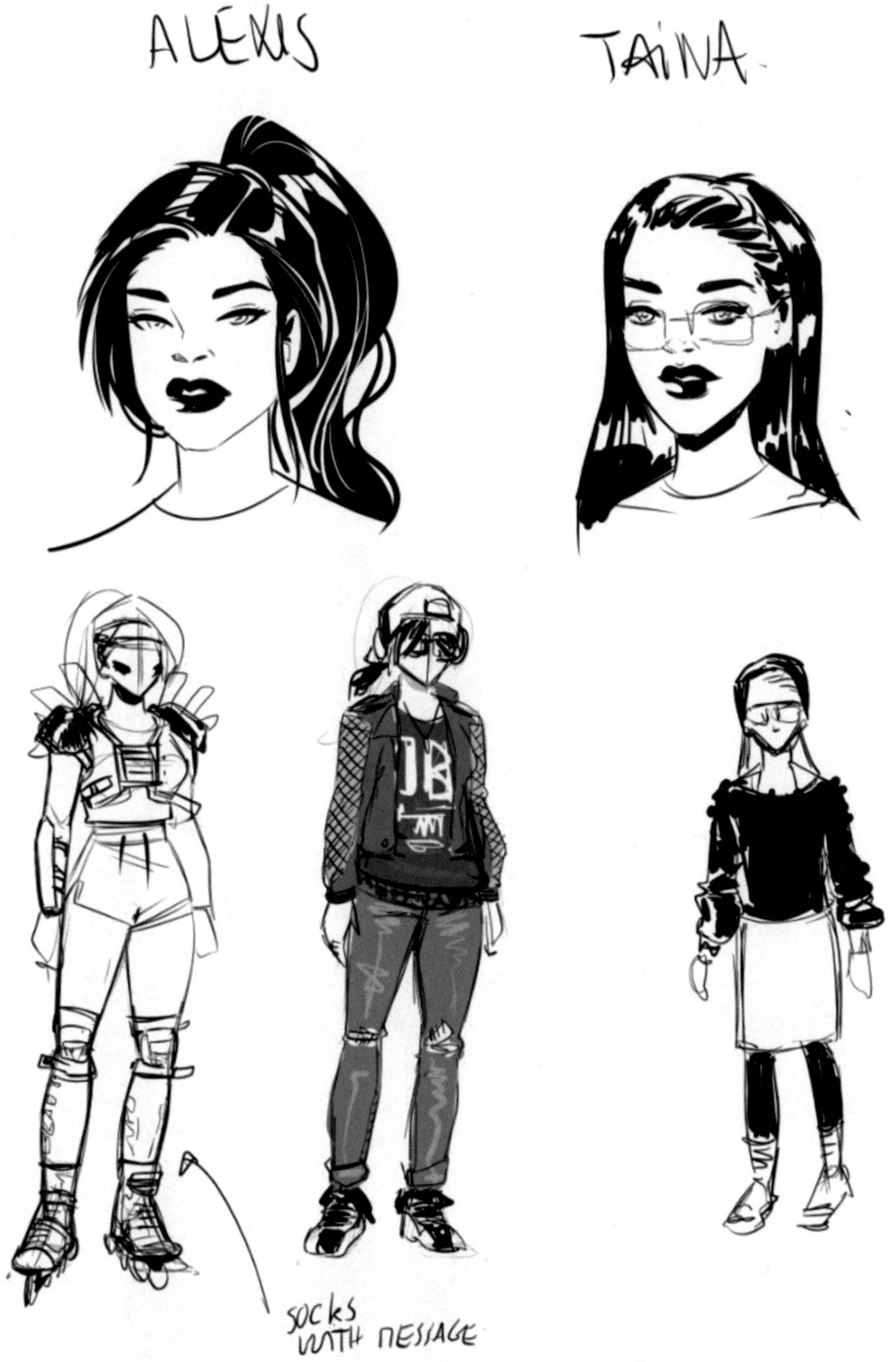
ALEXIS
TAINA
SOCKS WITH MESSAGE

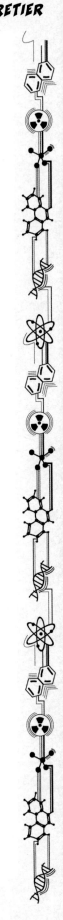

CHARACTER DESIGNS BY ELSA CHARRETIER

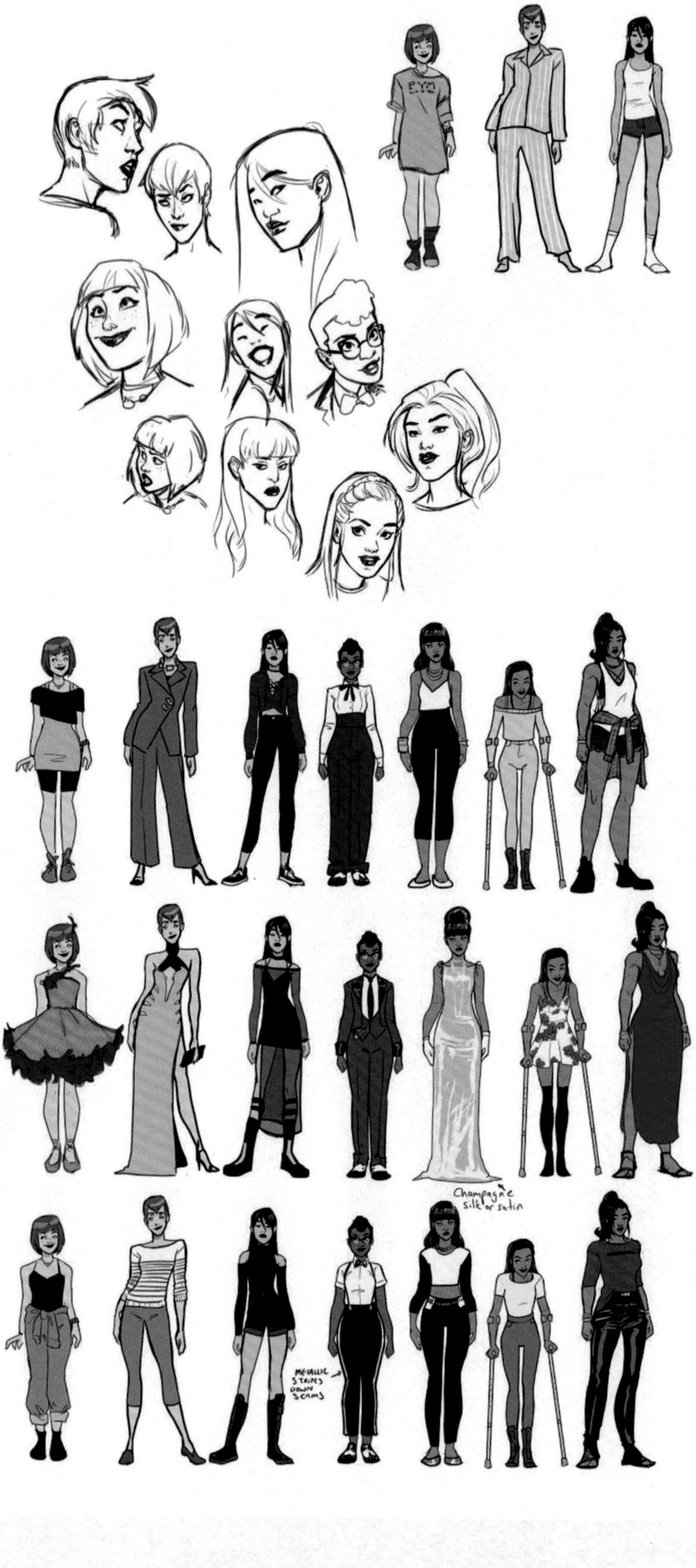

Champagne silk or satin
METALLIC STRIPES DOWN SEAMS

WASP SKETCH BY ELSA CHARRETIER

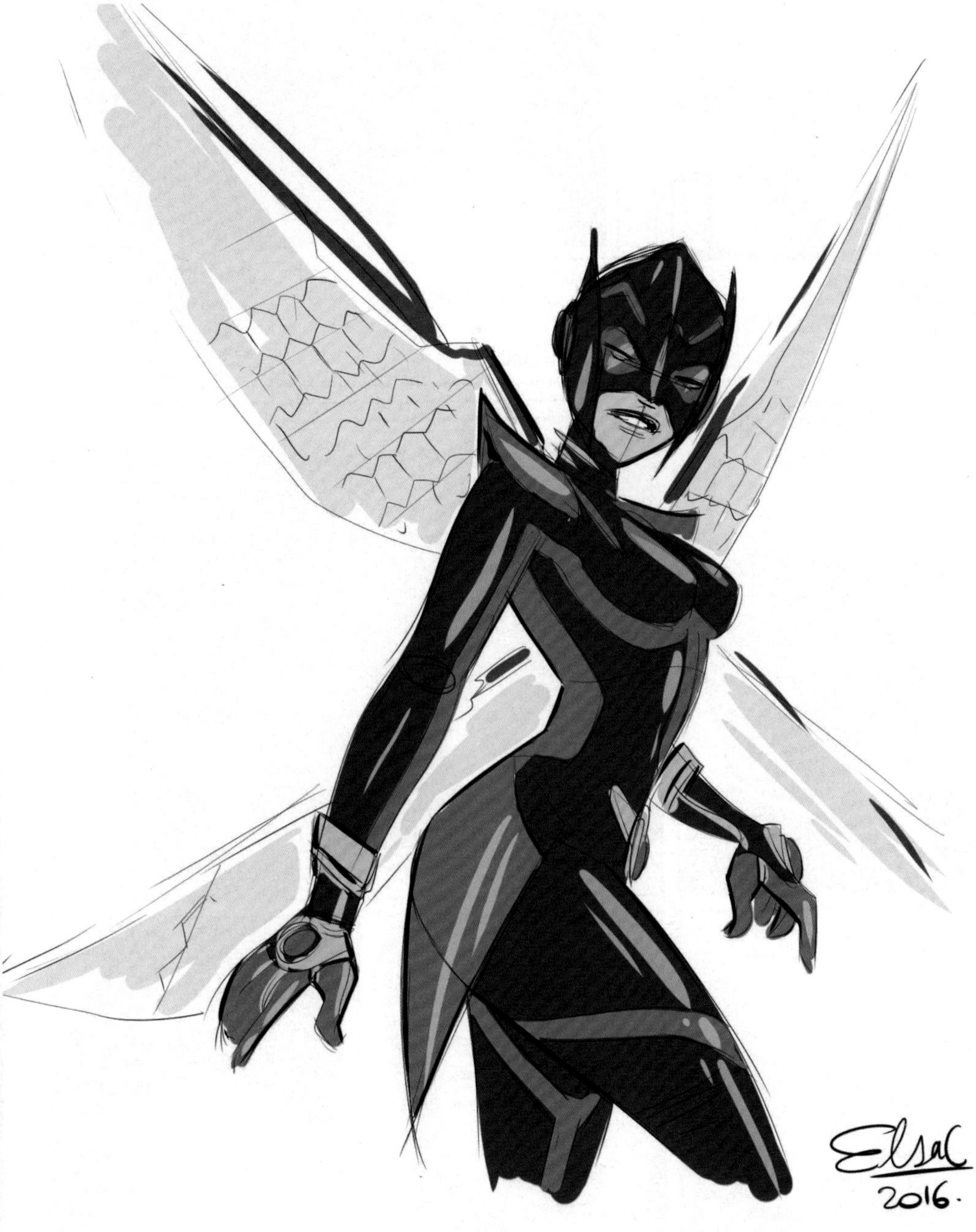
ElsaC
2016.

#5 PAGE 10 ART BY ELSA CHARRETIER

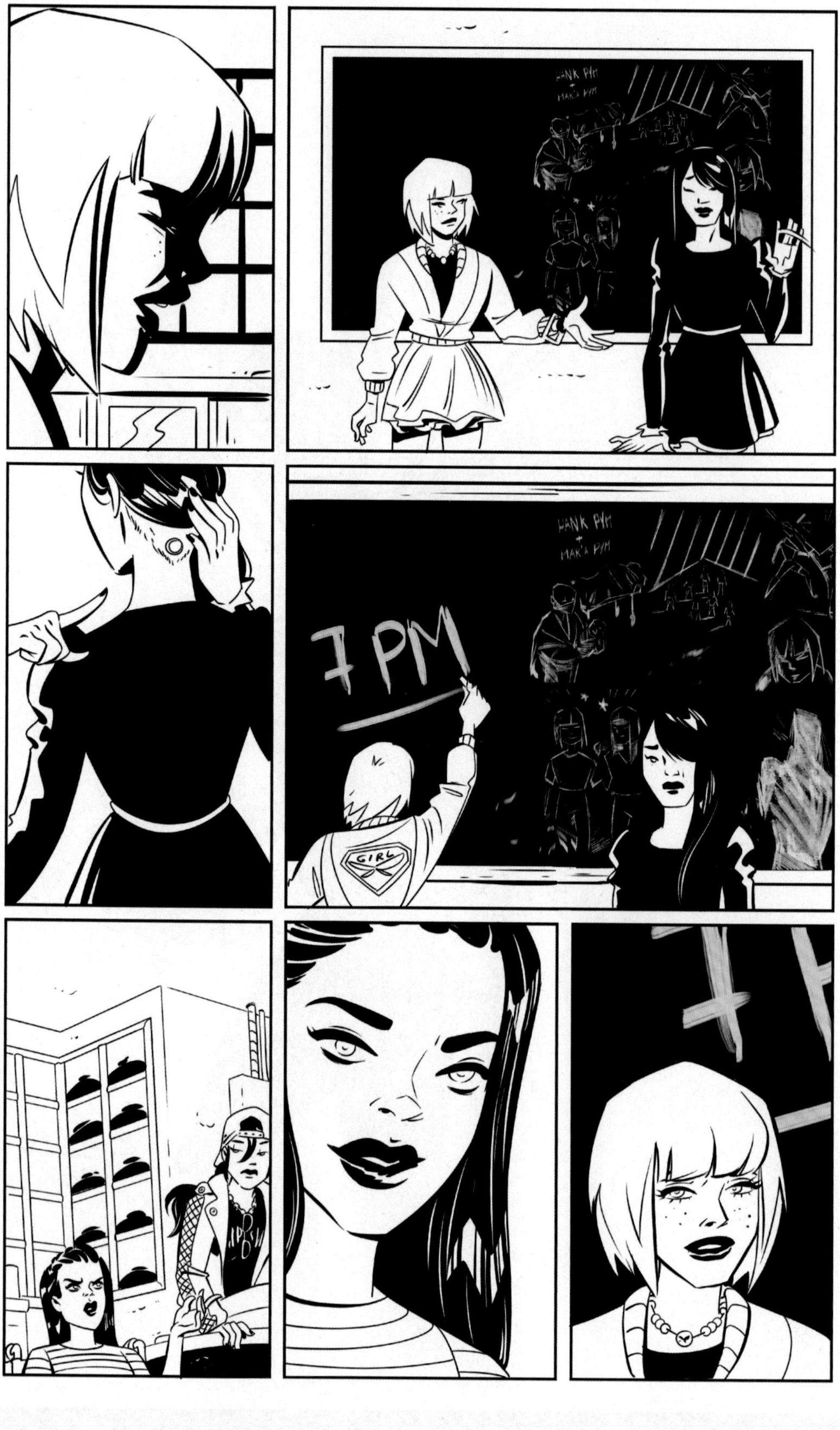
HANK PYM
+
MAR'A PYM
7PM
GIRL

#5 PAGE 11 ART BY ELSA CHARRETIER

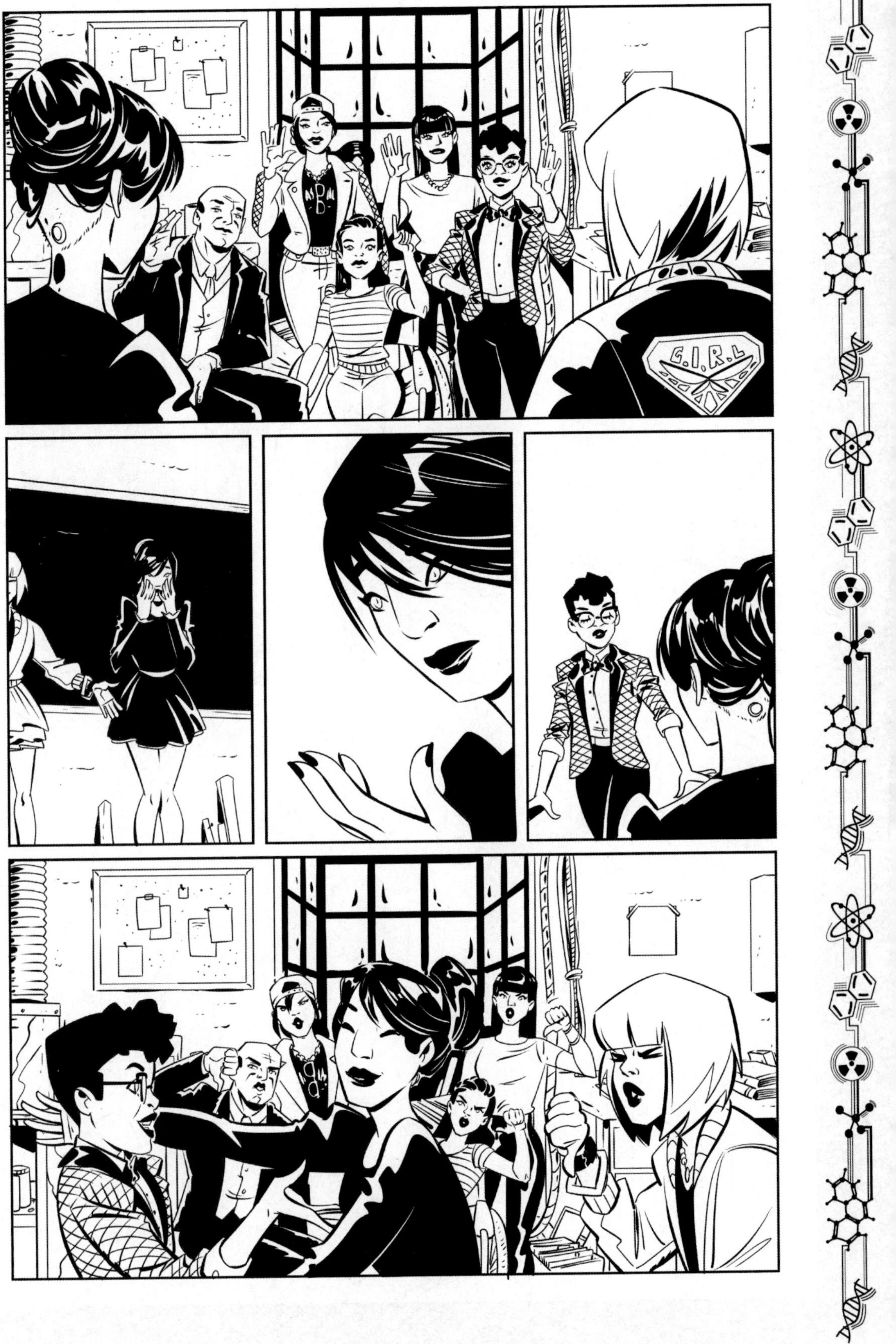
G.I.R.L

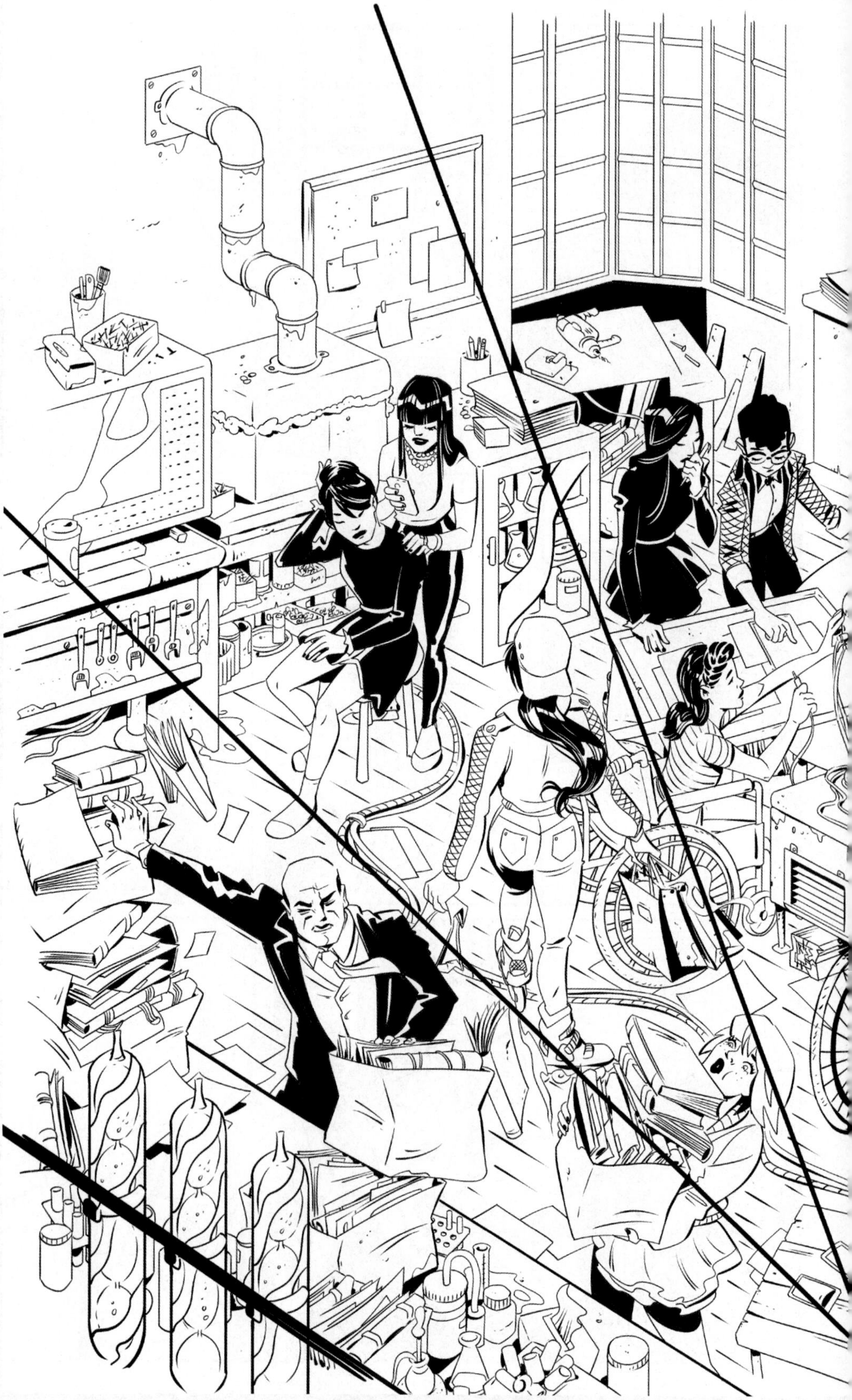

#5 PAGE 12-13 ART BY ELSA CHARRETIER

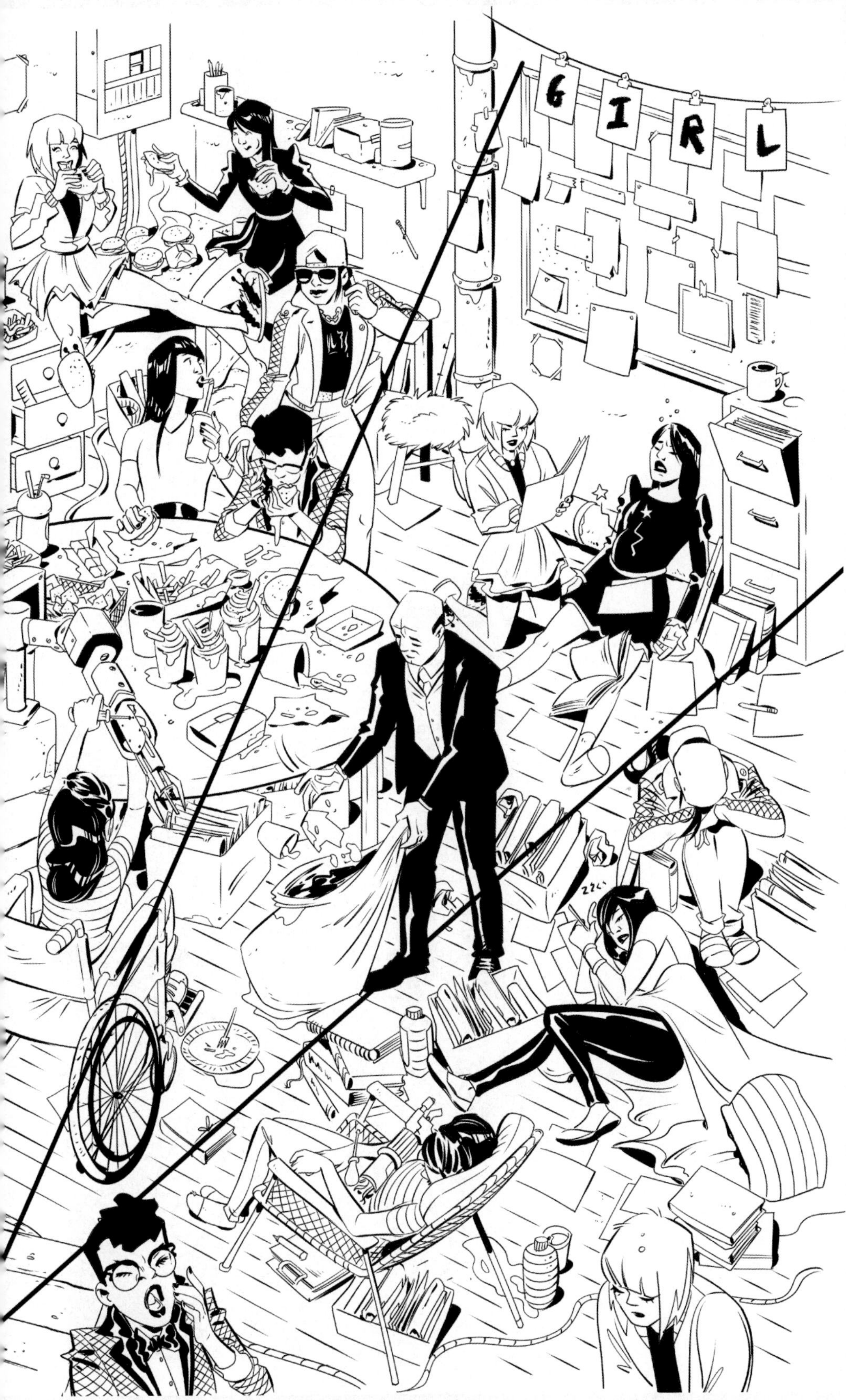
GIRL

#8 COVER PROCESS BY ELSA CHARRETIER

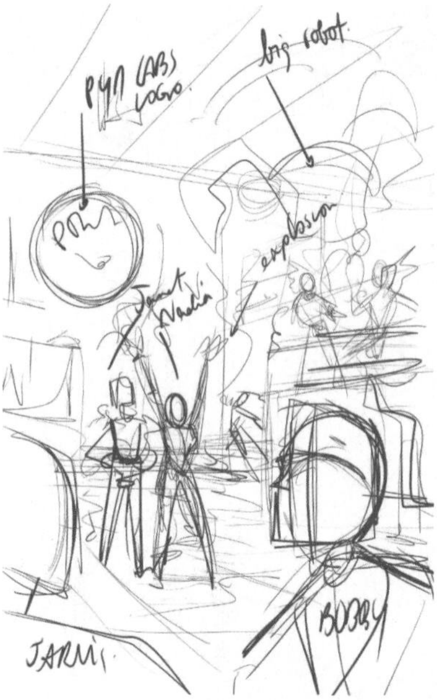

PYM LABS LOGO
big robot
explosion
BOBBY

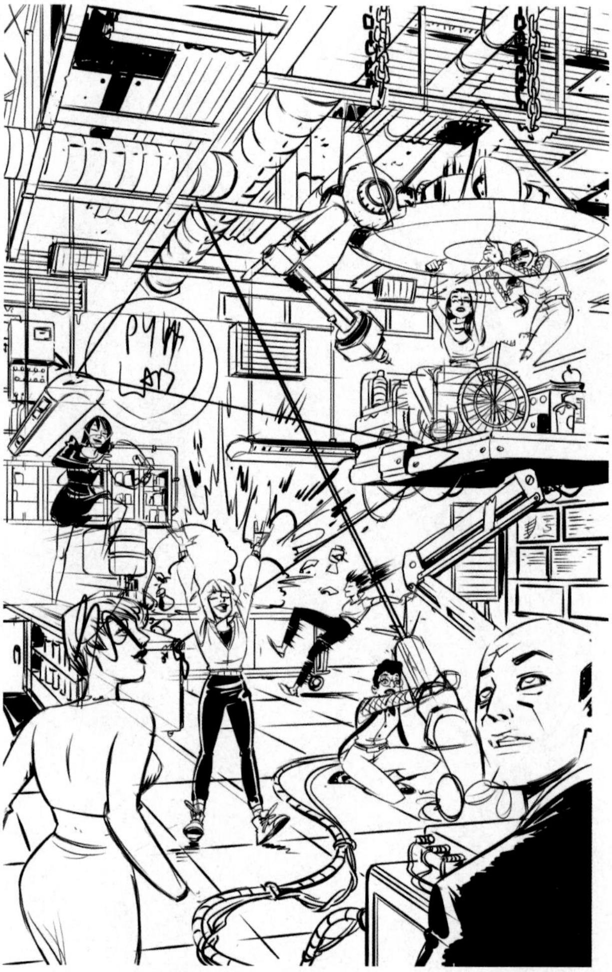

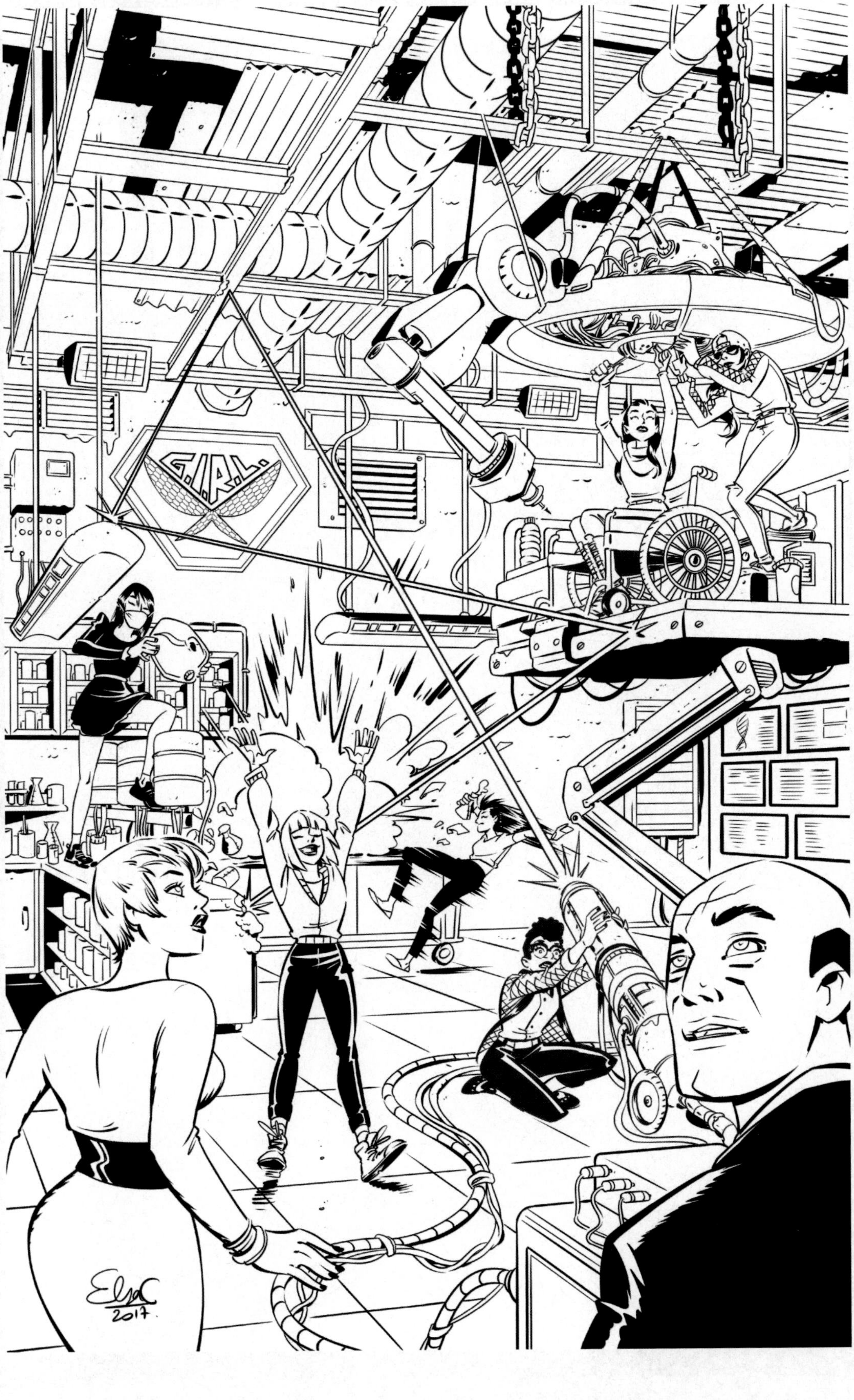
G.I.R.L.
2017

STAN LEE, ERNIE HART AND JACK KIRBY INTRODUCED JANET VAN DYNE IN THIS 1963 ISSUE OF THE LONG-RUNNING ANTHOLOGY SERIES *TALES TO ASTONISH* — AND A HEROIC LEGACY WAS BORN!

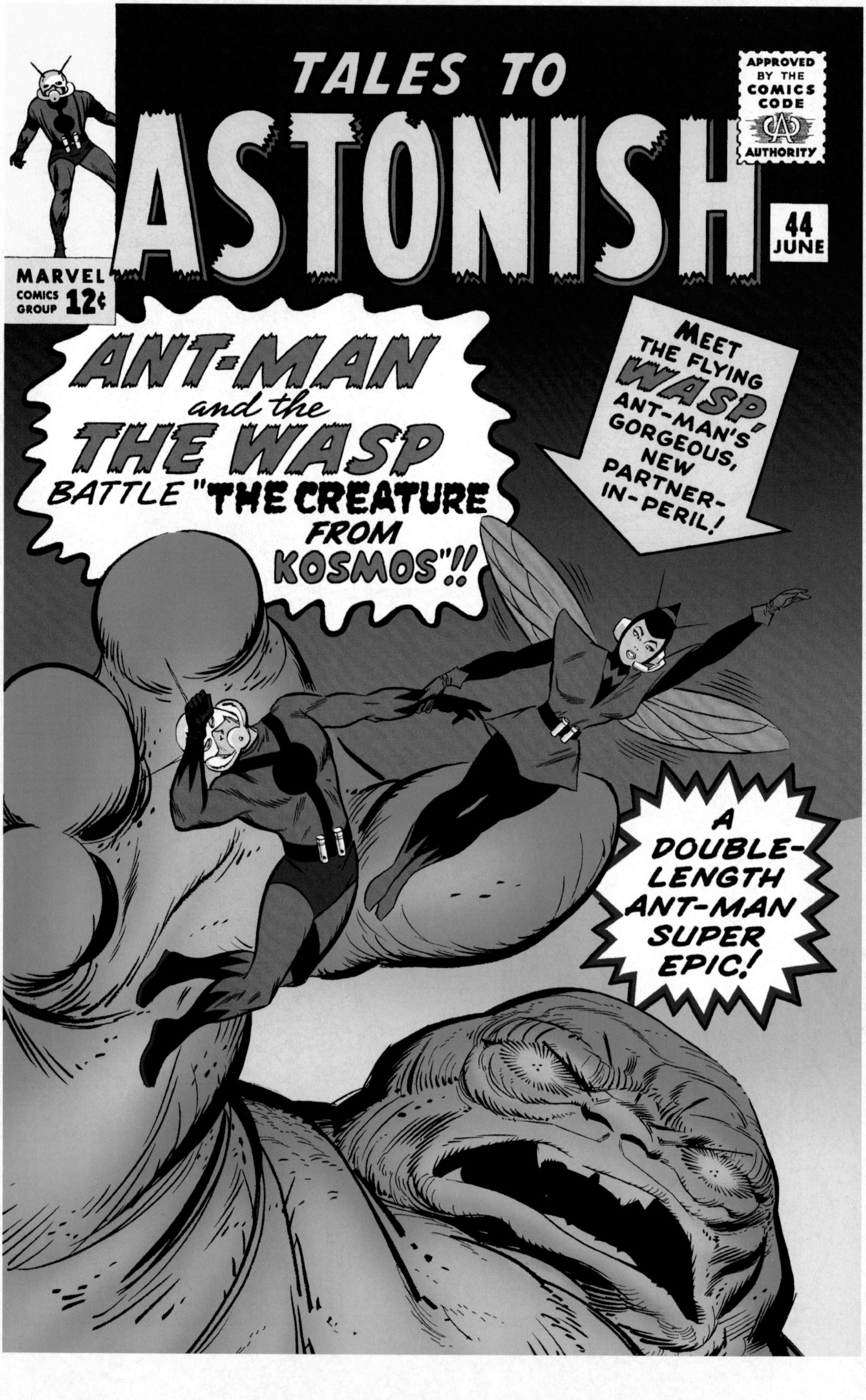

TALES TO ASTONISH
APPROVED BY THE COMICS CODE AUTHORITY
44 JUNE
MARVEL COMICS GROUP 12¢
ANT-MAN and the THE WASP BATTLE "THE CREATURE FROM KOSMOS"!!
MEET THE FLYING WASP, ANT-MAN'S GORGEOUS, NEW PARTNER-IN-PERIL!
A DOUBLE-LENGTH ANT-MAN SUPER EPIC!

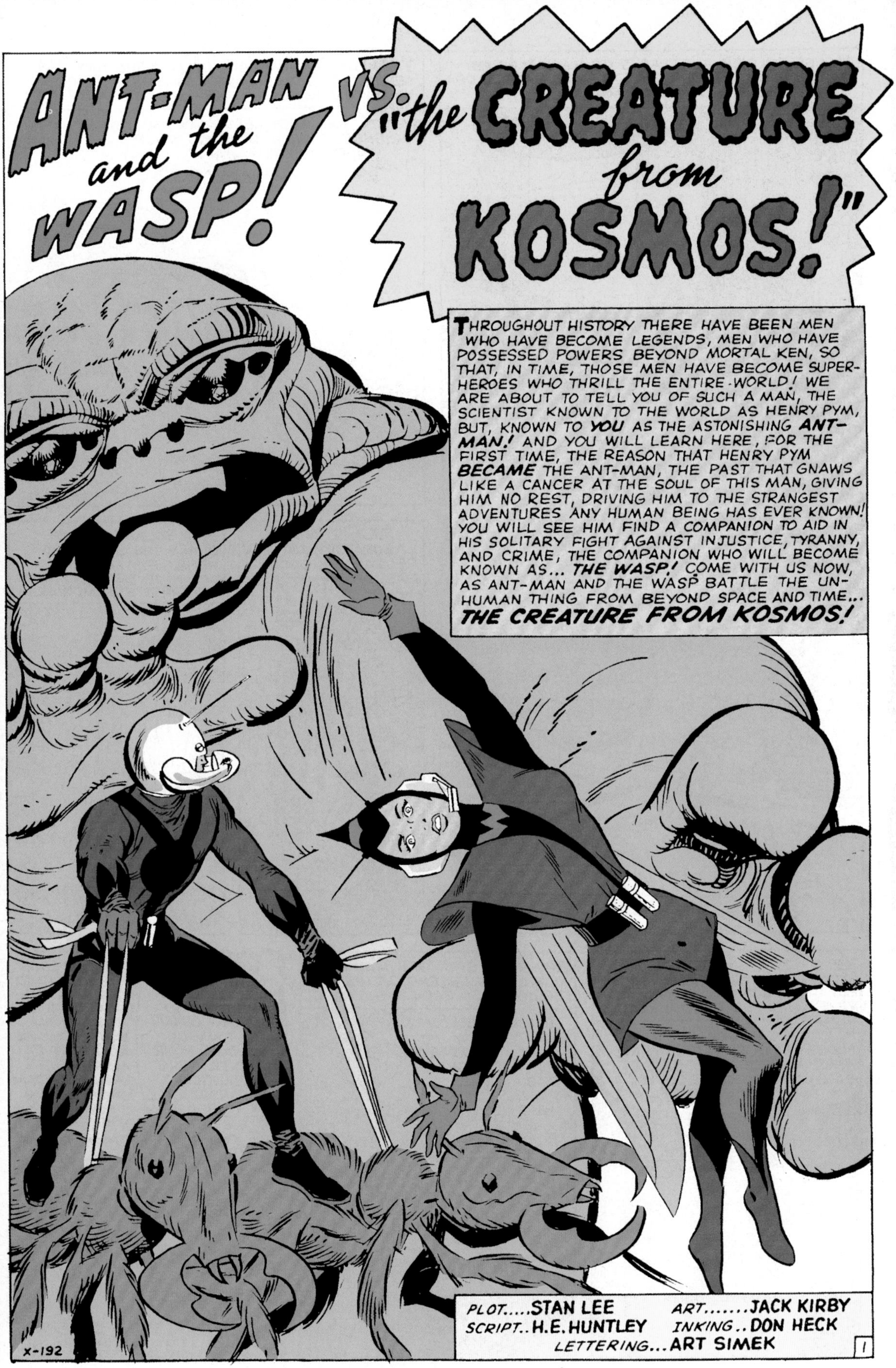
ANT-MAN and the WASP! VS. "the CREATURE from KOSMOS!"
THROUGHOUT HISTORY THERE HAVE BEEN MEN WHO HAVE BECOME LEGENDS, MEN WHO HAVE POSSESSED POWERS BEYOND MORTAL KEN, SO THAT, IN TIME, THOSE MEN HAVE BECOME SUPER-HEROES WHO THRILL THE ENTIRE WORLD! WE ARE ABOUT TO TELL YOU OF SUCH A MAN, THE SCIENTIST KNOWN TO THE WORLD AS HENRY PYM, BUT, KNOWN TO YOU AS THE ASTONISHING ANT-MAN! AND YOU WILL LEARN HERE, FOR THE FIRST TIME, THE REASON THAT HENRY PYM BECAME THE ANT-MAN, THE PAST THAT GNAWS LIKE A CANCER AT THE SOUL OF THIS MAN, GIVING HIM NO REST, DRIVING HIM TO THE STRANGEST ADVENTURES ANY HUMAN BEING HAS EVER KNOWN! YOU WILL SEE HIM FIND A COMPANION TO AID IN HIS SOLITARY FIGHT AGAINST INJUSTICE, TYRANNY, AND CRIME, THE COMPANION WHO WILL BECOME KNOWN AS... THE WASP! COME WITH US NOW, AS ANT-MAN AND THE WASP BATTLE THE UN-HUMAN THING FROM BEYOND SPACE AND TIME... THE CREATURE FROM KOSMOS!
PLOT.....STAN LEE ART.......JACK KIRBY
SCRIPT..H.E.HUNTLEY INKING..DON HECK
LETTERING...ART SIMEK
X-192
1

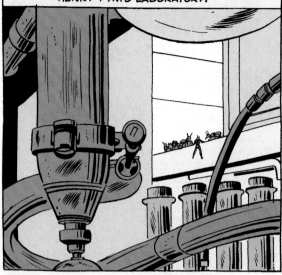

A HUGE SOLDIER ANT CLACKS ITS MANDIBLES AS THE ANT-MAN DISMOUNTS ON THE WINDOW SILL OF HENRY PYM'S LABORATORY!

THROUGH HIS CYBERNETIC HELMET THE TINY MAN SENDS ELECTRONIC-WAVE COMMANDS TO HIS HYMENOPTERA COMPANIONS...AND THE ANTS FAR AWAY!

YOU MUST LEAVE NOW, MY FRIENDS! I WILL CALL YOU WHEN THERE IS NEED AGAIN!

AND NOW, IT IS TIME TO RESUME MY *OTHER* IDENTITY!

ALONE IN HIS LABORATORY, ANT-MAN RELEASES HIS GROWTH GAS...

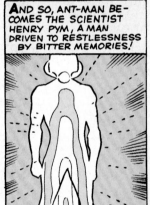

AND SO, ANT-MAN BECOMES THE SCIENTIST HENRY PYM, A MAN DRIVEN TO RESTLESSNESS BY BITTER MEMORIES!

HE IS TIRED... SO VERY TIRED! IF ONLY HE HAD HELP...HUMAN HELP! BUT IT IS HIS DESTINY NEVER TO REVEAL HIS SECRET TO ANY OTHER HUMAN...

I MUST ALWAYS BE ALONE! IT IS MY FATE! IF ONLY *MARIA* WERE HERE BY MY SIDE! TOGETHER WE COULD... BUT... MARIA IS *GONE*...

AND SO HE SITS, THIS MAN OF SCIENCE, OF LEGEND, AS HIS THOUGHTS GO BACK TO THE PAST...

HELLO, MRS. PYM ...MY BEAUTIFUL MARIA, MY LOVELY WIFE!

HELLO, MR. PYM, MY HANDSOME HUSBAND!

DARLING, DO YOU THINK IT WISE FOR US TO COME BACK TO HUNGARY ON OUR HONEYMOON! YOU AND YOUR FATHER WERE POLITICAL PRISONERS AND...

HUSH, MY LOVE! WE ESCAPED TO YOUR WONDERFUL COUNTRY! THEY WILL NOT KNOW ME NOW THAT I AM THE WIFE OF AN AMERICAN! I AM MRS. PYM NOW, NOT MARIA TROVAYA!

2

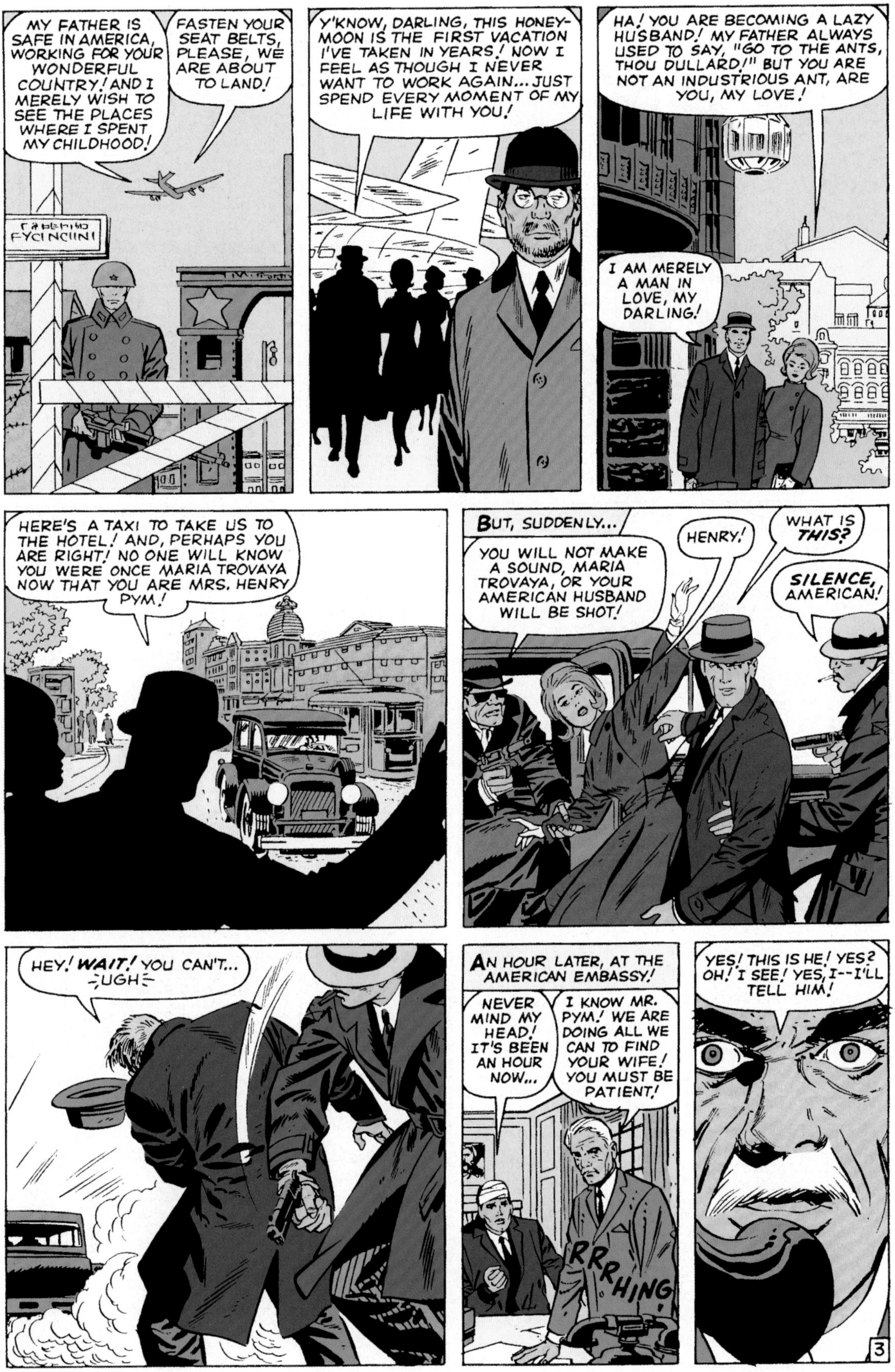
MY FATHER IS SAFE IN AMERICA, WORKING FOR YOUR WONDERFUL COUNTRY! AND I MERELY WISH TO SEE THE PLACES WHERE I SPENT MY CHILDHOOD!
FASTEN YOUR SEAT BELTS, PLEASE, WE ARE ABOUT TO LAND!
Y'KNOW, DARLING, THIS HONEY-MOON IS THE FIRST VACATION I'VE TAKEN IN YEARS! NOW I FEEL AS THOUGH I NEVER WANT TO WORK AGAIN... JUST SPEND EVERY MOMENT OF MY LIFE WITH YOU!
HA! YOU ARE BECOMING A LAZY HUSBAND! MY FATHER ALWAYS USED TO SAY, "GO TO THE ANTS, THOU DULLARD!" BUT YOU ARE NOT AN INDUSTRIOUS ANT, ARE YOU, MY LOVE!
I AM MERELY A MAN IN LOVE, MY DARLING!
HERE'S A TAXI TO TAKE US TO THE HOTEL! AND, PERHAPS YOU ARE RIGHT! NO ONE WILL KNOW YOU WERE ONCE MARIA TROVAYA NOW THAT YOU ARE MRS. HENRY PYM!
BUT, SUDDENLY...
YOU WILL NOT MAKE A SOUND, MARIA TROVAYA, OR YOUR AMERICAN HUSBAND WILL BE SHOT!
HENRY!
WHAT IS THIS?
SILENCE, AMERICAN!
HEY! WAIT! YOU CAN'T... UGH
AN HOUR LATER, AT THE AMERICAN EMBASSY!
NEVER MIND MY HEAD! IT'S BEEN AN HOUR NOW...
I KNOW MR. PYM! WE ARE DOING ALL WE CAN TO FIND YOUR WIFE! YOU MUST BE PATIENT!
RRRHING
YES! THIS IS HE! YES? OH! I SEE! YES, I--I'LL TELL HIM!
3

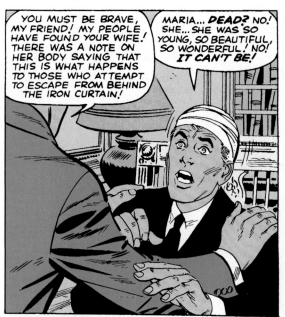

YOU MUST BE BRAVE, MY FRIEND! MY PEOPLE HAVE FOUND YOUR WIFE! THERE WAS A NOTE ON HER BODY SAYING THAT THIS IS WHAT HAPPENS TO THOSE WHO ATTEMPT TO ESCAPE FROM BEHIND THE IRON CURTAIN!

MARIA... *DEAD?* NO! SHE... SHE WAS SO YOUNG, SO BEAUTIFUL, SO WONDERFUL! NO! *IT CAN'T BE!*

THERE IS MORE! A MESSAGE FROM AMERICA! THE LABORATORY IN WHICH HER FATHER WAS WORKING BLEW UP! SABOTAGE IS FEARED!

THE FIENDS!! THE MERCILESS MURDERERS! WE MUST MAKE THEM *PAY!*

YOU HEAR? *WE MUST MAKE THEM PAY!*

CONTROL YOURSELF! MY PEOPLE WILL DO THEIR BEST...

DO THEIR BEST? *I'LL* FIND THEM! I'LL FIND THE ONES WHO DID THIS! I'LL MAKE THEM PAY! MARIA, I'LL FIND THEM... I SWEAR IT!

WAIT! PYM, YOU CAN'T!

THE YOUNG SCIENTIST WENT BERSERK, AND, WITHIN A FEW DAYS, LANDED IN JAIL ON THE VERGE OF A MENTAL AND PHYSICAL BREAKDOWN!

I... I COULDN'T FIND THEM! I DIDN'T KNOW... DIDN'T KNOW WHERE TO LOOK...

I'VE COME TO HAVE YOU RELEASED AND YOU WILL BE SENT HOME, MY BOY!

IN HIS LABORATORY IN AMERICA, HENRY PYM LIVED WITH THE TERRIBLE TRAGEDY THAT HAD MARRED HIS LIFE, STARING INTO SPACE, TRYING TO RECAPTURE EVERY MOMENT OF THAT WONDERFUL PAST THAT WAS NOW GONE FOREVER!

SHE SAID SOMETHING... MARIA SAID SOMETHING, BUT I CAN'T REMEMBER! WHY DID THIS HAVE TO HAPPEN? OH, MARIA, I... *WAIT!* I REMEMBER NOW!

I REMEMBER WHAT SHE SAID... "GO TO THE ANTS, THOU SLUGGARD!" YES, SHE WAS RIGHT! I SIT HERE DOING NOTHING WHILE THROUGHOUT THE WORLD, CRIMINALS PROWL, INJUSTICE IS RAMPANT, TYRANNY TRAMPLES THE UNDERDOG!

4

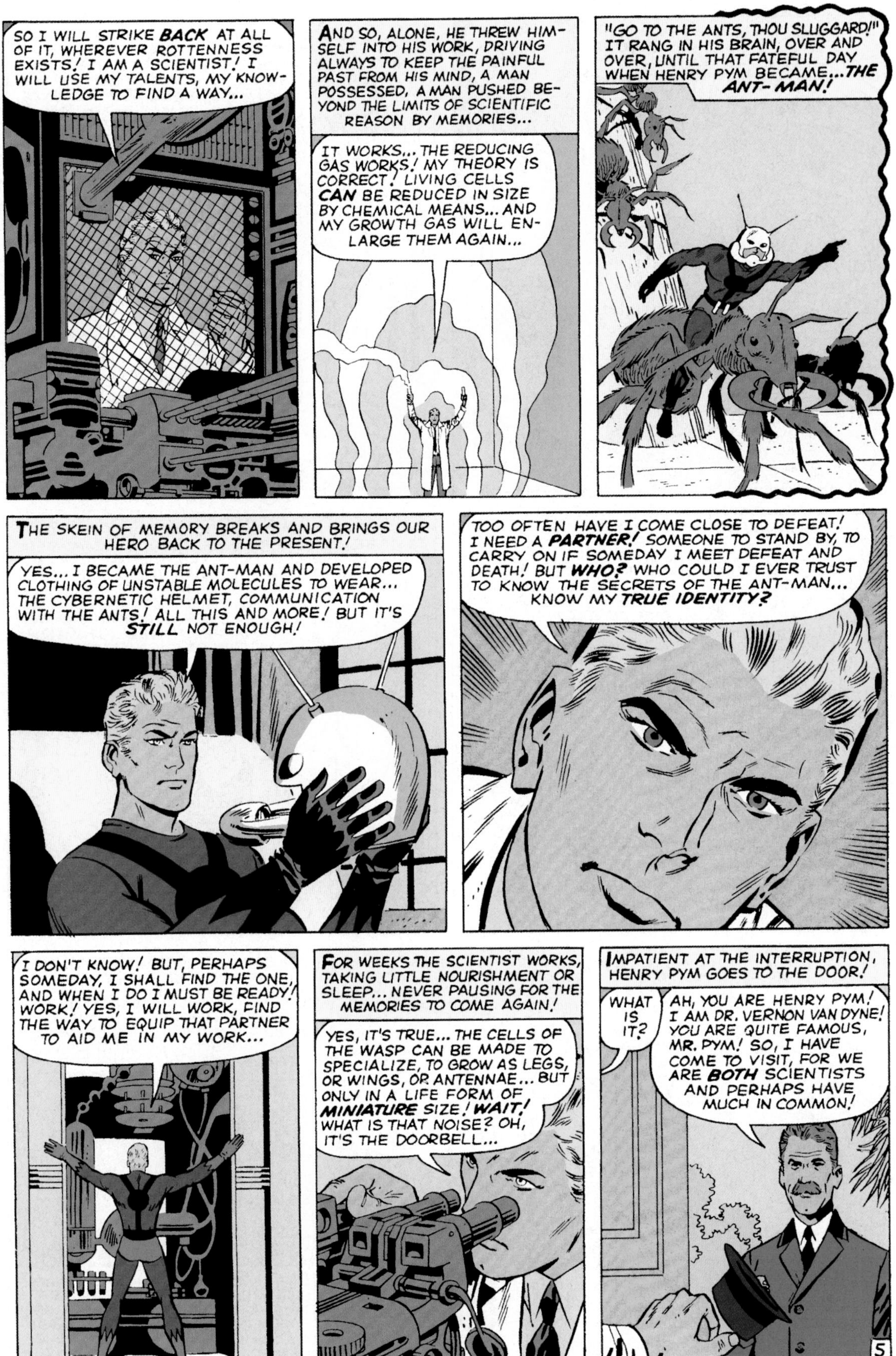
SO I WILL STRIKE BACK AT ALL OF IT, WHEREVER ROTTENNESS EXISTS! I AM A SCIENTIST! I WILL USE MY TALENTS, MY KNOWLEDGE TO FIND A WAY...
AND SO, ALONE, HE THREW HIMSELF INTO HIS WORK, DRIVING ALWAYS TO KEEP THE PAINFUL PAST FROM HIS MIND, A MAN POSSESSED, A MAN PUSHED BEYOND THE LIMITS OF SCIENTIFIC REASON BY MEMORIES...
IT WORKS... THE REDUCING GAS WORKS! MY THEORY IS CORRECT! LIVING CELLS CAN BE REDUCED IN SIZE BY CHEMICAL MEANS... AND MY GROWTH GAS WILL ENLARGE THEM AGAIN...
"GO TO THE ANTS, THOU SLUGGARD!" IT RANG IN HIS BRAIN, OVER AND OVER, UNTIL THAT FATEFUL DAY WHEN HENRY PYM BECAME... THE ANT-MAN!
THE SKEIN OF MEMORY BREAKS AND BRINGS OUR HERO BACK TO THE PRESENT!
YES... I BECAME THE ANT-MAN AND DEVELOPED CLOTHING OF UNSTABLE MOLECULES TO WEAR... THE CYBERNETIC HELMET, COMMUNICATION WITH THE ANTS! ALL THIS AND MORE! BUT IT'S STILL NOT ENOUGH!
TOO OFTEN HAVE I COME CLOSE TO DEFEAT! I NEED A PARTNER! SOMEONE TO STAND BY, TO CARRY ON IF SOMEDAY I MEET DEFEAT AND DEATH! BUT WHO? WHO COULD I EVER TRUST TO KNOW THE SECRETS OF THE ANT-MAN... KNOW MY TRUE IDENTITY?
I DON'T KNOW! BUT, PERHAPS SOMEDAY, I SHALL FIND THE ONE, AND WHEN I DO I MUST BE READY! WORK! YES, I WILL WORK, FIND THE WAY TO EQUIP THAT PARTNER TO AID ME IN MY WORK...
FOR WEEKS THE SCIENTIST WORKS, TAKING LITTLE NOURISHMENT OR SLEEP... NEVER PAUSING FOR THE MEMORIES TO COME AGAIN!
YES, IT'S TRUE... THE CELLS OF THE WASP CAN BE MADE TO SPECIALIZE, TO GROW AS LEGS, OR WINGS, OR ANTENNAE... BUT ONLY IN A LIFE FORM OF MINIATURE SIZE! WAIT! WHAT IS THAT NOISE? OH, IT'S THE DOORBELL...
IMPATIENT AT THE INTERRUPTION, HENRY PYM GOES TO THE DOOR!
WHAT IS IT?
AH, YOU ARE HENRY PYM! I AM DR. VERNON VAN DYNE! YOU ARE QUITE FAMOUS, MR. PYM! SO, I HAVE COME TO VISIT, FOR WE ARE BOTH SCIENTISTS AND PERHAPS HAVE MUCH IN COMMON!
5

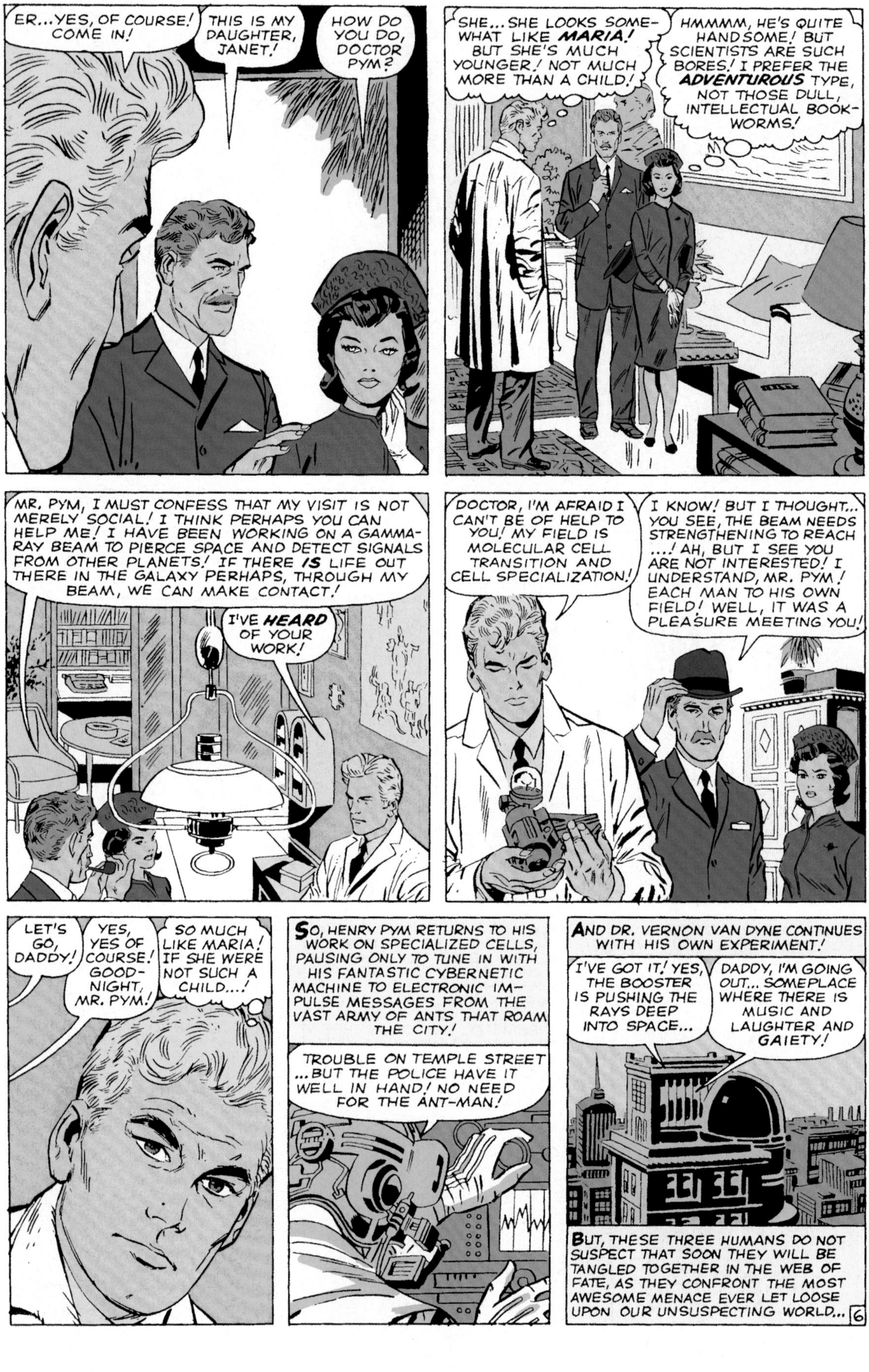
ER...YES, OF COURSE! COME IN!
THIS IS MY DAUGHTER, JANET!
HOW DO YOU DO, DOCTOR PYM?
SHE...SHE LOOKS SOMEWHAT LIKE MARIA! BUT SHE'S MUCH YOUNGER! NOT MUCH MORE THAN A CHILD!
HMMMM, HE'S QUITE HANDSOME! BUT SCIENTISTS ARE SUCH BORES! I PREFER THE ADVENTUROUS TYPE, NOT THOSE DULL, INTELLECTUAL BOOKWORMS!
MR. PYM, I MUST CONFESS THAT MY VISIT IS NOT MERELY SOCIAL! I THINK PERHAPS YOU CAN HELP ME! I HAVE BEEN WORKING ON A GAMMA-RAY BEAM TO PIERCE SPACE AND DETECT SIGNALS FROM OTHER PLANETS! IF THERE IS LIFE OUT THERE IN THE GALAXY PERHAPS, THROUGH MY BEAM, WE CAN MAKE CONTACT!
I'VE HEARD OF YOUR WORK!
DOCTOR, I'M AFRAID I CAN'T BE OF HELP TO YOU! MY FIELD IS MOLECULAR CELL TRANSITION AND CELL SPECIALIZATION!
I KNOW! BUT I THOUGHT... YOU SEE, THE BEAM NEEDS STRENGTHENING TO REACH ...! AH, BUT I SEE YOU ARE NOT INTERESTED! I UNDERSTAND, MR. PYM! EACH MAN TO HIS OWN FIELD! WELL, IT WAS A PLEASURE MEETING YOU!
LET'S GO, DADDY!
YES, YES OF COURSE! GOOD-NIGHT, MR. PYM!
SO MUCH LIKE MARIA! IF SHE WERE NOT SUCH A CHILD...!
SO, HENRY PYM RETURNS TO HIS WORK ON SPECIALIZED CELLS, PAUSING ONLY TO TUNE IN WITH HIS FANTASTIC CYBERNETIC MACHINE TO ELECTRONIC IMPULSE MESSAGES FROM THE VAST ARMY OF ANTS THAT ROAM THE CITY!
TROUBLE ON TEMPLE STREET ...BUT THE POLICE HAVE IT WELL IN HAND! NO NEED FOR THE ANT-MAN!
AND DR. VERNON VAN DYNE CONTINUES WITH HIS OWN EXPERIMENT!
I'VE GOT IT! YES, THE BOOSTER IS PUSHING THE RAYS DEEP INTO SPACE...
DADDY, I'M GOING OUT... SOMEPLACE WHERE THERE IS MUSIC AND LAUGHTER AND GAIETY!
BUT, THESE THREE HUMANS DO NOT SUSPECT THAT SOON THEY WILL BE TANGLED TOGETHER IN THE WEB OF FATE, AS THEY CONFRONT THE MOST AWESOME MENACE EVER LET LOOSE UPON OUR UNSUSPECTING WORLD...
6

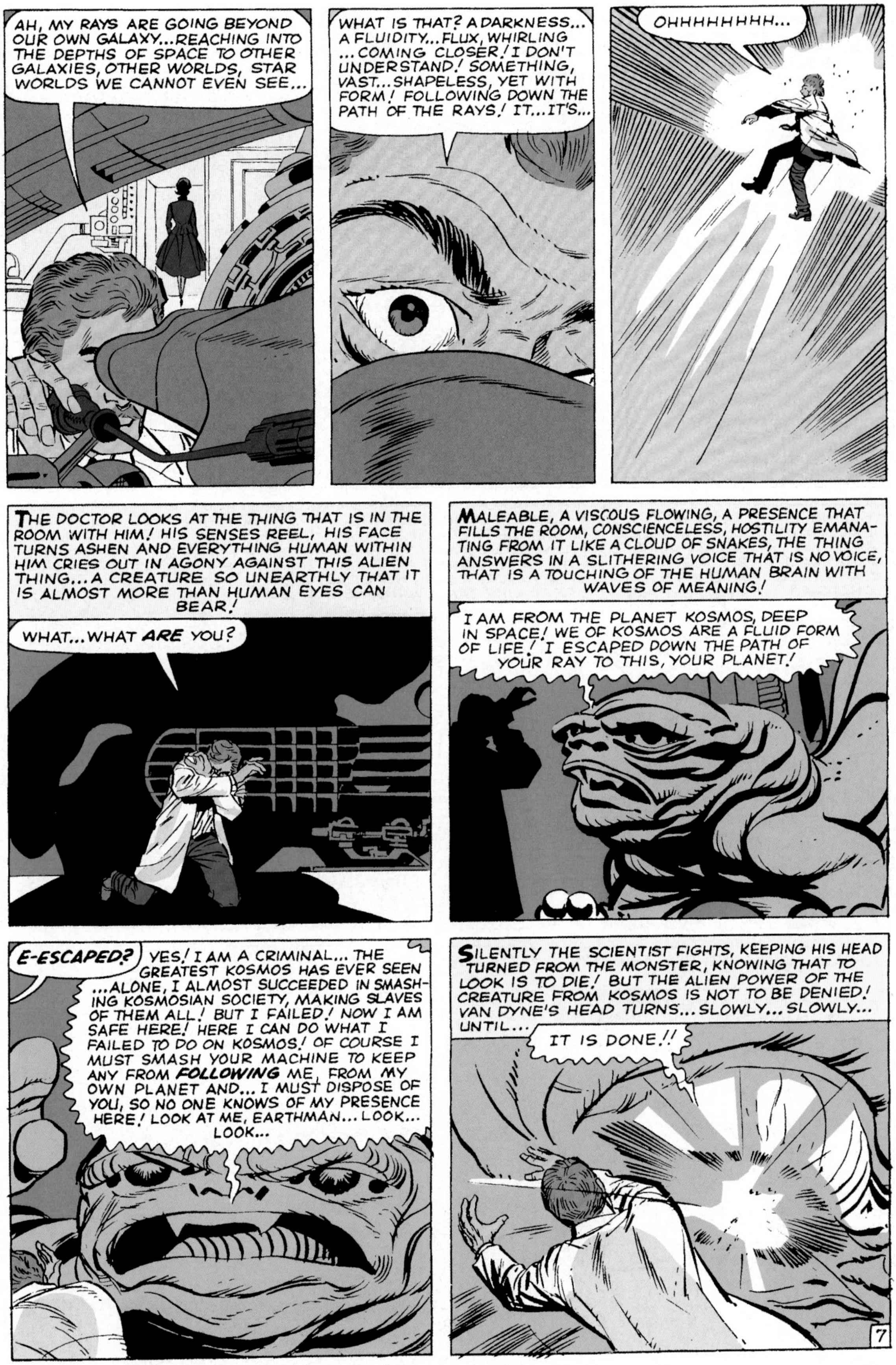
AH, MY RAYS ARE GOING BEYOND OUR OWN GALAXY...REACHING INTO THE DEPTHS OF SPACE TO OTHER GALAXIES, OTHER WORLDS, STAR WORLDS WE CANNOT EVEN SEE...
WHAT IS THAT? A DARKNESS... A FLUIDITY... FLUX, WHIRLING ...COMING CLOSER! I DON'T UNDERSTAND! SOMETHING, VAST...SHAPELESS, YET WITH FORM! FOLLOWING DOWN THE PATH OF THE RAYS! IT...IT'S...
OHHHHHHHH...
THE DOCTOR LOOKS AT THE THING THAT IS IN THE ROOM WITH HIM! HIS SENSES REEL, HIS FACE TURNS ASHEN AND EVERYTHING HUMAN WITHIN HIM CRIES OUT IN AGONY AGAINST THIS ALIEN THING... A CREATURE SO UNEARTHLY THAT IT IS ALMOST MORE THAN HUMAN EYES CAN BEAR!
WHAT...WHAT ARE YOU?
MALEABLE, A VISCOUS FLOWING, A PRESENCE THAT FILLS THE ROOM, CONSCIENCELESS, HOSTILITY EMANATING FROM IT LIKE A CLOUD OF SNAKES, THE THING ANSWERS IN A SLITHERING VOICE THAT IS NO VOICE, THAT IS A TOUCHING OF THE HUMAN BRAIN WITH WAVES OF MEANING!
I AM FROM THE PLANET KOSMOS, DEEP IN SPACE! WE OF KOSMOS ARE A FLUID FORM OF LIFE! I ESCAPED DOWN THE PATH OF YOUR RAY TO THIS, YOUR PLANET!
E-ESCAPED?
YES! I AM A CRIMINAL... THE GREATEST KOSMOS HAS EVER SEEN ...ALONE, I ALMOST SUCCEEDED IN SMASHING KOSMOSIAN SOCIETY, MAKING SLAVES OF THEM ALL! BUT I FAILED! NOW I AM SAFE HERE! HERE I CAN DO WHAT I FAILED TO DO ON KOSMOS! OF COURSE I MUST SMASH YOUR MACHINE TO KEEP ANY FROM FOLLOWING ME, FROM MY OWN PLANET AND... I MUST DISPOSE OF YOU, SO NO ONE KNOWS OF MY PRESENCE HERE! LOOK AT ME, EARTHMAN... LOOK... LOOK...
SILENTLY THE SCIENTIST FIGHTS, KEEPING HIS HEAD TURNED FROM THE MONSTER, KNOWING THAT TO LOOK IS TO DIE! BUT THE ALIEN POWER OF THE CREATURE FROM KOSMOS IS NOT TO BE DENIED! VAN DYNE'S HEAD TURNS... SLOWLY... SLOWLY... UNTIL...
IT IS DONE!!
7

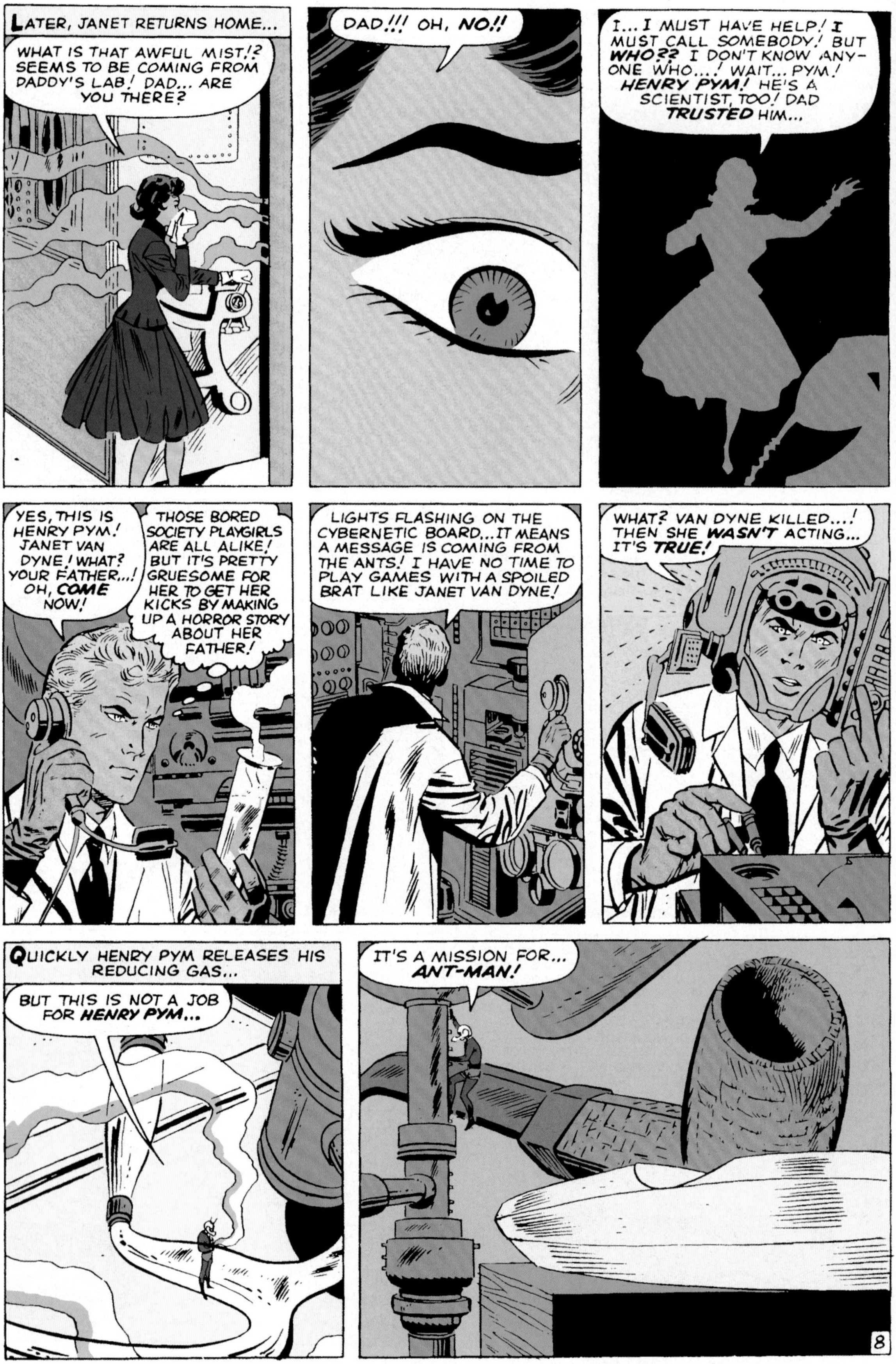
LATER, JANET RETURNS HOME...
WHAT IS THAT AWFUL MIST!? SEEMS TO BE COMING FROM DADDY'S LAB! DAD... ARE YOU THERE?
DAD!!! OH, NO!!
I... I MUST HAVE HELP! I MUST CALL SOMEBODY! BUT WHO?? I DON'T KNOW ANYONE WHO...! WAIT... PYM! HENRY PYM! HE'S A SCIENTIST, TOO! DAD TRUSTED HIM...
YES, THIS IS HENRY PYM! JANET VAN DYNE! WHAT? YOUR FATHER...! OH, COME NOW!
THOSE BORED SOCIETY PLAYGIRLS ARE ALL ALIKE! BUT IT'S PRETTY GRUESOME FOR HER TO GET HER KICKS BY MAKING UP A HORROR STORY ABOUT HER FATHER!
LIGHTS FLASHING ON THE CYBERNETIC BOARD... IT MEANS A MESSAGE IS COMING FROM THE ANTS! I HAVE NO TIME TO PLAY GAMES WITH A SPOILED BRAT LIKE JANET VAN DYNE!
WHAT? VAN DYNE KILLED...! THEN SHE WASN'T ACTING... IT'S TRUE!
QUICKLY HENRY PYM RELEASES HIS REDUCING GAS...
BUT THIS IS NOT A JOB FOR HENRY PYM...
IT'S A MISSION FOR... ANT-MAN!
8

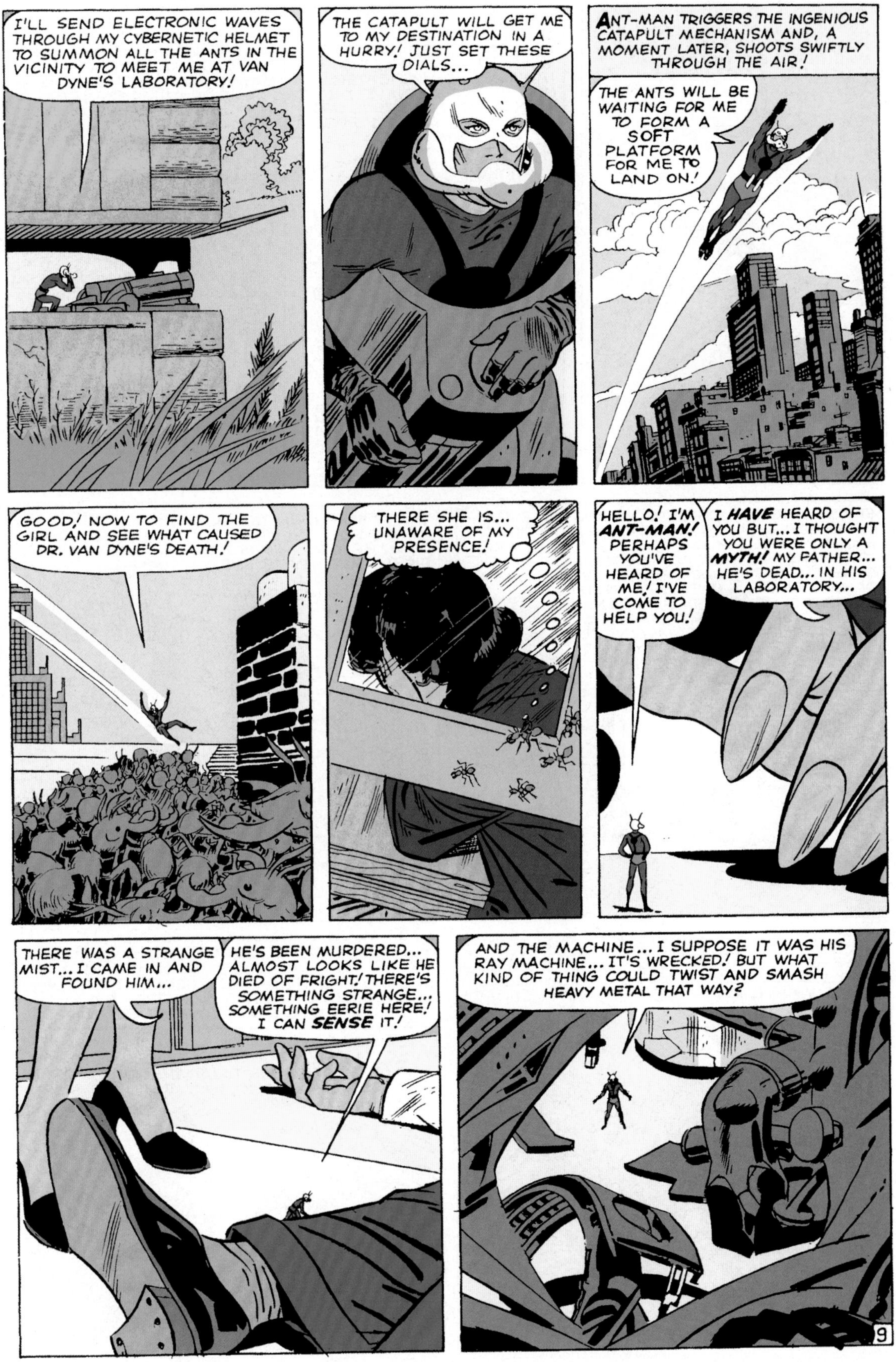

I'LL SEND ELECTRONIC WAVES THROUGH MY CYBERNETIC HELMET TO SUMMON ALL THE ANTS IN THE VICINITY TO MEET ME AT VAN DYNE'S LABORATORY!
THE CATAPULT WILL GET ME TO MY DESTINATION IN A HURRY! JUST SET THESE DIALS...
ANT-MAN TRIGGERS THE INGENIOUS CATAPULT MECHANISM AND, A MOMENT LATER, SHOOTS SWIFTLY THROUGH THE AIR!
THE ANTS WILL BE WAITING FOR ME TO FORM A SOFT PLATFORM FOR ME TO LAND ON!
GOOD! NOW TO FIND THE GIRL AND SEE WHAT CAUSED DR. VAN DYNE'S DEATH!
THERE SHE IS... UNAWARE OF MY PRESENCE!
HELLO! I'M ANT-MAN! PERHAPS YOU'VE HEARD OF ME! I'VE COME TO HELP YOU!
I HAVE HEARD OF YOU BUT... I THOUGHT YOU WERE ONLY A MYTH! MY FATHER... HE'S DEAD... IN HIS LABORATORY...
THERE WAS A STRANGE MIST... I CAME IN AND FOUND HIM...
HE'S BEEN MURDERED... ALMOST LOOKS LIKE HE DIED OF FRIGHT! THERE'S SOMETHING STRANGE... SOMETHING EERIE HERE! I CAN SENSE IT!
AND THE MACHINE... I SUPPOSE IT WAS HIS RAY MACHINE... IT'S WRECKED! BUT WHAT KIND OF THING COULD TWIST AND SMASH HEAVY METAL THAT WAY?
9

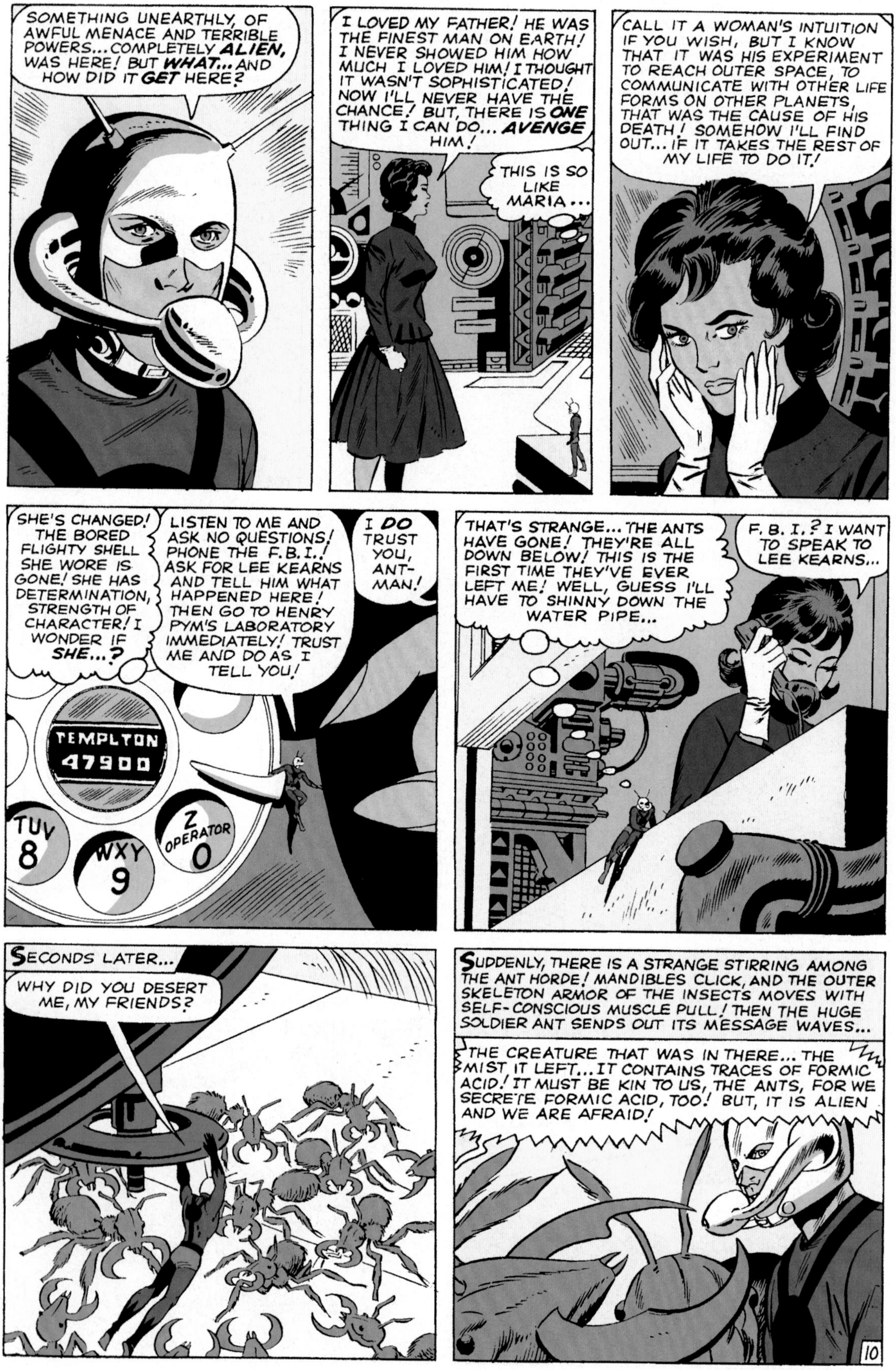

SOMETHING UNEARTHLY, OF AWFUL MENACE AND TERRIBLE POWERS... COMPLETELY ALIEN, WAS HERE! BUT WHAT... AND HOW DID IT GET HERE?
I LOVED MY FATHER! HE WAS THE FINEST MAN ON EARTH! I NEVER SHOWED HIM HOW MUCH I LOVED HIM! I THOUGHT IT WASN'T SOPHISTICATED! NOW I'LL NEVER HAVE THE CHANCE! BUT, THERE IS ONE THING I CAN DO... AVENGE HIM!
THIS IS SO LIKE MARIA...
CALL IT A WOMAN'S INTUITION IF YOU WISH, BUT I KNOW THAT IT WAS HIS EXPERIMENT TO REACH OUTER SPACE, TO COMMUNICATE WITH OTHER LIFE FORMS ON OTHER PLANETS, THAT WAS THE CAUSE OF HIS DEATH! SOMEHOW I'LL FIND OUT... IF IT TAKES THE REST OF MY LIFE TO DO IT!
SHE'S CHANGED! THE BORED FLIGHTY SHELL SHE WORE IS GONE! SHE HAS DETERMINATION, STRENGTH OF CHARACTER! I WONDER IF SHE...?
LISTEN TO ME AND ASK NO QUESTIONS! PHONE THE F.B.I.! ASK FOR LEE KEARNS AND TELL HIM WHAT HAPPENED HERE! THEN GO TO HENRY PYM'S LABORATORY IMMEDIATELY! TRUST ME AND DO AS I TELL YOU!
I DO TRUST YOU, ANT-MAN!
TEMPLTON
47900
TUV 8
WXY 9
Z OPERATOR 0
THAT'S STRANGE... THE ANTS HAVE GONE! THEY'RE ALL DOWN BELOW! THIS IS THE FIRST TIME THEY'VE EVER LEFT ME! WELL, GUESS I'LL HAVE TO SHINNY DOWN THE WATER PIPE...
F. B. I.? I WANT TO SPEAK TO LEE KEARNS...
SECONDS LATER...
WHY DID YOU DESERT ME, MY FRIENDS?
SUDDENLY, THERE IS A STRANGE STIRRING AMONG THE ANT HORDE! MANDIBLES CLICK, AND THE OUTER SKELETON ARMOR OF THE INSECTS MOVES WITH SELF-CONSCIOUS MUSCLE PULL! THEN THE HUGE SOLDIER ANT SENDS OUT ITS MESSAGE WAVES...
THE CREATURE THAT WAS IN THERE... THE MIST IT LEFT... IT CONTAINS TRACES OF FORMIC ACID! IT MUST BE KIN TO US, THE ANTS, FOR WE SECRETE FORMIC ACID, TOO! BUT, IT IS ALIEN AND WE ARE AFRAID!
10

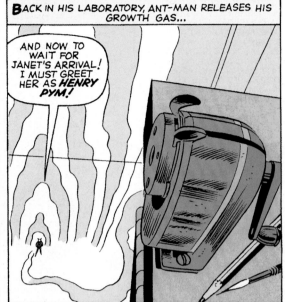

WELL THEN, TAKE ME BACK TO MY LABORATORY, QUICKLY! THEN YOU WILL SPREAD OUT, TRY TO FIND SOME TRACE OF THIS CREATURE! AND SOME OF YOU WILL GO TO THE F.B.I. OFFICES AND SEND ME A MESSAGE OF WHAT THEY FIND OUT!

BACK IN HIS LABORATORY, ANT-MAN RELEASES HIS GROWTH GAS...

AND NOW TO WAIT FOR JANET'S ARRIVAL! I MUST GREET HER AS *HENRY PYM!*

SECONDS LATER...

JANET... AT THE DOOR! PERHAPS I WAS WRONG IN ASKING HER TO COME HERE, TO CARRY OUT THE PLAN I HAVE IN MIND! PERHAPS...

DOCTOR PYM! MY FATHER --HE--

I *KNOW!* AND I KNOW YOU WANT TO *AVENGE* HIS DEATH! ARE YOU REALLY SERIOUS? WOULD YOU RISK *ANYTHING* FOR JUSTICE? I MUST KNOW!

I *MEANT* WHAT I SAID! I SHALL DEDICATE MY LIFE TO FINDING HIS MURDERER! COMING HERE, I HAD TIME TO THINK! I WISH I COULD HELP TRACK DOWN *ALL* THE CRIMINALS, THE HUMAN WOLVES WHO PREY ON HONEST PEOPLE! I SUPPOSE YOU THINK I'M JUST A FOOLISH FEMALE, BUT...

COME IN HERE, INTO MY LABORATORY, AND SHUT THE DOOR!

I'M GOING TO TELL YOU WHAT NO ONE ELSE IN THE WORLD KNOWS! IN SO DOING, I PUT MY *LIFE* IN YOUR HANDS! BUT, I TELL YOU BECAUSE I NEED A PARTNER... AND I HAVE *CHOSEN HER!* I AM... *THE ANT-MAN!*

YOU...? BUT, OF COURSE! HOW ELSE COULD YOU HAVE KNOWN ABOUT... BUT YOU SAID YOU HAVE CHOSEN A... *PARTNER?*

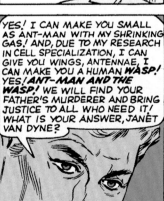

YES! I CAN MAKE YOU SMALL AS ANT-MAN WITH MY SHRINKING GAS! AND, DUE TO MY RESEARCH IN CELL SPECIALIZATION, I CAN GIVE YOU WINGS, ANTENNAE, I CAN MAKE YOU A HUMAN *WASP!* YES! *ANT-MAN AND THE WASP!* WE WILL FIND YOUR FATHER'S MURDERER AND BRING JUSTICE TO ALL WHO NEED IT! WHAT IS YOUR ANSWER, JANET VAN DYNE?

YES! I SAY, *YES!* SHOW ME HOW AND I WILL STAND BESIDE YOU ALWAYS... TO AVENGE MY FATHER'S DEATH! I SWEAR IT!

11

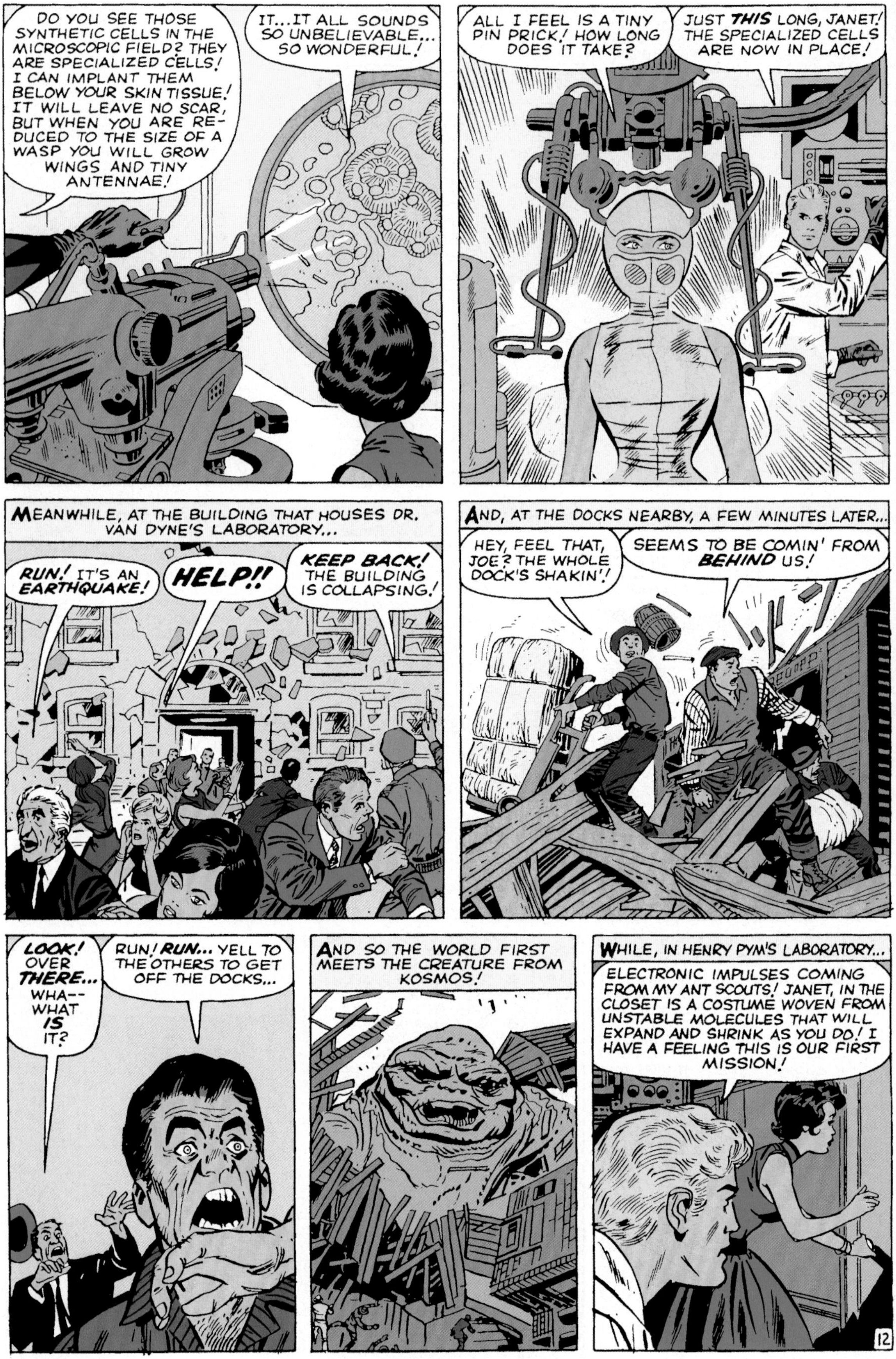
DO YOU SEE THOSE SYNTHETIC CELLS IN THE MICROSCOPIC FIELD? THEY ARE SPECIALIZED CELLS! I CAN IMPLANT THEM BELOW YOUR SKIN TISSUE! IT WILL LEAVE NO SCAR, BUT WHEN YOU ARE REDUCED TO THE SIZE OF A WASP YOU WILL GROW WINGS AND TINY ANTENNAE!
IT... IT ALL SOUNDS SO UNBELIEVABLE... SO WONDERFUL!
ALL I FEEL IS A TINY PIN PRICK! HOW LONG DOES IT TAKE?
JUST THIS LONG, JANET! THE SPECIALIZED CELLS ARE NOW IN PLACE!
MEANWHILE, AT THE BUILDING THAT HOUSES DR. VAN DYNE'S LABORATORY...
RUN! IT'S AN EARTHQUAKE!
HELP!!
KEEP BACK! THE BUILDING IS COLLAPSING!
AND, AT THE DOCKS NEARBY, A FEW MINUTES LATER...
HEY, FEEL THAT, JOE? THE WHOLE DOCK'S SHAKIN'!
SEEMS TO BE COMIN' FROM BEHIND US!
LOOK! OVER THERE... WHA-- WHAT IS IT?
RUN! RUN... YELL TO THE OTHERS TO GET OFF THE DOCKS...
AND SO THE WORLD FIRST MEETS THE CREATURE FROM KOSMOS!
WHILE, IN HENRY PYM'S LABORATORY...
ELECTRONIC IMPULSES COMING FROM MY ANT SCOUTS! JANET, IN THE CLOSET IS A COSTUME WOVEN FROM UNSTABLE MOLECULES THAT WILL EXPAND AND SHRINK AS YOU DO! I HAVE A FEELING THIS IS OUR FIRST MISSION!
12

CYBERNETIC UNITS IN THE MACHINE TRANSLATE THE INCOMING SIGNALS INTO HUMAN SPEECH, AS JANET VAN DYNE DONS HER NEW COSTUME...

F.B.I. SAYS VAN DYNE KILLED BY STRANGE ELEMENT AKIN TO FEAR... ENTIRE SYSTEM RUPTURED! F.B.I., POLICE, MILITARY CALLED OUT TO FIGHT ALIEN MENACE! VAN DYNE HOUSE SMASHED AS THOUGH BY GIANT HAND! DOCKS NEARBY UPROOTED, SMASHED!

ALIEN THING ADVANCING TOWARD GEORGE WASHINGTON BRIDGE! POLICE CLEARING MANHATTAN! MILITARY STANDING BY, READY TO FIRE!

THIS IS IT, JANET! THAT IS THE THING THAT KILLED YOUR FATHER! SOMEHOW YOUR FATHER'S SPACE PROBE MACHINE BROUGHT THAT UNEARTHLY MENACE DOWN TO OUR PLANET!

HERE, DON THIS BELT! THE CYLINDERS CONTAIN YOUR REDUCING AND GROWTH GASSES! PRESS THE BOTTOM BUTTON...LIKE THIS!!

I SEE!

THE MIRACULOUS VAPOR ENGULFS THEM AND THEY SHRINK... SMALLER... SMALLER... SMALLER...

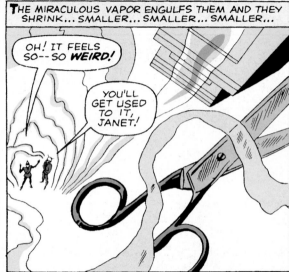

OH! IT FEELS SO--SO *WEIRD!*

YOU'LL GET USED TO IT, JANET!

AND, AS SHE SHRINKS TO MINUTENESS, GOSSAMER, DAINTY WINGS SPROUT FROM JANET'S SHOULDERS AND TINY, DELICATE ANTENNAE ADORN HER FOREHEAD! THE LOVELY GIRL HAS TRULY BECOME... *THE WASP!*

THE SPECIALIZED CELLS... THEY *WORK!!* I CAN HEAR THINGS THROUGH MY ANTENNAE!

THE VOICES OF THE INSECT WORLD... AS I HEAR THEM THROUGH MY CYBERNETIC HELMET! COME, NOW YOU WILL TRY YOUR *WINGS!*

SHOT INTO SPACE BY HIS CATAPULT, ANT-MAN FINDS HIS COMPANION CLOSE BESIDE HIM AS HE FLIES SWIFTLY THROUGH THE AIR!

THIS IS *EXHILIRATING!* WHERE ARE WE GOING?

TO THE GEORGE WASHINGTON BRIDGE! I'VE ORDERED THE ANTS TO GATHER THERE!

ANT-MAN... I THINK YOU'RE *WONDERFUL!* I WANT YOU TO KNOW, IN CASE THIS CREATURE KILLS US, AS IT DID MY FATHER, I--I'M FALLING IN LOVE WITH YOU!

13

NO! YOU MUSTN'T SAY THAT, JANET! YOU'RE ONLY A CHILD! LET'S GET THIS STRAIGHT... I CHOSE YOU AS MY PARTNER SIMPLY BECAUSE I THOUGHT YOU HAD A REASON, AS I HAVE, TO FIGHT FOR MANKIND!

I NEVER WANT TO LOVE AGAIN! I--I COULDN'T BEAR IT IF I HAD TO LOSE A LOVED ONE-- TWICE!

SO I'M ONLY A CHILD, AM I?? WELL, MISTER ANT-MAN... WE SHALL SEE!

SHE IS SO LIKE MARIA...HER BEAUTY,... HER SPIRIT!! I MUST BE CAREFUL LEST I DO FALL IN LOVE WITH HER!

THIS IS MY PARTNER, THE WASP! YOU WILL BE TO HER AS YOU ARE TO ME! NOW, MY FRIENDS, TOGETHER WE WILL DEFEAT THIS STRANGE MENACE FROM SPACE!

WE CANNOT AID YOU THIS TIME, ANT-MAN! THIS CREATURE... THERE IS SOMETHING ABOUT IT THAT PREVENTS US FROM APPROACHING IT! WE CANNOT!

SUDDENLY, THE EARTH SHAKES AS THE MILITARY BATTERIES OPEN FIRE! THE CREATURE FROM KOSMOS HAS APPEARED!

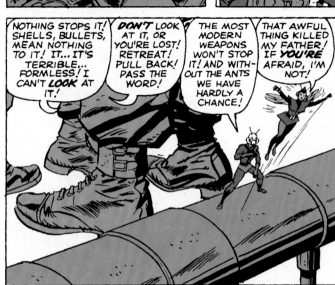

NOTHING STOPS IT! SHELLS, BULLETS, MEAN NOTHING TO IT! IT...IT'S TERRIBLE... FORMLESS! I CAN'T LOOK AT IT!

DON'T LOOK AT IT, OR YOU'RE LOST! RETREAT! PULL BACK! PASS THE WORD!

THE MOST MODERN WEAPONS WON'T STOP IT! AND WITHOUT THE ANTS WE HAVE HARDLY A CHANCE!

THAT AWFUL THING KILLED MY FATHER! IF YOU'RE AFRAID, I'M NOT!

THE WASP FLIES STRAIGHT TOWARD THE TOWERING, SOULLESS MONSTROSITY...

WASP, COME BACK! YOU FOOL CHILD! COME BACK!

I'LL SHOW HIM I'M NOT A CHILD!

14

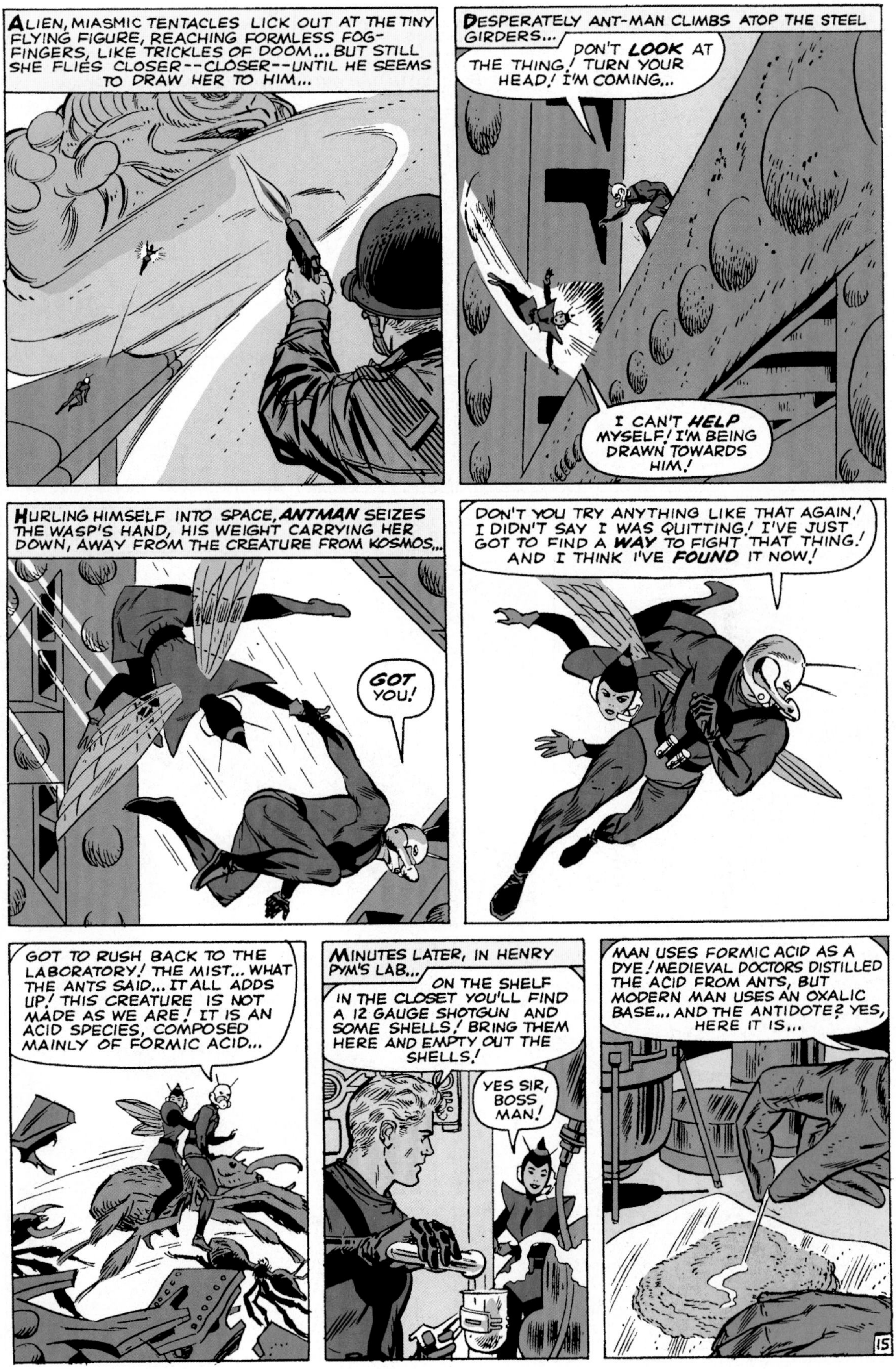

ALIEN, MIASMIC TENTACLES LICK OUT AT THE TINY FLYING FIGURE, REACHING FORMLESS FOG-FINGERS, LIKE TRICKLES OF DOOM... BUT STILL SHE FLIES CLOSER--CLOSER--UNTIL HE SEEMS TO DRAW HER TO HIM...
DESPERATELY ANT-MAN CLIMBS ATOP THE STEEL GIRDERS...
DON'T LOOK AT THE THING! TURN YOUR HEAD! I'M COMING...
I CAN'T HELP MYSELF! I'M BEING DRAWN TOWARDS HIM!
HURLING HIMSELF INTO SPACE, ANTMAN SEIZES THE WASP'S HAND, HIS WEIGHT CARRYING HER DOWN, AWAY FROM THE CREATURE FROM KOSMOS...
GOT YOU!
DON'T YOU TRY ANYTHING LIKE THAT AGAIN! I DIDN'T SAY I WAS QUITTING! I'VE JUST GOT TO FIND A WAY TO FIGHT THAT THING! AND I THINK I'VE FOUND IT NOW!
GOT TO RUSH BACK TO THE LABORATORY! THE MIST... WHAT THE ANTS SAID... IT ALL ADDS UP! THIS CREATURE IS NOT MADE AS WE ARE! IT IS AN ACID SPECIES, COMPOSED MAINLY OF FORMIC ACID...
MINUTES LATER, IN HENRY PYM'S LAB...
ON THE SHELF IN THE CLOSET YOU'LL FIND A 12 GAUGE SHOTGUN AND SOME SHELLS! BRING THEM HERE AND EMPTY OUT THE SHELLS!
YES SIR, BOSS MAN!
MAN USES FORMIC ACID AS A DYE! MEDIEVAL DOCTORS DISTILLED THE ACID FROM ANTS, BUT MODERN MAN USES AN OXALIC BASE... AND THE ANTIDOTE? YES, HERE IT IS...
15

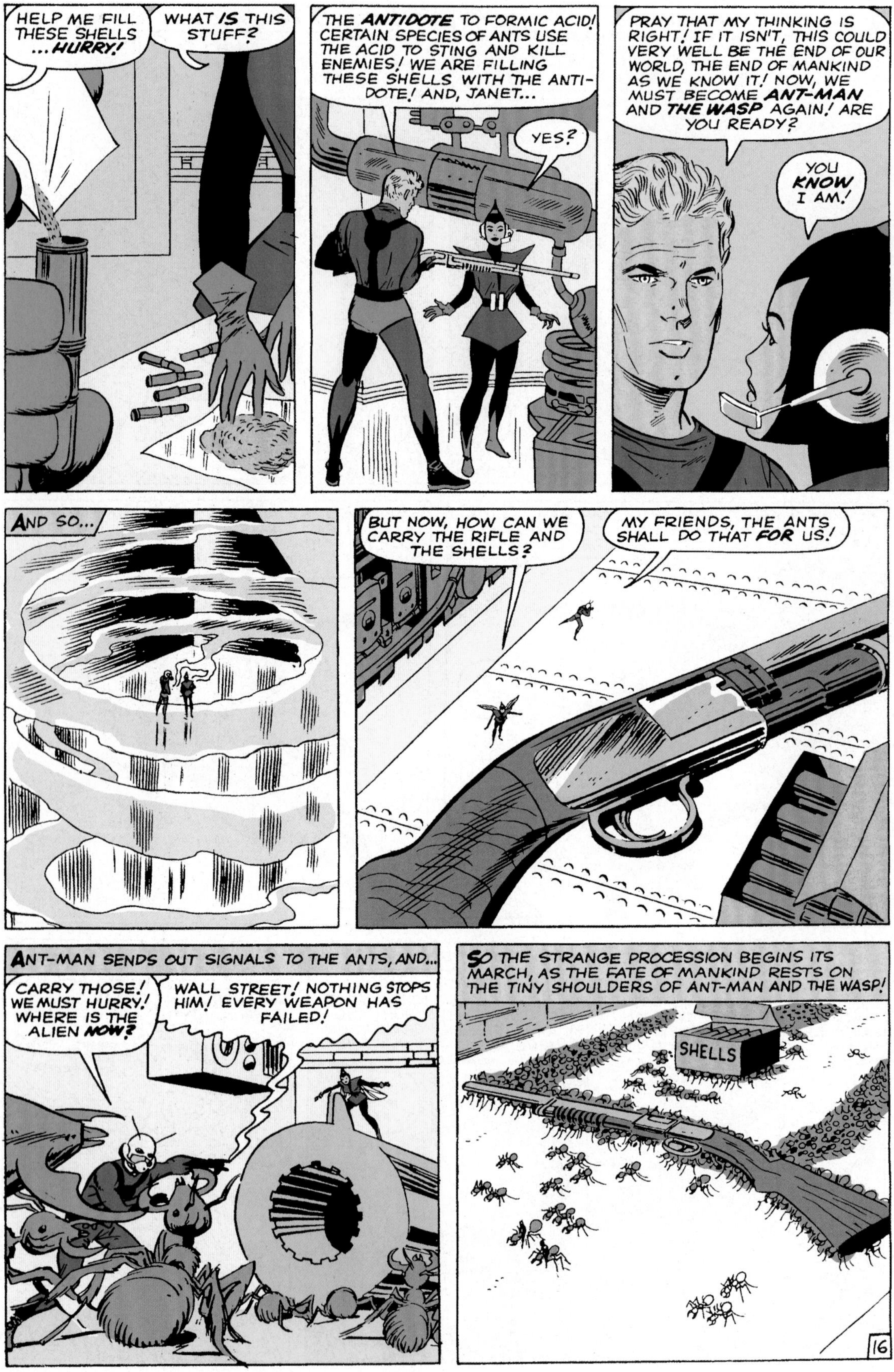

HELP ME FILL THESE SHELLS ...HURRY!
WHAT IS THIS STUFF?
THE ANTIDOTE TO FORMIC ACID! CERTAIN SPECIES OF ANTS USE THE ACID TO STING AND KILL ENEMIES! WE ARE FILLING THESE SHELLS WITH THE ANTI-DOTE! AND, JANET...
YES?
PRAY THAT MY THINKING IS RIGHT! IF IT ISN'T, THIS COULD VERY WELL BE THE END OF OUR WORLD, THE END OF MANKIND AS WE KNOW IT! NOW, WE MUST BECOME ANT-MAN AND THE WASP AGAIN! ARE YOU READY?
YOU KNOW I AM!
AND SO...
BUT NOW, HOW CAN WE CARRY THE RIFLE AND THE SHELLS?
MY FRIENDS, THE ANTS SHALL DO THAT FOR US!
ANT-MAN SENDS OUT SIGNALS TO THE ANTS, AND...
CARRY THOSE! WE MUST HURRY! WHERE IS THE ALIEN NOW?
WALL STREET! NOTHING STOPS HIM! EVERY WEAPON HAS FAILED!
SO THE STRANGE PROCESSION BEGINS ITS MARCH, AS THE FATE OF MANKIND RESTS ON THE TINY SHOULDERS OF ANT-MAN AND THE WASP!
SHELLS
16

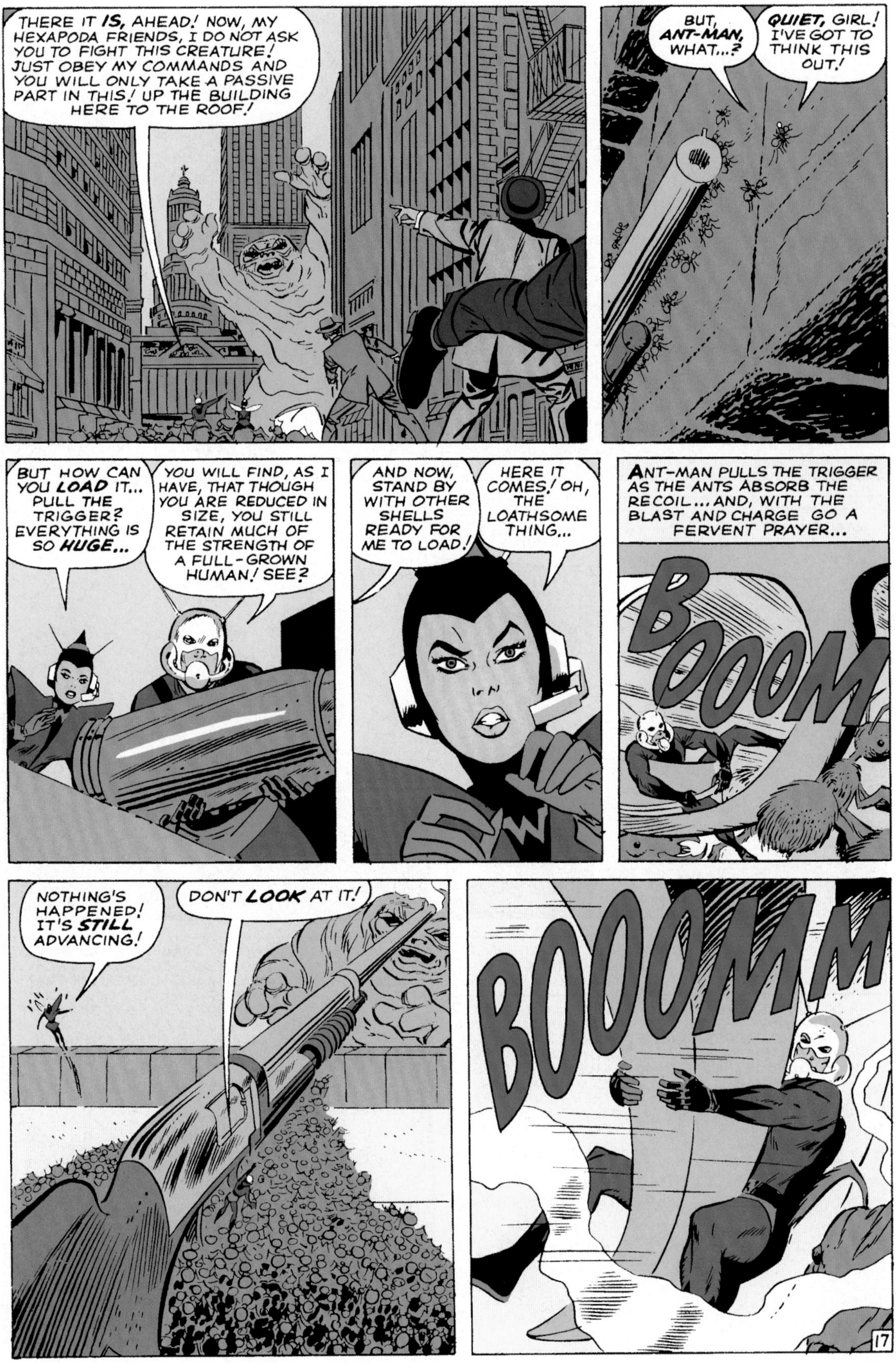
THERE IT IS, AHEAD! NOW, MY HEXAPODA FRIENDS, I DO NOT ASK YOU TO FIGHT THIS CREATURE! JUST OBEY MY COMMANDS AND YOU WILL ONLY TAKE A PASSIVE PART IN THIS! UP THE BUILDING HERE TO THE ROOF!
BUT, ANT-MAN, WHAT...?
QUIET, GIRL! I'VE GOT TO THINK THIS OUT!
BUT HOW CAN YOU LOAD IT... PULL THE TRIGGER? EVERYTHING IS SO HUGE...
YOU WILL FIND, AS I HAVE, THAT THOUGH YOU ARE REDUCED IN SIZE, YOU STILL RETAIN MUCH OF THE STRENGTH OF A FULL-GROWN HUMAN! SEE?
AND NOW, STAND BY WITH OTHER SHELLS READY FOR ME TO LOAD!
HERE IT COMES! OH, THE LOATHSOME THING...
ANT-MAN PULLS THE TRIGGER AS THE ANTS ABSORB THE RECOIL... AND, WITH THE BLAST AND CHARGE GO A FERVENT PRAYER...
BOOOM
NOTHING'S HAPPENED! IT'S STILL ADVANCING!
DON'T LOOK AT IT!
BOOOMM

SUDDENLY THE HORRIBLE MIST FILLS THE AIR... A SOUNDLESS SCREAMING VIBRATED INTO NOTHINGNESS...

IT--IT'S STOPPED! IT SEEMS TO BE FALLING APART... WAVERING... SECTIONS ARE BLOTTING OUT...

IT WORKED! YOUR ANTIDOTE WORKED!

LIKE ROTTING TENDRILS OF SOME EVIL, ALIEN PLANT, THE CREATURE FALLS, WRITHING, VANISHING AS THE FORMIC ACID ANTIDOTE CHARGES ENTER THE NOXIOUS SUBSTANCE THAT WAS THE ALIEN BEING OF THE CREATURE FROM KOSMOS...

BOOOOOM!

IT--IT'S VANISHING! IT'S FADING AWAY!

YES! WE'VE WON... WE'VE WON!

ER... WE--WE'D BETTER GET BACK TO THE LAB! AND FROM NOW ON YOU MUST NOT DISPLAY SUCH EMOTION! IT-- IT ISN'T PROPER!

HE'S BLUSHING... AND PRETENDING THAT HE DIDN'T FEEL ANY EMOTION AT ALL!

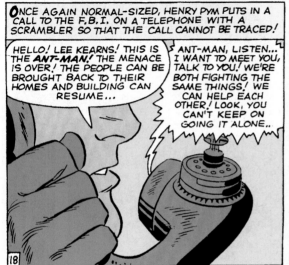

ONCE AGAIN NORMAL-SIZED, HENRY PYM PUTS IN A CALL TO THE F.B.I. ON A TELEPHONE WITH A SCRAMBLER SO THAT THE CALL CANNOT BE TRACED!

HELLO! LEE KEARNS! THIS IS THE ANT-MAN! THE MENACE IS OVER! THE PEOPLE CAN BE BROUGHT BACK TO THEIR HOMES AND BUILDING CAN RESUME...

ANT-MAN, LISTEN... I WANT TO MEET YOU, TALK TO YOU! WE'RE BOTH FIGHTING THE SAME THINGS! WE CAN HELP EACH OTHER! LOOK, YOU CAN'T KEEP ON GOING IT ALONE..

18

I'M NOT GOING IT ALONE, KEARNS ...NOT ANYMORE... NOT EVER AGAIN!

NO, MY DARLING! I WILL ALWAYS BE BESIDE YOU! AND SOMEDAY I WILL MAKE YOU REALIZE THAT YOU LOVE ME AS I LOVE YOU! BUT, UNTIL THAT DAY COMES, IT WILL BE AS YOU WANT IT...JUST PARTNERS... THE ANT-MAN AND THE WASP FIGHTING SIDE BY SIDE!

THE END